HIGHLY EMBELLISHED TRUTH & SOME POETRY

Just Folks Three

Jerry W. Engler

*Illustrations
Sheri Lauren
Schmidt*

Just Folks
Highly Embellished Truth & Some Poetry
©2008 Jerry W. Engler

Published by 6-mile roots
1429 260th
Marion, KS 66861

Printed in the U.S.A.
Print Source Direct
Hillsboro, Kansas

Library of Congress Control No.: 2008910224

ISBN: 978-0-9771255-2-4

Dedication

Highly Embellished Truth and Some Poetry: Just Folks Three is dedicated to the love and persistance taught by the author's parents, Wayne S. and Patricia A. Engler

Table of Contents

Foreword

The contents of Jerry Engler's *Highly Embellished Truth and Some Poetry: Just Folks Three* evoke a familiar Midwestern quality often discerned in the earnest conversations that occur around pot-bellied stoves, scarred oak tables or well-worn sales counters in general stores, grain elevator offices, and parts shacks across the broad American mid-section. The characters that populate Engler's stories reverberate in a collective culture that prizes simplicity and integrity over machination and a fast-forward society that has forgotten its roots. Firmly grounded in the fiber of Americana, stories like "Payback Time for Mean Dean" and "The Saint Louie Bird Call" derive truth from a morality as rich as loam and as timeless as the river. In balance, the poems excite our senses ("First Day Mowing") and engage our intellects ("Oh My Father") in language simple and compelling. Pull up a box. Stoke the stove. Jerry Engler has a few things to say.

Merle Bird, Kansas author and editor

Author's Introduction

Thank you for your interest in Highly Embellished Truth and Some Poetry: Just Folks Three.

Chances are, if you are looking at this book, you may also have seen Just Folks: Earthy Tales of the Prairie Heartland and A Heartland Voice: Just Folks Two. So, I also thank you for your interest in those books.

I hope you enjoy the transition of having some of my poetry included with my newer short stories in this edition when the first two books had only short stories.

I owe a special continuing thanks to the artist for the Just Folks series, Sheri Lauren Schmidt, who also is my daughter. Sheri has shown inspiration and attention to detail in doing the inside sketches and cover art for the book. We have developed a method for her work. I try my best to leave her alone, which isn't always easy for a person with a history for meddling. She reads what I have written to come up with the inspiration for what she draws all on her own.

I acknowledge the efforts made by my wife, Belinda, my brother, Greg, my children and grandchildren, Sheri, Carl, Amber, Aiden, Ron, Shanna, Jesse, Abigail, Benjamin, Mark and Stefanie, plus a whole con-glomeration of cousins and friends, who have continued to offer their support and enthusiasm for Just Folks books.

My father, Wayne Engler, always told us that "All you can do is the best you can do."

You may find that sentiment most poignantly expressed in the poem about him entitled "Oh My Father."

I hope that somehow you might find the same value imparted in my work.

Jerry W. Engler, October, 2008

Ignacio Rode

The old warrior's bones lie less than a hundred miles west of the Arbuckle Mountains, Oklahoma's natural central gateway from Texas, where he was kept with the remnant of his group at Ft. Sill into the first years of the Twentieth Century.

Geronimo, a Chiricahua Apache nation war and spiritual leader, had still been considered by the Army questionably dangerous to turn loose when he had become only a romantic legend to the public. The tragedies of his bloody battles against Mexicans and Americans, and his personal losses of wives and children were lost to the memories of most people. His name became a paratroop battle cry and a comic book title.

But some people never forgot the person of the name. Some people always did revere Geronimo.

In 2006, 97 years after Geronimo's death, the white-bearded, broad faced man was sitting down to a breakfast of bagels and black coffee in a typical motel lobby south of the Arbuckles where a continental breakfast was advertised. It was too late in the morning for most people to still be there, so he was alone. He was staring, bleary-eyed and tired when a door opened, and a young, square-built, muscular young man with long black hair and obviously sun-enhanced, healthy, glowing copper-brown skin, came in.

Although he seemed too young and vigorous to be very interested in meeting an older man, the black-haired man smiled with deep crinkles around his eyes. "Good morning, Sir," he said. "Is there much breakfast left? I am very late."

"Well, there's not much, but these bagels looked good."

"Then I will have bagels and coffee, too."

"You might as well sit down with me, if you'd like," said old white beard. "I think we'll be the only ones here. Did you sleep late, too? I don't think I made up for staying up late even if I tried."

"No, I am a steel foreman. I don't know if we are going to work more, or if we are going back to Texas. My crew and I are waiting for a final decision. We're working on the highway, and the company contracting with us wants us to cut back on the steel to save costs. I won't do that. My company won't do that. We use quality steel, and we build quality products. If they don't want to stick to the original specs, we will go home. They will take our name off the project."

"Boy, that doesn't sound good. I don't like the sound of them cutting quality when people depend on it."

"No, we don't either. Tell me, what do you do?"

"I'm a writer. I've been here for book signings. I've enjoyed traveling Oklahoma. It's been interesting meeting members of the Indian nations, and seeing how much of their cultures they have retained."

"I'm Apache myself, actually seven eighths Apache and one eighth Mexican. What do you write?"

"Books of short stories. You're the first Apache I've met. But I don't think there are many Apaches in Oklahoma, are there? Did you come from Arizona or New Mexico?"

"No, I'm from Southern Texas, down on the Mexican border. Is that one of your books—may I see it?"

"Sure."

"It looks good. If I told you a story of my family, would you use it in a book you do later?"

"Maybe. I'd be interested in hearing it anyway."

"Would you be sure to tell it just as I tell you? It has been handed down for many years."

"Well, I write fiction, some of it a lot of highly embellished truth."

"You could embellish a little bit to fill in gaps, but I'd want the story to stay much the same. I would like some people in the world to hear what my family heard. Please try, but I leave it to you. OK?

"OK, I'd like to hear your story. I won't promise anything, but I'm interested."

"In the family, we call our story 'Ignacio Rode.' We have always called it that because Ignacio did that, Ignacio rode. He was my great great grandfather. I never knew him, but my parents and grandparents handed the story down, that Ignacio rode."

"Ignacio is a Mexican name, isn't it. So, this is where your one-eighth Mexican ancestry came from, from Ignacio?"

"No, Sir. My Mexican ancestry is from one of my great grandmothers. I am, as I said, one-eighth Mexican and seven-eighths Apache. You can decide what Ignacio was, and so can your readers if you ever write this. "

"What about Ignacio's wife? Wasn't she Mexican?"

"The family said she grew up where Ignacio did, Sir. Ignacio said he was a Mexican. He and his wife herded goats and sheep. They lived in a village on the Southern Texas border, the same area I come from. Ignacio said he was a Mexican, but when the time came, Ignacio rode. He was a Mexican who wore his hair like I do, but much of the time it was tied into a large bun under his sombrero. He kept a spotted mare when often the other people around him were too poor to own a horse."

"Hey, I just remembered I've heard of the Fort Sill Apaches. Were your people ever some of them?"

"No, Sir. Like I said, I come from Southern Texas. The Fort Sill Apaches were the followers of Geronimo who had also been in prison in Florida with him, and their families of course. They kept their families there. The only thing I know about Fort Sill is when Ignacio rode."

"OK, so you are from Southern Texas, so was Ignacio, and Ignacio rode. It sounds like it's mysterious."

"Not very mysterious, Sir. Now, Ignacio kept a Christian cross on his wall, and under it was where he hung his medicine bag of leather with leather thongs except when he wore it around his neck. He kept things of his youth and significant spiritual things from later in it. At night Ignacio would hold the bag while he prayed on his knees before his cross. It's buried with him along with the picture."

"The picture?"

"Yes. Once when Ignacio was growing old, someone in the night brought him a picture of Geronimo--a new photograph. He kept it on the wall with the cross and the medicine bag. Sometimes when he prayed, he would hold the picture against his chest. He would whisper a word that sounded like Goyathlay in English. Sometimes he would hold a stone from the bag with the picture.

"Then one night, someone else came to whisper to Ignacio outside his door. Ignacio told his family that Geronimo the Apache was dead. Then Ignacio rode. Now when we say, Ignacio rode, it sounds maybe like he galloped very fast. But Ignacio rode his little spotted mare like a man should ride who has to travel a great distance.

"He travelled very lightly, only a blanket for a saddle, his big knife and a canteen at his belt, a bedroll with some dried goat meat behind him, his hair gathered under his sombrero. He loped his little mare, then walked her. Often he walked in front of her while she rested. They stopped to sleep in daylight hours, and the mare grazed. Both of them ate mesquite beans, and he pealed prickly pear for them. Ignacio rode, but he rode differently than many people would. He rode up all of Texas into Oklahoma, and still saved his little mare's strength in case she was called on to do more. Ignacio knew how to ride to cover many miles in a hurry while your horse stayed strong.

"Yes, Ignacio rode. He rode as a man should. He knew how to ride a horse to save it for work or for war when a big moment arrived.

"He went to Fort Sill to see the grave himself in the military cemetery. He was about to get off his horse to pray there when a white officer on a big black horse rode up beside him. Ignacio didn't try to ride away as many men would when he heard the officer coming. It might have made him seem like a bad man. The officer asked him, 'Are you Apache? I don't recognize you.'

"Ignacio replied, "Soy Mejicano. No comprendo Ingles, pero maybe little bit.'

"The officer looked at him long and hard, his forehead wrinkling above his eyes while Ignacio smiled at him. It was difficult to smile at him because the officer had the hard, experienced blue eyes of a hundred campaigns. 'You come, come with me,' said the officer. They rode side by side, the officer on his big black horse, Ignacio on his little spotted mare.

"They went to where two elderly Apache men stood in front of a building. The officer asked one of them to look at Ignacio. Ignacio looked deep into the other man's black eyes like water pouring into his inward being. Then the other man spat on the ground, and said, 'Mexican!' Obviously despising Ignacio, he rejoined his companion, and they ignored the officer and the Mexican.

"'I fear Los Indios,' Ignacio said to the officer shrinking back on his horse.

"'Come on, come on,' said the officer riding toward the borders of the post, Ignacio at his side. 'Now get out of here, and never come back. Understand? Vamoose!'

"Then Ignacio rode far to the north and the west only at nighttime before he made a big loop to return to Southern Texas. Yes, Ignacio rode. But during that first day, he took time for the prayer the officer had interrupted even if he was no longer at the grave."

"So, he really was an Apache, huh? That other Indian recognized him, and covered for him."

"I don't know, Sir. I can't tell. You decide for yourself, and let your readers decide for themselves, too."

"But you said you are seven-eighths Apache."

The younger man stood smiling with all his large, square, white teeth showing while the bearded man leaned over the table toward him. "I have told you everything I have been told, Sir. I only know that Ignacio rode."

Oh My Father

Oh my Father,
what am I to say
to you who woke
with the thousands of dead
around you many mornings,
so much so,
that you tell me,
being around the dead
doesn't bother you.
I fear death
as I know we all do,
even with faith,
as you must too,
because you tell me
the Ten Commandments include
"Thou shalt not kill,"
so you must be going to hell,
you say.

Oh my Father,
I know in my heart of hearts,
the discernment knowledge,
that Lord Jesus Christ
has a special place for you
for the nobility of soul
that sacrificed for all of us,
listed most reliable
in a high school year book,
known for reliability, gentle wisdom,
and your incredible honesty,
your entire life.
Your human soul more valued
in our living God's eyes
than any nation,
yet you were uplifted
for being willing
to lay your life down.

Oh my Father,
what can I say
when I was a protected one

5

while you saw friends die
before the Viche guns,
saw the crushing defeat of Kasserine,
then went from Tunis
up the bloody spine of Sicily
for Patton's glory,
went under the blasts from Bertha
for the nights on Anzio,
where you learned to say
"When it's your time to go,
it's your time to go."
You saw the horror on Monte Casino,
then went into Rome into Florence,
throughout the valley of the Po.
You saw Mussolini and his mistress
hanging in the square,
more than 20 days dead,
awful pieces of meat.
From another man's stiffened fingers,
you took your Luger.

Oh my Father,
you who saw
a thousand years of death
in only four of war,
need to know you are saved
by the grace of our ever-living God,
and not judged
by what you did in war
or as a good man afterward.
But what can I say without being
your weeping child again,
for you to comfort again,
for you were given dominion over me,
and it was me who grew up in peace
under the steadfast protection
of one who knew the worst tragedies
of our turning terrible
but beautiful world.

Oh Father, save my Father,
and give him the peace
that passes understanding.

We're Not Lion,
Somethin's Happenin'

There's a danger in saying "nothing ever happens here," especially on days that dawn with a chill, pristine atmosphere, where the sky is that unbroken sheet of soul-pleasing, deep blue behind a white sun.

The forces of this dimension must hear such statements because they do things like roll out the storm clouds to stomp the foolishness of the being who said such a thing, or they cause the hearts of men to join in follies like making stupid rules.

Nearly every community, whether a village or a giant city, has on its books a stupid rule, or a rule that sounds stupid, but made perfectly good sense at the time it was created.

Most of them probably were made on those days where the day was so clear the humans couldn't see beyond the fogs of their minds.

It must have been Johnny Beauregard who first said it, shuffling in his chair with a cup of coffee to his lips, as he looked out the Deerhead Tavern's front window to the piercing sunshine bathing Main Street. Yes, it was Johnny who first sighed out the words, "You know, nothing ever happens here. This has got to be the deadest town around."

"You got that right," said Charmin' Carmen. "Only, why don't you put in that nothin' unusual ever happens here, and that I like it that way in case God is listenin' in. Makes it easier to just sell a few horses. Then I come in here to sit on my fanny drinkin' coffee in the mornings while bozos say 'nothin' ever happens here.' Here comes Doc. I heard his door swing shut next door. Now that's somethin' happenin'."

"That ain't nothin' happenin'," said Johnny, as pink swirling fog surrealistically enveloped the folds of his brain.

"Yeah, I don' know, but I'd guess maybe if I knew somethin', that is dependin' on your definitions or some such thing or other for sure, that Johnny's right. I lived here my whole life, and nothin' ever really happened except normal stuff," said Buck Barnsworth, who never had guessed that everybody else hadn't necessarily lived a life like his, even in the same town. The fog was getting deeper.

"How you doin', Doc?" asked Charmin Carmen as the stocky veterinarian sat down to stare out the window with the others.

"Oh, OK, Carmen. Beautiful day, isn't it? I don't have hardly anything going on today, and I hope nothing happens to spoil it. Every once in a while it's good to have a laid-back day, isn't it, fellows?" asked Doc, whose brain usually operated in unusual clarity.

"I don't know, Doc," said Buster Noggins. "I guess I'm with the others. I'm kind of bored today. For a winter day, it's turnin' out pretty

7

warm, but it was still too frosty this morning even for the fish to be bitin'. Tell you what, I'm goin' home to check my telephone messages one more time. If there's nothin' there, I'll be back again."

"You boys are just lucky to be living in a place where there's fish to bite at any time," said Doc, taking a big swig of the hot, black liquid.

They sat there for five minutes, just looking out the window. Nobody said a word, and nobody new came in.

Finally Harrison Washington, owner of the Deerhead, sat down to interrupt the silence. "Kind of quiet today, isn't it, boys? The guys last night didn't make any big messes, so there wasn't much to clean up. There's not many people coming in. It's nice to have it quiet every once in a while."

"Nothin' ever happens here," said Johnny.

After another five minutes, Mrs. Ava Lagerty came up the sidewalk out front with her Pekinese, Gilifont, on a leash. Gilifont wetted on the utility pole while Mrs. Lagerty tried to appear not to be looking at him, and while all the men looking out the Deerhead window did look at him. "There you go," said Johnny. "That's about as good as it gets. Nothin' else ever happens around here."

Mrs. Lagerty and Gilifont moved on to be replaced at the pole by Gilbert Wittesage and his Malemute, Fang.

"At least it ain't cats you got to look at, Doc," said Carmen. "Everybody knows how Doc hates a darn cat."

"I don't hate 'em, Carmen," said Doc. "I'm just allergic to them. Most folks can just take their cat business to another veterinarian. It's good when nothin' happens if it involves the cat business. It's a good day for walkin' dogs, it seems."

Gilbert Wittesage and Fang had been replaced at the pole by Wilbur Walacant and his fat half-breed Blue Heeler, Jill, named after an old girl-friend of his which he thought nobody else knew, but which everybody did know.

"That old Jill was hell," said Johnny, "but I guess we've talked about her a thousand times before. Nothin' new ever happens around here."

"Well, this might bring something new," said Harrison, looking across the street by the hardware store where Gilbert and Fang already had come around the block. Fang was rearing on his hind legs looking back from where they had come while Gilbert was pulling on the leash with all his might to keep the powerful dog from getting away.

Wilbur and Jill had no trouble catching up with and passing Gilbert and Fang. Wilbur walked in his longest stride while Jill puffed and trot-ted, both of them glancing back down the walk behind them anxiously from time to time. Finally both men and their dogs moved on.

Then Mrs. Lagerty came trotting with Gilifont, pulling on the leash trying to run at a gallop in front of her with his tail tucked between his rear legs. She looked anxiously across the street to the men watching out the front window of the Deerhead, then jerked Gilifont to the side to come trotting across the street, and up the steps to the Deerhead front door.

"Mrs. Lagerty, what's wrong?" cried Harrison as the lady flopped backwards into a chair, her gray curls bouncing as she breathed a deep heaving sigh.

"It was awful," she finally gasped out. "It looked at us with those big, yellow eyes, and I thought Gilifont and I were goners. And that stupid, stupid man just kept saying, 'Don't worry, I got him. He won't hurt you,' as if everyone doesn't know they are killers."

"What are killers, Ma'am?" asked Doc even as he looked across the street to see the first appearance of the answer. And there it was, huge and golden with a brown-turning-to-black mane of hair around its head and shoulders.

The chubby little man with the black leash holding the powerful male African lion looked incapable of doing anything if it decided to take off, but bob and bounce across the ground hanging onto the leash as it bounded away.

"That thing," said the woman. "It looked at us."

Harrison seated Mrs. Lagerty at another table, and sat listening to her solicitously while the men at the main table, looking out the window at the man leading the lion across the street, sat in silence. When the man disappeared outside the range of the table, the men continued to sit in silence for a moment.

Finally Johnny Beauregard said, "That might have been somethin' happenin' here."

They could see people looking outside windows across the street, and the one new car that drove in there backed out, and left. Then, just like magic, the lion came into view again on their side of the street just outside the window, the pink-skinned chubby man, with the fringe of gray-brown hair below his bald head, behind it as the big cat sniffed at the utility pole. The lion turned his tail to the pole, and bunched its muscles to mark its scent there.

Something caught the man's attention next to the Deerhead. He pulled a small notebook from his shirt pocket, and stood there writing something down.

"Oh, Good Lord, no," groaned Doc Frenchie leaning his head down to the table to rest his forehead on his hand."

"What, Doc, what's wrong?" asked Johnny.

"It's the guy with the lion," said Carmen. "He's writin' down the contact information off Doc's door I betchaya. He needs a veterinarian, I'd guess."

"If something's got to happen in this town, why does it have to be the biggest cat possible looking for a veterinarian," said Doc, still shaking his head.

"Kitty, kitty, kitty," called Johnny tapping at the window.

"Stop that," growled Doc.

"I don' know, I just don' know for sure if I'm seein' what I'm seein' for sure, but it sounds like the rest of you might see it. I think there's a lion out there," said Buck.

It was then that the little bald man looked up at them from pin-point blue eyes that seemed too small for his head, and smiled at them through the glass.

At about the same moment, there was a crash from the kitchen that made them all jump as though the lion had come in. But it was Buster Noggins, followed closely by Harrison Washington who was stammering, "What's the matter with you comin' in the back door that way, turnin' over all the stuff we had against it?"

"There's a lion out there, that's why," said Buster. "You didn't think I'd come in the front way past him, did you?"

The man with the lion outside was beckoning to them with a wiggling finger while he pointed at the front door with the other hand that held the leash loosely in its grip. The lion looked up at them a moment too, its yellow-brown eyes gleaming brightly in the brilliant sunshine. Then it yawned, revealing its huge, pointed teeth.

"Go see what he wants, Johnny," said Charmin' Carmen the horse trader.

"Yeah," said Doc. "And if he's looking for the veterinarian, tell him that's an old sign. The veterinarian died two years ago. I'll buy your coffee for the next two weeks if you tell him that, Johnny."

"You guys are nuts," said Johnny. "Look at the teeth on that guy. Think of how much horse meat he must chew down in a night with those teeth."

"Think so, do you?" asked Carmen. "Must take a quarter of a horse to feed him every day, wouldn't you figger, Doc. Why that might be $100 worth of horse every day of the week. Maybe I ought to go out there with you, Johnny."

"Think of your reputation, Carmen. How can you tell everybody about your quality horses if you're buying for horse meat on the side?" said Doc.

Carmen puckered his lips, "I could just say I got a new sideline in the quarter-horse business."

"Go on, Johnny, get out there," said Doc. "And remember, I'm not around." The door closed behind Johnny. The men still inside watched as the short chubby man gestured at Johnny to come on down.

"I'll go out too," said Buster Noggins. "Maybe I can give Johnny encouragement from the sideline. After all, I used to be a rodeo clown.

Gettin' pushed around in a barrel by a mad bull probably isn't much better than facin' down a lion."

Johnny took about four steps down. The chubby man was taking him by the hand, and pulling him the rest of the way down. He spoke to the lion, and he spoke to Johnny. Then the lion was rubbing his big body against Johnny like any common house tabby while Johnny froze in place with his arms hanging at his sides.

Buster stayed behind Johnny a couple of steps higher looking over Johnny's black hair to see the lion.

A police car drove up with flashing lights, and Deputy Owen Reuben got out on the side of his car opposite all of them while he held his firearm in the air talking.

The chubby man was talking quickly to the deputy with hand movements that suggested reassurance. He stuck the lion's leash in Johnny's hand, and leaned across the hood of the police car to talk to the deputy who finally holstered his weapon.

Then Johnny was nodding his head to the chubby bald man, who followed Buster Noggins' lead into the Deerhead.

"Doc, Doc," said Buster. "It was Johnny that told him you was in here. Johnny's so scared with the lion and the cop that he would have ratted on his own mother, which come to think of it, he did, which is why his daddy left town. Anyway, this here is Thedro Whadwhipple, the papa of the lion out there."

"Actually Richard III just thinks of me as his papa since I hand-raised him from a cub," said Whadwhipple. "I like English history, so I named him Richard III, the Lion-Hearted if you're an anglophile also. Anyway, Little Ricky, I call him that for pet-name reasons, seems to have a bit of toothache, and I needed a veterinarian to take a look at it.

"Don't worry about your friend, Johnny, out there. Ricky really is quite friendly, although there's always the cautionary that he is a wild animal and could become ferocious if pushed too far. That's why I cautioned your deputy there. Isn't it funny how all cats like to rub on their prey, but also rub to show affection.

"Now, Dr. Frenchie, I guess the name is. I suggest you help me check Little Ricky before your people get too excited. The good deputy there was warning me that your city council already has your city attorney, O. B. Goodfellow, drawing up an ordinance about the situation. I've bought the motel out north of town where Little Ricky and I will live. We just came to town because Main Street looked like such a pleasant place to stroll, and because we needed you."

"Guess you got me, Whadwhipple," said Doc. "Let's get out there, and get your cat into my office before someone makes a stupid mistake."

"You'll need to give Ricky a tranquilizer, I might as well warn you now, Doctor. Little Ricky doesn't like injections by needle. I suggest when you stick him that Johnny and I stand on either side of his head since he seems to like both of us. He'll stay perfectly calm if we do that, and he doesn't have to watch the needle go in. He's sensitive that way, you know.

"You'd do well to have the deputy stay away. He's too frightened and frightening to Ricky. See Ricky drawing his lips back out there. He really doesn't care for the deputy and his lights. I'd have to be running out there to keep him from going nuts if he didn't like Johnny so well. I figure we have about 10 minutes before that happens anyway."

"Oh, I think we got a little time here, Whadwhipple," said Doc. "I'm allergic to domestic cats, you know, so I might be to a lion. This will cost you extra."

"I have money. That's no matter," said Whadwhipple.

Carmen licked his lips again at the mention of money. "So, do you think you'll be needin' quite a bunch of horse meat, Mr. Whadwhipple?"

"No, Little Ricky eats a special balanced dry meal lion food with all the drinking water he needs free choice on the side. It keeps him content so that unfortunate things don't happen, like perhaps swallowing the pekinese back there."

"I'll only ask one more thing, Whadwhipple," said Doc. "Can you give him some sort of hand signal to get old Richard III to give that loud lion cough once? Then maybe you can get him to roar right after I give the shot, and before I look at the tooth, so that Johnny is still right there by his head?"

"Easily. We have many hand signals," said Whadwhipple.

Outside, he let Johnny keep the leash, and the two of them stepped out on either side of Little Ricky, with hands on his mane as they walked into Doc Frenchie's office, the other coffee drinkers stopping to sit in Doc's waiting room.

When the lion coughed and roared, they all jumped. The crowd that was beginning to gather out front began to find reasons to go back home or into the Deerhead.

Deputy Reuben Owen got back in his car, and said to nobody in particular that his handgun wouldn't have had much effect on a lion anyway.

Doc sent Buster Noggins out to go to Johnny's house. What few people were left asked if anything was wrong, but all Buster told them was that Johnny needed a change of clothes.

Doc pulled a piece of chicken bone out of the gum between Little Ricky's teeth.

"Richard III, have you been getting into the garbage again?" asked Whadwhipple.

Buster Noggins and Charmin' Carmen went with Doc and his wife Marcelle to the hospital that night for Doc to get an emergency steroid injection. His eyes had swollen shut from contact with a cat.

The human doctor explained that being exposed to a lion was probably equivalent to exposure to 50 house cats. "Doc to doc, Dr. Frenchie, there's a lot more cat there."

Sometimes when travelers stay at the motel out north of town, they tell the girls serving breakfast at the Deerhead in the morning how they could have sworn they heard a great rumbling roar of a large animal from someplace in the night.

The Kaw Town City Council passed an ordinance making it illegal to walk a lion on Main Street, years later agreed upon by the people who rediscovered it as one of the strangest rules they had ever seen in a city.

Several months after the incident, the coffee drinkers were sitting on a steamy April morning, looking out the window of the Deerhead, when Johnny Beauregard said, "You know, nothin' ever happens in this town." Doc Frenchie had half a cup of chilled down coffee left that he threw in Johnny's face before getting himself a refill.

"I just didn't want him to completely lose his memory," he said.

"Poor Johnny," said Buck Barnsworth throwing his own cup of coffee on the thin-faced man too. "I think I get it, maybe I do, but I really don' know for sure."

That night the Methodist Church steeple got hit three times in a row by lightning.

A farmer had Doc Frenchie come out to see that his cow had triplet calves the next morning.

Johnny Beauregard had three mosquito bites lined up in a perfect row on his nose by evening.

And, none of that's a lion.

13

The Lilac Bush:
A Centering Of Soul

From the middle of the lilac bush,
from that hidden secret hollow
amidst the green growth coolness
of summer's respite,
the world goes by,
on one side cars kicking
gravel on occasional flights,
and on the other,
a bantam cock attempting
to herd white rocks,
a flash of green, gold and black
storming around the peaceful
cackling feathery clouds.
From the middle of the lilac bush,
you can be when
and where you want to be.
Each daydream climbs unseen,
as you are unseen
by the nervous bantam cock
or anyone else
who comes into the yard
or calls for you
wondering where that
dreaming child could be.
Even now you can
draw it around yourself,
and from the middle
of the lilac bush
let speeding cars
and nervous cocks
and their cackling charges pass
while you climb
in clouds unseen.
From the middle of the lilac bush,
from that hidden secret hollow
amidst the green growth coolness
of summer's respite,
the world goes by,
on one side cars kicking

gravel on occasional flights,
and on the other,
a bantam cock attempting
to herd white rocks,
a flash of green, gold and black
storming around the peaceful
cackling feathery clouds.
From the middle of the lilac bush,
you can be when
and where you want to be.
Each daydream climbs unseen,
as you are unseen
by the nervous bantam cock
or anyone else
who comes into the yard
or calls for you
wondering where that
dreaming child could be.
Even now you can
draw it around yourself,
and from the middle
of the lilac bush
let speeding cars
and nervous cocks
and their cackling charges pass
while you climb
in clouds unseen.

Crank One Long For Central

[Author's Note: Kids were kids even back in the rural and farm areas in the 1930's, 1940's, 1950's and early 1960's when the telephone service was much different than it is today. The phones were wooden boxes with batteries inside, a ringing crank, receiver on a line and a speaker mouthpiece. The lines frequently were put up with help from the local people on poles cut from local timber. They were more susceptible to weather than today's lines.]

"Hello, Central?

"Hello, hello...hello, hello. Yes, I can hear you fine, Central. Can't you hear me? Well, hang on, hang on, I'll be back in a minute.

"Whew, that was a lot of work. Can you hear me now, Central?

"Well, yes, I am a little out of breath. I had to get the Sears Catalogue and rearrange it on top of the chair with the Spiegel's and the Montgomery Wards, and then climb all the way back up here again. My Daddy calls the Montgomery Wards the Monkey Wards. That's funny, ain't it, Central? Yeah I like that one too. Cracks me up. Sometimes Daddy's pretty funny. Most times Mommy says he's just being Daddy.

"I could hear you really good on the receiver, Central, but was tryin' to stand up here on tippy toes at the mouthpiece so I probably wasn't quite close enough to it so you could hear me, Central. Now I got all these catalogues stacked on the chair, and I've climbed up here close enough so I'm right at the mouthpiece.

"Who am I? Why, Central, this is Jimmy, Jimmy Schleighbottem. Well, yes I am Ned and Sadie's little boy, they're my Daddy and my Mommy. No, Mommy doesn't know I'm up here on all these catalogues, but this is an emergency, Central. Mommy and Daddy aren't home. I wouldn't be allowed to use the phone if it wasn't an emergency cuz of some other things I did, of course unless I'm callin' Grandma. I'm allowed to call Grandma any time I want, and especially if Mommy and Daddy aren't here cuz sometimes things look a little spooky if they ain't here, Central. Course, I'm not scared of much anything, been highly beneficial that way, not even scared of sharp knife blades, Central.

"What's that got to do with it? No, this emergency ain't anything to do with me getting cut up. You see, Central, the knife blade has to do with me carving on this here telephone, it being such pretty brown wood and all. Tom Bosnick claims his brother carved both their initials

in a cedar fence post, and I thought this might be about the same. But it ain't, Central. Mommy said it ain't anywhere near the same thing, and I'm never to try to do anything to the telephone again. Heck, I only took a little nitch out of it, maybe scratched it up a little it's such hard work.

"Know what I think it really might have had to do with, Central? I don't think Mommy liked it that I used her good butcher knife for the carving, and climbed up on all these here catalogues to do it. There was

17

somethin' about it that seemed to bother her powerful like I might have hurt the knife or something. Heck, Central, that knife is tough. My brother and I drove it clear through a piece of wood one time with Daddy's hammer, but I guess we better hadn't be doing that she's so sensitive about her knife. She even put it on a higher shelf. Now I have to get a chair to climb the cabinet to get it, Central. Of course, let's just let that be our little secret, and not tell Mommy about it. OK? What? You don't think I ought to be doing that either because I could what? Heck, Central, I'm smarter than that. I ain't going to stick a knife in my belly.

"The only other thing I ever done with that old knife is stick it in the electric socket, liked to scare me to death, and Daddy said I wasn't burnt worse because the wooden handle insulated me. Mommy screamed while the fire was sparking.

"Heck, Central, she screamed worse than that cuz of this old telephone. Lightening hit the wires, and came out the phone's mouthpiece, and shot clear across the kitchen. Whenever it lightenings now I go to the living room, and curl up in the easy chair. Lightening don't get you in the easy chair.

"Oh, you're in a hurry cuz you got other stuff to do? That's just the way with all you grown-ups, always hurrying. You ought to dig around with us in the dirt in the back yard sometime, Central, then you'd find out what real work is. That's what Daddy said after we showed him his tools we buried. That was one of the times he was only a little bit funny.

"Oh, I'm sorry, you say I either got to tell you what the emergency is or hang up cuz someone else might need to talk to you. Well, Central, I was just trying to be nice to you, and talk to you a little first. I didn't know you wouldn't like talking to me. Oh, you say you do like talking to me, it's just that you might have to work?

"Well, Central, one reason I thought you might like to talk to me is because Mommy says you must be awful lonesome being an old maid who likes to listen in on everybody else talking on the phone.

"No, Central, I don't think that's insulting.

"Heck, that's the other reason my brother and I are in trouble when it comes to this old telephone. You see, we like to get up here, and listen to the Bohunk sisters talk their gibberish. Central, they talk English like you and me unless someone listens in on them, and they switch to the gibberish, 'Gib, gib, gib, yippy, yippy, yippy.' We just like to hear'em talk it, Central. Mommy says we shouldn't even call them Bohunks like Daddy does, but call them Checks (Czechs). That's silly isn't it, Central? What do they have to do with banks? Silly old Mommy. Sometimes she's funny. too, but not very often.

"No, no, just wait a minute. I don't want to hang up. I really do have an emergency, and yes, OK, OK, I know you want me to get on with it. What? First you have to transfer another call, do you, Central? You say just hang on? You're not too terrible excited about a kid with an emergency, are you, Central?

"Oh good, you're back, Central? I was afraid you might not come back on, and then I'd have to ring you again. Really, you mean the phone company wouldn't let you hang up on a kid that says there's an emergency? Why, they're just a pretty good phone company, ain't they, Central?

"OK, OK, I'll get down to it, Central. Lordy, you don't have to throw a tizzy like Mommy says that Ginette Cooper does.

"Why I don't know the difference between gossip and gospel, Central?

"Well, I would have if you hadn't interrupted me. You need to be more courteous, Central. Mommy's always telling me that too.

"Now, listen, here's my emergency. I think you can help me. What, you have to transfer another phone call right in the middle of my emergency? Don't that beat all, Central?

"Oh, you're back. You're getting quicker, Central. Me too. Daddy says I just get quicker all of the time, like the time... What? Oh yeah, the emergency.

"Well, Central, Miss O'Brian, my new first grade teacher, that is I'm new, she's old. Anyway, she says today that we all have to give her our home phone number this very day. When it comes my turn to tell her my phone number, I was really proud cuz I've known my phone number since I was lots littler. She bends over to me when my turn comes, and says, lookin' over the tops of her glasses and smellin' pretty good, 'Now, Jimmy, what's your phone number.'

"So, Central, I comes right out with it, and tells Miss O'Brian that my phone number is two shorts. Well, Central, she tilts her head down even further giving me that 'stupid little Jimmy look with her thick, curled lips,' and she says 'Now that ain't your phone number,' only she don't say ain't cuz Miss O'Brian don't ever say ain't, I know that already. She's a real proper acting sort of a grown-up except for when she slapped me for telling her she stole my crayons.

"Then she says to me, 'So, Jimmy, what's your Grandma's phone number?' Ain't that some piece of hell, Central? She even knows my Grandma. So, I tells her, my Grandma's number is three longs. Then I tell her the one Bohunk sister my Grandma talks to a lot is one long just to show her I know lots of numbers. She romped me then for callin' the sisters Bohunks. Heck, Central, them Bohunk sisters can't help it if they's Bohunks. Live and let live, my Daddy says.

"Yes, yes, go ahead, and transfer your next call. Too bad you can't let a few of those calls go so we can get this finished up, Central.

"Ah, good, you're back. That time it sure took you a while, Central. I even got down, and went to urinate while you were gone. Yes, I can use big words like urinate cuz Mommy says that's the proper way to talk, not like Daddy does. Oh, you knew I was gone cuz you left once more for another call. Gosh, Central, you are getting busy.

"Well, no, listen here, the best part of my phone numbers was you. I told Miss O'Brian that you crank one really long ring for central. I thought that might set her back. But she said, 'No, Jimmy. You have another number. You get it right away when you get home, and you let me know what it is.'

"So, Central, you being the expert, I figured you know if I got another number, and you'd know how to get Miss O'Brian, so we could give it to her. See, it's really her emergency, and not mine. I'm plenty happy with two shorts. And, Mommy ain't here, so I can't ask her, but I don't suppose she knows there might be another number anyway because she always says two shorts, too.

"Well, no, Central, I didn't know it would cost Mommy and Daddy an extra dime to call Miss O'Brian. You're right. That is a lot of money. And you don't think you ought to place a pay call for me without them here to say OK? I see your point, Central. You're thinking ahead. I've heard Mommy even say that sometimes Daddy can be an old tightwad.

"And just for my information I do have another number? Well, go figure. It's 1922. Hold on, Central, I got to climb down, and get a pencil and paper to write that down. What do you mean you don't have time? After all the time we already talked, you don't have time now for me to write the darned phone number down? You think Mommy will know the number anyway? I don't know about that, Central. She always seemed to figure two shorts was good enough for me. I don't really think Mommy knows numbers, Central. You better hang on while I get my pencil.

"Now there's no need to get cranky with me, Central. Huffy, huffy, but if you like, yes, I can have Mommy call you back if she needs too. I'll even tell her just crank one long for central, Old Crank."

Click.

First Day Mowing

By the second round
you have the feel
of more
than an ocean of prairie.
Nine feet of hand-sharpened
sickle stays hungry
for the taste
of wounded bluestem
while you stay high
in the tractor saddle
breathing easy
into the south wind
under a fiery sun.

It's when you
turn into the north
that the tractor speed
matches the soft breeze,
and the sweet pungent smells
steep your brain,
or burn the nose
if the sickle
clacks in struggle
against a renegade patch
of wiregrass with ragweed
that's on the shallow ground.

On the even soil
the grasses are uniform,
the mower's a well-fed shark
slicing happily
through little blue,
big blue and gramma,
slowing for a bigger bite
on the switch,
or gulping in struggle
on slough grass in the draws.

The dog grins up at you
from his place
on the left or behind;

he knows the sickle's big bite
that cottontails flee.
He's there for mercy
if a bunny's bloodied,
a dog's dining day out.

By the time
you're four hours
into your voyage
when the rake man's there
to check the drying
from your beginning,
you've found your sea legs,
wobbling over to him
from the tractor,
and your eyes are reading
the sickle's challenges
in rippling waves of green.

Prowling For Kitty Cat Barbe-Coon

Spring's just wonderful, Roland, and you know what I'm thinking of doing?" Ricky asked from where he sat sprawled on the porch front steps with his elbows propped back on the porch deck.

"The day really is nice, warm sun and all," Roland answered from where he laid his scrawny frame in the lawn chair. "And I'm feeling all lazy-like, kind of sleepy. So I don't know if I even want to know what you're thinking, Ricky, on a day like this."

Ricky looked up dreamily, with that far-away and long-ago look in his eyes. "Well, you see, Carol said I did such a great job at Valentine's that she fixed me a special barbecued steak dinner for St. Patrick's, and you know, I love barbeque."

"Uh huh, think I better be going home now," said Roland as he tightened his eyelids down in sudden irritation.

"No, no wait. You're going to love this, I promise you. You're involved."

"No, I ain't ever wanting to be involved again. I want to wake up now. This sounds like the beginning of a nightmare I have from time to time."

"Anyway, Carol says we ought to celebrate every holiday that comes along, no matter how small, we're having such a fun time now. She said I get the next one, April 1, April Fools' Day, because as long as she's known me, that's just naturally been my day."

"I think that woman just called you a fool, Ricky. You know, she always has been perceptive."

"No, no, no, she hasn't done any such thing. My wife knows I always like to play tricks and jokes on folks on April Fools'. You just wait. The best is coming."

"Yes, I suppose it is. But I'm just getting up now. Nap time is over."

"Sit still. You see, I have to add, Carol also said I'm the best kind of fool--sweet, innocent and loving--then she leaned over, and called me 'Sweetie.'"

"Oh, so that's the best part. Carol's a fool too?"

"No,no,no. You know, I grew up poor. When I was young, we ate all kinds of meat, anything my Daddy could catch."

"Uh huh. Well, you ain't your Daddy. Let's remember here we're upscale, middle class folks. Isn't it nice to have all that chicken, beef and pork? How about a turkey sandwich? We can quit having nightmares now."

"It will be really special because I got me a hankering, Roland, a real desire to eat coon once like when I was a kid."

"You ate coon? Yuck. You don't mean raccoon, I hope, not the warm fuzzy kind with the black mask you see in the cartoons."

"You have it part right, Roland, but I mean the snarling, furry up-a-tree kind you hunt with hounds. You and me, we'll run through the night air with some boys who really know how to hunt, listen to the dogs bay the coons. We'll barbeque those coons we caught ourselves, surprise the girls. You know, coon tastes just like beef."

"Yeah, just like opossums taste like pork, and frog legs and most everything else you catch is said to taste like chicken. The best solution is to go to the grocery store, and buy some beef. Besides, your folks might have cooked coon, but I bet you don't know how."

"Opossums! You're right, Roland. I nearly forgot about opossums. I'll bet those dogs will run some opossums they track down up the trees too. We'll barbeque opossums with the coons. I've been talking about how to cook them with Mrs. Violet Bureauford, an old-timer from down the street. Her son, DuAllen, runs coon hounds, and really knows how to do it all."

"I don't know. We're good friends, Ricky, but I don't know if I want anything to do with this," said Roland, rolling his big almond-brown eyes in his slender face for emphasis.

"Violet says you skin the coons, and of course the opossums, too, since we'll be going for them, too."

"Ricky, opossums look a lot like big rats."

"Don't talk like that. You'll enjoy it all. Then after you skin'em, you boil'em outside in a big cooker. See, we'll have a campfire, all outdoorsy. Then you skim the fat off, and you boil them again. Then you skim the fat off again, and then you cook it like beef. It's really, really good."

"Why do you keep skimming the fat off?"

"That's where most of the bad flavor is. You don't want them to taste gamey."

"I repeat. That's why we have jobs, so we aren't poor anymore so we can buy beef. It's really, really good. And, maybe this DuAllen has dogs, but I don't know anything about coon dogs, and neither one of us even owns a rifle."

"No matter, Roland. This is why we have jobs. We can pay people to help us be cool, and have fun, and we have friends. DuAllen has a rifle, and those dogs of his are all under his control, ferocious good trackers. And if that isn't enough, our sheep farmer friend, Leon Gambel, said he can bring this other guy along who's kind of uncanny, better than a dog himself. He's also a crack shot, and between him and DuAllen, we can just ease back, and watch. The guy's name is Oswald K. Underfoot, and he's becoming notorious for his hunting abilities among the sheep

24

farmers--even got a cougar that wasn't there for Leon. Leon wants to bring him because he thinks he needs friends. As for DuAllen, he says for $20 we can come along and keep all the coons we get."

"Notorious, huh? I never heard of this Ozzie fellow."

"No, Roland, never call him Ozzie. Leon said it's very important to call the guy by his full name, Oswald K. Underfoot. He made me repeat the name several times. And it's also very important never, never to say anything about him being spooky."

Roland raised his eyebrows, "Oh boy, coons, opossums and Looney Tunes all in the same night."

"Now, Roland, Carol and your wife went out together and bought us matching red flannel shirts for the hunt, and we'll wear our tan, duckcloth coats. It's gonna be fun."

By the time they got out there for the night of hunting, even Roland, fired up by Ricky's constant chatter, was beginning to believe that it could be a little fun.

The sun was setting in a clear sky, promising a bright, moonlit night, as Ricky's car dropped off the last street bricks to continue down another two miles of dirt road to a tall, two-story Victorian era white, frame house. In the front yard was what looked to Roland like an uncommonly well-made, tall scarecrow dressed in tan duckcloth clothes with a pack of tri-colored black, tan and white hounds around it.

Only the scarecrow proved to be the 6-foot-6-inch toothpick tall figure of DuAllen Bureauford swaddled deeply in clothes, his chinless, bush-haired, heavily eyebrowed face poking out.

"So, here we are for the coon hunt, Duallen," Ricky said.

"Yup," said DuAllen.

"This is my good friend, Roland."

"Yup, spose so," DuAllen replied, his yellow-brown eyes looking Roland up and down in an unusual pattern, as though each eye could look in a separate direction from its partner, from a still focused, unsmiling face as they shook hands. "Late, ain't ya? Me and the dogs been waitin' 15 minutes, and they're gettin' anxious. I said 5 p.m. See, it's 5:15."

"Couldn't help it. Had to do some chores for the family, you know," said Ricky. "Didn't think the time would matter that much to the coons. Say, these dogs are interesting. I didn't know coon hounds could be so short-legged as this one here. Some of the others are, well, a little on the short-legged side too."

"They're mongrels, just like me, to maximize their herterozygosity for vigor. That's Ma Belle, the dam of the pack, half coon hound and half beagle, which kept her black and tan with good tracking ability. She always tracks the coons to see you through to a good hunt," DuAllen said, continuing to stare at Roland with one eye, the other eye wander-

25

ing toward Ricky. "You guys trying to be twins or somethin' with your matching clothes? Kind of strange, cuz you don't look alike."

Another car pulled up, and while a square-built, blond-haired man and a small, dark man got out to approach, Roland whispered into Ricky's ear, "This DuAllen's a little peculiar, isn't he?"

DuAllen shook hands with blond Leon, but when he held out his hand to Oswald K. Underfoot, he was thrown off to find himself looking down into eyes darker than his own with eye brows equally bushy.

"Wuz you ever in the Nam?" Oswald K. Underfoot squinted one eye, and screwed his face up suspiciously to look up at DuAllen.

"Why, yes, I was, artillery," DuAllen answered squinting an eye to return the expression."

"Yeah, but you're too tall ever to have gone down holes after Charlies, and you wasn't infantry. Still, you might be somethin', not like these other fellas here.

"So, this is your platoon is it, DuAllen Bureauford, snuff, snuff?" Oswald K. Underfoot said, looking down at the dogs while stretching his hands out to his sides.

"What are you doing, Underfoot, trying to smell me or something?" DuAllen asked.

"The name's Oswald K. Underfoot, and don't you forget it," the little man grimaced. "You get out on patrol, you might need me."

"Oswald K. Underfoot and I didn't bring any equipment, DuAllen," said Leon. "Ricky said you'd have everything, but if you need something, Oswald K. Underfoot has a truckload of things he could bring. Say, aren't those coon hounds a little short legged, especially that little female there?"

Oswald K. Underfoot dropped to all fours, sniffing noses with Ma Belle. "She's just fine. She takes point with the platoon all the time, I can tell. Me and Ma Belle are gonna be fine."

"I got enough of everything to take care of us," DuAllen said. "Here's a sack for each of you to carry for coons and whatever opossums we pick up too. Don't like opossums much. They don't climb the trees to get away from the dogs like the coons. They just play dead so the dogs will leave them alone, so all you get to do is whack them, and throw them in the bag. They're cheap meat though.

"I got my rifle, and one box of shells is plenty," he said, waving a .22 rifle with no stock in front of them. "And one of you needs to be my pole man," he added, waving a 10-foot cut-wood staff."

"DuAllen," said Ricky, "how are you going to use a rifle with no stock?"

"The dogs tree the coon, the pole man puts one end of the pole on the ground, and points the pole at the coon. I lay my single shot along the pole, and bingo, it usually only takes one shot if the pole's held steady.

No sense wasting shells. Here," he said, shoving the pole at Roland," you be the pole man. Now, no more jawing, the river and the woods are waiting, let's get them coons."

He released the hounds from their station beside him with a single word, "Yaaa." Ma Belle was in front at a gallop with nose to the ground, her dozen offspring behind her, Oswald K. Underfoot trotting behind the dogs, the men walking quickly behind.

"Say," whispered DuAllen, leaning over to Roland's ear, "This Oswald K. Underfoot's a little peculiar, isn't he?"

"Aren't we all, aren't we all?" Roland replied, staring at the .22 that looked partly dismantled swinging back and forth in the tall man's hand. Roland had given up on his pleading sideways glances at Ricky to go home.

They heard the "owwl, owwl, owwl," of baying hounds switching to excited barking signaling a treed coon not far away in the distance. A moment later came a higher pitched "yeowl, yeowl, yeowl" along with them.

"What the heck is that yeowling with my dogs?" DuAllen asked, stopping to scratch at an eyebrow.

"Uh, I think that would be our friend, Oswald K. Underfoot," said Leon.

"How could he get so far ahead of us?" puffed Roland. "This doggone pole keeps catching on the brush."

"He's like a banshee out of a fantasy story," added Ricky.

"Oh, Oswald K. Underfoot is capable of things you wouldn't believe. Get a look at the cougar-claw necklace under his coat if you can," said Leon.

It was a big, nice boar coon snarling down from the upper tree branches at the pack of yapping dogs and the little man jumping up and down under him.

"Steady there, steady with the pole, Roland," DuAllen said." And crraack went the .22 with the coon dropping like a rock to the ground. Oswald K. Underfoot threw him in a sack while dancing like a mystic Celtic sprite.

The night wore on with the hounds and Oswald K. Underfoot showing little wear while the hunters grew tired with carrying two coons to every sack along with the occasional opossum.

"This is great, this is just great, Roland," said Ricky, the sweat beginning to roll down his forehead under the load. "This fresh air is making me hungry. I can almost taste the coon now. Hey, you other guys are expected to bring your families over to eat, too. You too, DuAllen."

"I can always eat coon," said DuAllen.

"I think I'm sick. All I want to do is sleep, and wake up again, or wake up right now if I am asleep," said Roland.

"Have you all noticed how the coons snarl down at us, staring down from their little black masks, and how Oswald K. Underfoot growls back at them," said Leon.

"That Oswald K. Underfoot is peculiar," said DuAllen.

"Almost spooky," said Ricky, Roland nodding in agreement.

"Just don't let him hear you say anything like that," Leon shuddered.

"Just one more coon ought to do it," said DuAllen.

They made their way to the river bank, where the dancing dogs and man cavorted under one last tree, a tall thin-stemmed whip of a tree that swayed back and forth in the wind channeled down the water.

As they approached, they could hear the furry animal in the top of the tree snarling loudly and furiously at the dogs, "Reeowr."

"Why, that's no coon," said DuAllen, his eyebrows rising in surprise. "That's the biggest old tomcat I ever did see--big old yellow tiger stripe with that broad head."

"Just get the dogs and let's go," said Ricky. "The cat will get down if we leave him alone."

"No, no, I can't do that. I have to bring him down. I won't ever be able to get the dogs away with him up in the tree. I got to shoot him."

"You can't aim along this pole with him swaying back and forth so much," Roland said.

"That's right. But I got a method for everything. You just stand here, and I lay the barrel on your shoulder, snug alongside your neck, and I get the sway of it to pick him off. Steady now. Don't wince."

"I'm not wincing, I'm just closing my eyes," said Roland. "I'd rather leave him alone. I've had enough of this. Poor old tomcat."

Crrack, crrack, crrack, went the rifle, time after time, Roland gritting his teeth, and soon the box of shells was empty.

"I'll be, I've never missed like that before," said DuAllen.

"What are we going to do now?" asked Ricky.

"Reeowr," growled the cat, baring his teeth and laying back his ears at the dancing, baying dogs.

"Hss, I'll get him," snarled Oswald K. Underfoot, baring his teeth, and pushing his forefingers back along his ears. "Just empty a sack for me to get him." Then he locked his heels into the tree trunk, and began pulling himself up with his hands and arms in a shinnying climb.

When he got to the top of the tree, it went whipping around in a huge circle, and there was a furious chorus of snarls and counter-snarls. "Reeowr, eeor, yaaawh, snap, arrgh." Then there was one last terrible "Heereeowroyay."

"Good lord, what was that last cry?" asked Ricky.

"I can't hear anything. My ears are ringing," said Roland.

"That was Oswald K. Underfoot," said Leon.

"Near as I can tell," said DuAllen, "the tomcat had his teeth in

Oswald K. Underfoot's ear, and Oswald K. Underfoot had his teeth in the scruff of the cat's neck. The cat had his claws in Oswald K. Underfoot's head, but Oswald K. Underfoot had his fingers around the cat's body. That was peculiar." Miracuously, only a small bead of blood was trickling down Oswald K. Underfoot's neck when he hit the ground with a bulge in the bag bouncing one side out, and then the other.

Later, on a soft, humid spring day, both the fragrance of blooming trees and tangy barbecued meat permeated the air where people gathered to eat around redwood picnic tables on the newly mowed grass.

"This is just great, Roland," Ricky said, "Everybody, even our wives, said they'd at least try eating the coons. Hey, what's that you're eating? That's not coon."

"No, Ricky, somebody brought a marinade chicken. I'm just going to stick with that. I don't feel like eating coon."

"Gosh, some friend you're being, Roland. I thought you'd at least eat a little of the coon. Are you that weak stomached?"

"Ricky, did any of you guys know what Oswald K. Underfoot did with the tomcat? I watched him, but I never could see. I just don't feel like I can eat that barbecue without knowing that tomcat isn't in there."

"I see what you mean, Roland. Hey, I think I'll try some of that chicken, too. It doesn't look bad at all--kind of loosen me up for some of the coon later, maybe. Let's don't say anything to the others, don't want to ruin their enjoyment. Wonder if tomcat tastes more like chicken or more like beef."

Ricky stood for a while longer, thoughtfully munching on a piece of chicken. "You know, Roland, it was thoughtful of somebody to bring chicken because maybe not everyone would want to try eating coon or opossum other than just trying a little piece. Your Nancy's thoughtful that way. So, she bought the chicken, right?"

"No, Ricky, Nancy didn't bring the chicken."

Carol, who was walking by just then, heard them talking. "No, boys, you'll never guess who brought the chicken. It was your friend, Oswald K. Underfoot. Isn't he thoughtful and kind of cute, too? We've been talking to him. They say he has something for me, too."

Ricky gagged.

Roland dropped his plate on the ground.

Then, hearing the sounds of conversation rise in the background, they turned around to see at the other side of the yard, Oswald K. Underfoot placing a big yellow tomcat in Carol's arms.

"He gentled up really nice," said Oswald K. Underfoot. "But then, I have a different way with cats. I thought he ought to belong to you, Miss Carol, you're so nice," the little man said turning the deepest red possible for a dark person.

29

"You can call me Ozzie if you want to. But you're the only one who can."

"Well, isn't that peculiar," said DuAllen Bureauford, who seemed to be able to focus on the cat in the woman's arms with one eye while focusing on the chicken all over Ricky's shoes with the other.

You'll Be Back Again

The soft pungent wind
of summer's wet heat
is tumbling off the meadows
through the hedge rows
reminding me on its return
that you'll be back again, my child,
you'll be back again.
I can see your eyes a sparkling,
laughing through the breeze,
your hair flowing over your forehead,
your hand upon my cheek once more,
your body next to mine,
as we used to be before.
Yes, you'll be back again, my child,
I feel it in my heart,
the choke arising in my throat,
you'll be back again.

And in the fall, when the gray flocks
wing their rhythmic ways south again,
and the frost clings close to the grasses,
the beat of your heart
comes close to me,
and I know,
you'll be back again,
oh eye of my soul's longing,
you'll see your way home once more.
Should winter fall to spring,
the blossoms will return,
then you'll be coming back again,
I'm sure,
you will come back, my child.

And, if you've been here 10,000 times,
then find that I have gone,
remember, I'll be coming back again, my child
I'll be coming back.
You'll feel me in the churning throats
of spring's vast stormy clouds,
and in June's rising dew,
I'll whisper in your ear.

When snow blows down the frozen roads,
and you've nowhere to go,
know I'll be close at your side,
I'll come back again.

This is our land, our roots are here, my child,
God will it for a thousand years, my child,
we'll be back again.

Oswald K. Underfoot
Finds A Firefight Treasure

Sue Gambel walked down to the sheep lambing barn in the cool of a balmy, sunny morning sweet with the smells of the purple and greenleafed Hall's honeysuckle she had planted in great beds by its doors.

She let her husband, Leon, deal with the uglier aspects of farm life while she reveled in holding and helping with the newborn lambs, and tending her flower beds. Inside, her home was her domain, decorated and cleaned to her own pace of life with a niche allowed here and there for Leon to live in.

They had once been called the blonde twins by knowing neighbors, a little boy and a little girl who had grown up to marry. Now nothing much intruded to bother her life.

Might as well go in the barns to look at the lambs, she told herself. They would be frolicking in the mild morning chill. Leon would be out in a moment to feed all the sheep before he left for Kansas City to visit some men in the produce market north of downtown about the possibility of selling farm-raised lamb in shrink-wrap packaging to be wholesaled directly to stores, something that could be a value-added product for local farmers.

She was only halfway down the center aisle, between pens that extended outside for ewes with lambs a few days old, and lambing stalls to the inside for the newly born animals, when she saw a pile of furry tan animal laying next to the fence, nearly at the other end of the barn.

Sue paused before her curiosity overcame her, thinking she really might want to go back for Leon before she looked at whatever it was. It had the field-brown color of a wild animal. But, no, she would look at it anyway. After all, she was a grown woman with little to fear.

"Oh," she said, inhaling a breath of air involuntarily. It was a dead coyote, all stretched out life-like, its golden-brown hair still sleek, a small bead of blood visible at the tip of its black, pointed nose.

She thought for a moment that perhaps their Great Pyrenes sheep guard dog, Buddy, had killed it, but it was marvelously unmauled, and Buddy wouldn't bring it into the barn.

And then, "snuff, snuff," Sue heard a little too loudly in her left ear from something closer to her than it should be.

She froze in place, wondering if she dare scream for Leon. Or, perhaps she had been hearing things. The hairs on the back of her neck were rising.

"You are a woman. Why are you in Leon Gambel's sheep barn?"

asked a voice from only a foot behind her. "You smell good, don't smell like sheep."

"Uggh," Sue sucked wind in a small way as she turned to face a small, slender man who was tilting his head to look at her in a most bird-like way from under dark, bushy eyebrows. He was standing there patting Buddy's head, the dog that ought to be guarding her and the sheep.

"She's my wife, Oswald K. Underfoot," said Leon Gambel who had just entered the barn from up the aisle. "You just haven't met Sue because she's been in the house when you've been here. What are you doing here Oswald K. Underfoot?"

"Brought you a gift to pay for my keep, see. Sneaky, sneaky Leon Gambel, didn't even have to say you saw Oswald K. Underfoot's name on a bulletin board this time to get his help. I just came to help, brought you a gift for rent, see. Been out hunting Charlie, snuff, snuff, sneak up on him in the night before he kills sheep, brought him in to show Leon Gambel.

"Glad you have a wife, Leon Gambel. Don't suppose she was ever in the Nam. Not many women were.

"Oswald K. Underfoot, myself, I slept in a lambing stall last night, and Buddy the dog comes in to check me from time to time. I moan a little without the rest of the platoon, but I'd have gone down a hole to get this Charlie if I had to, always was good at going down the holes. Don't suppose a round boy like you ever did that did you, Leon Gambel? No, you wasn't in the Nam.

"I like this barn just fine, snug and tight. It will suit me. Charlie's shelling my position. Can't stand it, Leon Gambel, had to come to your place."

"What do you mean, shelling, Oswald K. Underfoot? There's no way there could be any shelling at your place. You're safe there. You must be having nightmares. The Vietnam War's been over for decades."

Oswald K. Underfoot's eyelids spread wide to show the whites around his dark eyes.

"KA-BOOM!" he hollered doing a jumping jack to clap his hands above his head so hard that Sue jumped involuntarily, and Buddy whined.

"KA-BOOM, they go, and soon they will come screaming in black pajamas with the coyotes and bobcats and pumas to bite poor Oswald K. Underfoot back, and yeow, yeow, yeow I will go," Oswald said, clinching his long white teeth together in an open grimace. "Oswald K. Underfoot will live here until they stop shelling."

"Oswald K. Underfoot, what's really going on? Slow down, and say it in plain ordinary life terms what's happening over at your place. You can't really come here to live, you know."

Oswald K. Underfoot gulped slowly, closed his eyes, and struggled to speak very slowly.

"Yes, Leon Gambel, Oswald K. Underfoot understands you need reality. I will try to say it in Leon Gambel's world instead of Oswald K. Underfoot's world.

"It's the rock quarry. I live next to the rock quarry. They are dynamiting a new vein of rock at the rock quarry. And, they are just going to keep shelling me and shelling me until they get me, and I can't hardly stand it. Now, you have Sue Gambel to hold on to at night. Oswald K. Underfoot has nobody, they're dead or discharged. So, I must come to live in your sheep barn for a little while before I sneak over there some night to kill one of those charlies even if he's a good man with a family at home, maybe even an American. Now, that is it, Leon Gambel, God almighty, amen, roger that, over."

"OK, Oswald K. Underfoot, I understand. But today, I am going to Kansas City, and Sue doesn't feel like she can have you stay here without me," Leon looked at his wife, who was slowly nodding her head. "You ride to Kansas City with me. You can see some sights, and have a little fun, OK? We'll eat out. I'll buy."

"Oswald K. Underfoot will go to a big city? Ride point man in Leon Gambel's car?"

Oswald K. Underfoot ground his teeth together locking the palms of his hands around his chin while he stroked his long nose with an index finger. "OK, I'll go, and I promise to have lots of fun."

"Nice to have met you, Mr. Underfoot," said Sue.

"Aaah," the little man hollered. "You call me Oswald K. Underfoot, not Oswald, not Ozzie, but Oswald K. Underfoot. Mr. Underfoot was my father."

"OK, Oswald K. Underfoot," said Sue blinking her eyes at her husband in puzzled exasperation.

And Leon had a chance for the next exasperations of his day on the trip to Kansas City.

Oswald K. Underfoot rocked back and forth on the front seat of Leon's car as they drove down the interstate going "ssss, ssss," every time they came near a semi-truck.

"OK, Oswald K. Underfoot, try to take it easy," said Leon, who was beginning to wonder about the wisdom of the trip. Why don't you lay your hatchet on the floor? I know I said you could bring it. But this is America. Nobody out there is going to hurt you, understand?"

They got off at Broadway to head down to the produce market with Oswald K. Underfoot down on the floor on his knees with the hatchet propped in front of him on the seat. "Are we about there, Leon Gambel?"

"Yes, we're here, Oswald K. Underfoot. Do you think you could just walk around the market for a while on your own while I go in to visit with the Picolet brothers? See, it's a nice, peaceful place, kind of fun looking at everything. See, there's a booth with flowers in it to look at, and down on that corner they're selling peaches. It's a neat place. You have $20 with you to spend on whatever you want. If you need help, see that nice old gentleman in the white broad-brimmed hat and pin-striped suit. He can help you."

"He looks like he might have been a general."

"Well, he is kind of a general, of this place anyway."

"Well, Leon Gambel, I can have fun. I brought $200, not $20. Oswald K. Underfoot can have a lot of fun in the city."

"OK, Oswald K. Underfoot. This might take me a couple of hours, but I'll be back, OK? The old gentleman is almost always there at that booth, see? You just watch that place, watch him. I'll be back there to meet you. So, you watch for me. Leave your hatchet in the car. We'll lock it up so nobody messes with it."

"OK, I will watch for you, and I will have fun."

Leon was tired by the time he got done talking with the brothers, tired from the tension of discussion, tired from the tension of the trip down with Oswald K. Underfoot. He looked around for the little man while he walked up to the man with the aristocratic finely cut features in the pin-striped suit.

"Excuse me, sir," Leon interrupted the old man's thoughts politely. "I came down here with kind of a strange little fellow with bushy black eyebrows, parked over there, and I was wondering..."

"Yes, I saw him, talked to Mr. Spook, or whatever his name was. He's the one who asked me what my command in the Nam was."

"Yes, that would be the one."

Joey in there told him about the burlesque district, and he got a taxi to go there real soon after you left him. Said to tell you he'd be back real soon when he thinks he's had fun."

"Oswald K. Underfoot in the burlesque district? You're telling me he got a taxi cab all by himself, and just left like that when I have to meet him here to go home?"

"Yeah, I think I am tellin' you somethin' like that. How'd your sheep deal go with the Picolet brothers?"

"How did you know about that?"

"Nothing much goes on here that I don't know about. It may look big, but we're all one big, happy family. I know you drove in that side of the market, and circled to the west, and that's your green Chevy down there. That little spook had a hatchet you made him leave on the floor—smart move that. Bernie in the flower booth was wondering about moving on him until he laid it down. Don't worry about your little friend. He's just nuts, not terminal. Have a Coke with me until he gets back."

Leon Gambel drank a Coke. He ate a sample of peaches. He carried a basket of peaches to his car to take home. He heard what each of Joey's sisters either did for a living, or the husbands and kids they had to put up with. The sun began to glow red in the western sky. Then a yellow cab pulled up to the curb with Oswald K. Underfoot hanging out the window to watch for Leon. He had a half-shredded shirt and a swollen eye. He stepped out the back door of the cab followed by an enormous, fat arm with a snake tattooed on it that reached out to take his hand. The little man braced himself as the arm contracted to help raise out of the back seat a greatly obese woman with gold dangling earrings, black frizzy hair and several chins. She looked toward Leon with small, hard, shiny black eyes that periodically darted to the sides to look around.

"Oswald K. Underfoot, am I ever glad to see you," said Leon. "Where have you been? I was worried about you. What's happened to your shirt, and to your eye. That's going to turn black on you."

"Oh, I did just like you told me, Leon Gambel. I tried to have fun. I tried to see the sights. It has changed my life forever. And, I am out of $200 now."

"Changed your life?" asked Leon trying to take his gaze away from wondering if the frown lines around the cake-shadowed eyes of the fat woman who stared at him stoically could really be sunk a full inch into her face.

"Yes, Leon Gambel. I would like you to meet the woman I am going to marry after the three of us get home. She is Susie. I told her I was staying temporarily with you and Sue, and she said that sounded like a good name to her because her name can be Susie, too."

"Marry her? Leon asked as the big woman towering a head over him held out her huge hand with valentines tattooed on the knuckles. It swallowed his own hand in its grip. "Oswald K. Underfoot, how can you be getting married? You can't have known this, err, lady more than a couple of hours. Are you sure she's…"

Leon stopped talking as he saw the shiny black eyes fixated on him. The woman growled to him in a soft, low voice, "Mr. Gambel, Ozzie here is the best chance in life a girl like me ever gets."

"Ozzie? You called him Ozzie?"

"Yes, she did," said the little man, "but you still call me Oswald K. Underfoot, Leon Gambel. I have fallen in true love at first sight after a brief but meaningful conversation. Here I was, just walking through Kansas City after the cab takes me to where the burlesque is because Joey tells me that's the most different thing to see here that we don't have at home. I tell you the posters here made me blush even compared to that Taiwanese place that made Lieutenant Jones—well never mind. Let's just say it pains me that my poor little Susie had to grow up near places like that.

"I'm trying to hold a hand over one eye while I go past the posters so people won't see I'm looking at them when I see this cute little cafeteria called Ivan's. I go in, sit at a booth, and who do you think waits on me. Why, it was Susie here, my bride to be. I look Susie up and down, and I think to myself, wow, Oswald K. Underfoot, that's quite a lot of woman, and look at all those pretty tattoos.

"I was so spell-struck, I didn't know what to say, so I just sort of blurted out, blurted out like this, Leon Gambel," Oswald K. Underfoot said, hanging his head to one side with his tongue dangling out. "I blurted out, 'Hello there, are you Ivan?'

"Sweet Susie here looks at me, and says, 'Well, you're a smart aleck little blank, blank, blank, ain't you?'

"I say blank, blank, blank to you because I know, Leon Gambel, that you believe you are a nice man, and I haven't heard such words since my First Sergeant said them, and Susie can't help talking that way, and I was touched to the heart remembering my Fist Sergeant. She reminds me of my First Sergeant. She's so wonderful, I think she could have been in Nam.

"After I ate at Ivan's, we went for a walk, and before I know it, she's got her arm around me. We came back to Ivan's to announce our engagement, and all of Susie's other boyfriends jumped me because they didn't want her to leave. I decked three of them even if they ripped my shirt up. The last one hit me in the eye. Susie decked the other four. She said they shouldn't stand in the way of her true love. So, here we are. Let's go home."

Leon wondered all the way home, with the big woman staring glumly at him over the backseat while she held Oswald K. Underfoot against her one-armed, what Sue was going to say. When he had looked too long in the rear-view mirror, Oswald's Susie's black eyes snapped at him, and she said, "Just like I said, this is the best opportunity of my life, fella. Leave it alone."

He needn't have worried about how Sue would take it. After the first introduction, Sue took Susie by the arm to lead her to the house saying, "We need to talk."

Soon he could hear them laughing together, and they came out spouting nonsense about how romance works. Odd to hear a big woman giggle so sweetly. Even more odd to hear Oswald K. Underfoot giggle.

Suddenly Leon Gambel realized he was the odd person out. This feeling was reinforced when Sue spoke.

"Now Leon, you will call tomorrow to the quarry to see when the shelling, or dynamiting, will stop. Until that happens, you will sleep in the lambing barn with Oswald K. Underfoot, and Susie will sleep in the house like I do to keep things proper, and to keep the smell down. Then Oswald will go home while Susie stays with us for a time, so there is a proper courting period. When Susie and I decide the time is right and decent, Reverend Bixby can perform the marriage ceremony. Then Susie Leona Underfoot and Oswald K. Underfoot can go to their own place to live."

Leon Gambel was puzzling over the series of events and the behavior of his own wife as he carried his sleeping bag from the house. He kept doing so for the several days ahead in the lamb barn. He just made sure that every night Buddy the Pyrenes slept between himself and Oswald K. Underfoot.

You can't beat owning a good guard dog.

Twilight Window

Through the gray light
of the twilight window
I see the reflection
of your familiar silhouette
emblazoned with red-orange fire
in the angled rays
of the setting sun
shining in a halo
around your brown-gray hair.

Oh my Darling,
hold me softly.
Know only that
I'm growing old
for the twilight
also grips my spirits,
and the fire of life within me
begins to grow so very cold.

Yet I know
we still have days before us,
days of joy and days of pain.
Let us grasp our faiths together
as I strain to see
so very darkly
through the twilight window pane.

Oswald K. Underfoot Hears The Wedding Bells Chime

"We want a formal wedding, and we want at least a six-month courtship, Leon," said Sue Gambel looking her husband in the face with a tight, proud smile on her own face.

The huge fat woman with newly cut and frizzed black hair standing behind her tried the same kind of smile, but somehow it was coming out as a grimace, particularly with the way she was holding her big knuckles with the valentines tattooed on them tightly against her hips.

Leon Gambel took a slow, deep breath of the cool morning air laden with the scents of honeysuckle and sheep in the nearby pens. This new liaison of his wife with the woman who called herself Susie in honor of Sue, and who stood a head taller than even him was throwing him. He never knew how to react next.

But there was at least one thing he did know how to react to—— "Oswald K. Underfoot," he fairly snarled at the little, dark man behind him, "stop that giggling. Stop it now. A fellow can hardly think when you start giggling every time you see Susie."

"I can't help it, Leon, she's so purty, pretty, pretty Susie," Oswald K. Underfoot said while wrinkling his nose, and extending his face at the large woman with the heavily mascara-covered eyebrows and eye lashes.

Oh, God, was she. Yes, she really was sticking her tongue out at Oswald K. Underfoot to return the flirt. "OK, stop it. Stop it both of you, Oswald K. Underfoot and Susie, stop it. I really can't have you flirting while I'm trying to think around you. Just save your carrying on for when the two of you are alone. You're making me sick, ah, sick that I, ah, can't flirt with Sue like that in public because we've been married so long."

"Oh, is that right, Leon?" Sue said sticking out her tongue at him with a grin. But OK. That's OK. Knock off the flirting in front of Leon you two. It's too much for him."

"Doggone, if that ain't going to be tough, my little Susie Woozie."

"Stop it, I mean stop it," Leon stomped his foot so that even Buddy, the Great Pyrenes dog that guarded the sheep raised his head from the ground where he lay between the two men. "What do you mean a six-month courtship? The shelling, oh I mean the dynamiting at the rock quarry, is done for now. Oswald K. Underfoot can go home tonight. Look, I'm really, really tired from sleeping out there in the lambing barn. Buddy sleeps between Oswald and I but...."

41

"Oswald K. Underfoot's the name, Leon. Oswald was my father. I'm sick of you forgetting."

"That's tellin' him, Ozzie," said Susie, wrinkling her nose at the little man.

"Alright already, I understand--but I keep waking up at night to look over Buddy to see if Oswald K. Underfoot is still there. He doesn't make any noise. He just lays there breathing like a baby, no snuffling, no nightmares, no nothing."

"That's right, that's right. I don't have to dream back to the Nam any more to find my first sergeant. Susie looks just like him, my first sergeant incarnate."

"That's OK Oswald K. Underfoot. It's good that you aren't having nightmares any more," Leon tried to speak low in a soothing kind of voice. "But other times, I wake up, and Buddy and Oswald K. Underfoot are both gone, out making the rounds together to make sure no coyotes are coming up on the sheep in the night. So, I go back to sleep, and then wake up, and they're both back asleep again. Somehow I can stand the dog doing this, but, oh Lord, don't tell me I'm sleeping out there for six more months."

"No, of course not, Sweetheart," Sue Gambel, said. "You were just out there temporarily to watch over Oswald K. Underfoot. He will be going home now for the duration of the courtship, and you'll come back in the house. Since Annette is away at school now, Susie will stay in her room."

"Susie? Susie will be staying in Annette's room? For six whole months?"

"Of course, Sweetheart. Where else would you expect her to go?"

Susie snorted once in response at that, nodding at him with her big hands on her hips again, the very emblem of the proper woman doing the right thing.

"This all does bring up one more thing though," said Sue gazing past Leon in a hard-eyed way at Oswald K. Underfoot."

"Oswald K. Underfoot, do you have plumbing?" Sue asked.

"Expects I do, expects I do just like anyone else," Oswald K. Underfoot said, his lower lip beginning to tremble. "That's kind of an embarrassing question to ask, Mrs. Sue, but I always have been able to pass water pretty much like anyone."

Sue raised her eyebrows, and gave a disgusted guffaw. "No, Oswald K. Underfoot, your house, I'm asking if your house has plumbing?"

"You mean like pipes with water coming through them, and a proper toilet what flushes everything to the outside?"

"That's exactly what I mean."

"Well, Mrs. Sue, I guess that means no," Oswald K. Underfoot replied tapping his thumb nervously on his cheek. "I guess my house doesn't have those things."

"I thought as much. You seem to carry a slight odor, Oswald K. Underfoot, a lot of the time as a matter of fact. Do you take baths?"

"Sure I take baths, lots of them. I got me a tin tub that I pump water into by hand from the well out in the front yard, and it works real good to scrub myself out there as long as visitors don't come to make me keep my privates under the water. Other times, I just take a dip in a pond or a creek. Susie ain't gonna fit well in my little tub, but I'm a guessin' I could buy a stock tank for her."

At that, tall black-haired Susie clapped her hands together, and said, "Hah!"

"As for the necessities of life, Mrs. Sue," Oswald K. Underfoot said, flushing very red for a dark man, "and I do mean going to the bathroom, the toilet is what I mean, I usually just do that wherever I'm at as long as nobody can see me that ain't a man. I mean, I wouldn't want girls to see me going."

"Susie has to have plumbing, Oswald K. Underfoot," Sue said in a fierce tone through clenched teeth. "That's part of what you are going to be doing during the six months."

"Yes, Ozzie, I want plumbing," said Susie, shaking her broad head again.

Sue continued, "And, Oswald K. Underfoot, you aren't going to get away with reporting the progress of the plumbing yourself. Leon will go to your place weekly to see how it is coming along. You can't do it yourself. It has to be done by real plumbers. Your electrical wiring will have to be checked, too. Remember, Leon will be checking on you."

"I will?" Leon protested. "But, Sue, I have lots to do. These sheep need care, and growing the feed doesn't happen by accident. I'm sure Oswald K. Underfoot has relationships with other people who can help him."

"Just do it, Leon."

"I don't have relationships with anybody else. You are my one true friend, Leon Gambel," Oswald K. Underfoot said.

"In the meantime," Sue added, "Susie and I will be preparing for the wedding. We will set up seats and refreshments here on the yard when the day comes. The Reverend Bixby will perform the ceremony, only, Oswald K. Underfoot, if we ever take you to church again, you have to quit asking the pastor if he was ever in the Nam. I don't want you to alienate the man. Also, whenever he says the word 'love' during the service, you are to quit standing up to share that you have fallen in true love. Everybody knows it by now. As a matter of fact, just quit saying it."

"I kind of liked hearing my little Ozzie say it," Susie said making a frown.

"OK," said Sue, "Your little Ozzie can say it to you in private any time he wants to, but not publicly."

"Hey, nobody calls me Ozzie, but Susie, Sue Gambel, you hear. You call me Oswald K. Underfoot."

"You just shut up, Oswald K. Underfoot. Save that garbage for Leon or whoever you want to. By this time I'm calling you anything I want to. Got it?"

"Yes Mam, Mrs. Sue, got it," Oswald K. Underfoot replied trying his best to give a conciliatory smile while scowling to the side, "but not you Leon Gambel."

"OK, back to the wedding again. Like I said, it will be here in the yard. I will be Susie's maid of honor, and I'll get a few of the other women to be her bridesmaids. Susie doesn't want any of her people here from Kansas City because she doesn't want any fights. Leon, you will give Susie away, be her surrogate father."

"Hey, I wanted him to be my best man," said Oswald K. Underfoot. "That's right. I wanted Leon Gambel and his dog, Buddy, to share being best man."

"You want my dog to share being best man with me?" Leon asked puzzedly.

"That's right. I can't decide which one of you I like better."

"That's no problem, Oswald," Sue said. "Oswald," she repeated his name pointedly, "you can have whoever you want for best men. I like Buddy too.

"Leon, after you give Susie away, you just move up behind Oswald. That's pretty much the preliminaries you need to know for the wedding.

"Susie and I will take care of getting her wedding gown and the bridesmaid dresses. You guys can decide where you rent tuxedos. And, get a black bow tie for Buddy too. It will look fine against his white hair.

"Oswald, you can't make anything for the wedding out of animal skins. I won't have it. But you will pay for everything until you run out of funds, then Leon and I will pick up the tab."

"No, Sue, we can't do that," said Leon.

"We will do it, Leon," she replied. "It will be one of our wedding gifts to them. There won't be any loans here unless Oswald wants to show his regards by not charging you to kill problem coyotes any more."

"I'll kill anything for Mrs. Sue, except Susie," the little man said grinning at Leon.

"That's settled then. Now you two men go to town with the truck, and buy a platform porch swing for the front porch for Susie and Oswald's courting. Oswald, you don't kiss Susie anywhere during this time except on the front porch, and don't you dare make a pun out of that. You only kiss her on the face, Oswald. "

"Yes, Mrs. Susie," Oswald said, tapping his cheek with his thumb again.

That was only the beginning, and the rest turned into a long, long six months for Leon Gambel. First of all, the contractor said Oswald K. Underfoot's little house would have to be jacked into the air to put a new foundation under it before plumbing could be installed. Then the contractor said, as evidenced by the hunks of wood that fell from the house, the whole thing was only fit for demolition.

Fortunately, Mr. Ediger at the rock quarry was very happy to see him with Oswald K. Underfoot. He set it up right away to buy Oswald K. Underfoot's 20 acres with the house for additional quarrying. In so many words, he let Leon know that not only was it good to have a little more rock source, but it also would be perhaps even better to not have Oswald K. Underfoot there hollering at his workers while he shook a rifle in the air. Yes, he'd been to the Nam himself, and he didn't want the sheriff's men hauling Oswald K. Underfoot away. No, he would just ignore that the little house was there, and give full land price anyway because the rock quarry equipment could knock the little house down in short order.

Leon explained carefully to Oswald K. Underfoot for the next two days they stayed in the lambing barn again that he couldn't use the remaining $9,000 to buy dogs and more weapons.

The banker said Leon had to cosign the note for Oswald K. Underfoot to buy a mobile home and a mobile home lot. This was because even though Oswald K. Underfoot had the down payment, it wasn't acceptable to list killing domestic animal predators as his only occupation even if people did pay him to do it, and he was good at it. He also questioned Oswald K. Underfoot's mental capacity, and made the mistake of calling him Mr. Underfoot which came close to Leon's also being responsible for Oswald K. Underfoot's jail bond. But the banker said he had been in the Nam too, and that Leon could just take Oswald K. Underfoot away with him if he would be responsible for his behavior.

Leon did call Sue to ask her opinion about signing the note.

"Heck yes sign the darned thing," she said. "Just do anything you have to do for us to get this over with. I will make sure Oswald K. Underfoot pays that note off if I have to hound him into hell."

The courtship itself really tested Leon's limits. The couple spent hours cooing and giggling together on the platform swing. He never did find out what Oswald K. Underfoot meant when he said, "Ookie, ookie, ookie," and they both giggled.

Leon found Susie nearly repulsive the way she would put her arm around Oswald K. Underfoot's slim waist, and then work it up to his neck to pull him close to her bosom in a strangle-hold murmuring, "my little Ozzie."

Then there was Sue poking him in the ribs in the middle of the night saying, "What are they doing out there? What are they doing now?"

"My God, Sue, they aren't teenagers, and Buddy's out there. He can watch Oswald K. Underfoot and Susie if he can watch the sheep."

The warm fall drifted into cold winter, and then back to spring again. Praise God, Leon told himself, the end is near. No more of Sue's and Susie's nylons hanging in the bathroom together, no more Underfoots at his dinner table, and no more of those loud popping kisses when they parted company. Goodness sakes, how did the woman kiss like that. It sounded like she could pop "little Ozzie's" noggin off. Leon shuddered at the sound. Then he shuddered whenever he thought of the sound. Then he started shuddering whenever he saw the couple together. Please, God, it has to end soon.

He had to admit that Susie looked more attractive in her indigo blue wedding dress, and his Sue looked absolutely delectable in her matching bridesmaid indigo blue dress too.

"Well, do you like them?" Sue asked. "Do you like our dresses?"

"They are stunning, Sweetheart. I don't think any other color could have looked so good," Leon said. "I suppose she couldn't have worn white anyway."

"Of course not, silly. White would have emphasized her weight. Indigo blue slims her down."

"I see."

Buddy didn't like the bath. He sputtered after he bit at the soapy water, and got some down his gullet. But he did rather enjoy all of the attention from the women when they brushed his white hair out. As a matter of fact, the big dog began to hold still, enjoying everything, until the men came along with the bow tie.

Leon slipped the elastic with tie attached over Buddy's neck, and then the Great Pyrenes promptly rolled over, and began trying to rub the tie off on the carpet. "No, Buddy! Sit! Still! Leon grew evermore harsh.

But then Oswald K. Underfoot knelt down at the dog's side, raised his ear, and whispered into it for what seemed like a good 10 minutes. Buddy sat perfectly still then while they arranged the tie into just the right position.

"What did you say to Buddy? How did you get him to do that?" Leon asked.

Oswald K. Underfoot smiled in a wolfish way that Leon usually only saw when the little man was going hunting. "Oh, there are things that animals know how to say to each other that you wouldn't know about Leon Gambel. Buddy will be fine now."

And, he was.

46

The CD player played the opening cords of Hear Comes The Bride as Leon walked Susie to the head of the aisle along which sat nearly 40 guests. All eyes were on the bride. Only Leon was distracted a moment by the sight of Duallen Bureauford wearing high buckle overshoes, and seeming to be able to look up the aisle with one eye while looking down it with the other. It had been raining at Duallen's place. But then, Duallen's place always was a little different than a place belonging to someone else.

At the head of the aisle stood Sue looking regal in indigo blue with three of her friends who had agreed to be bridesmaids as an opportunity to be in a wedding, as a favor, and in order to get new dresses.

"It might be fun," they had said.

"And, it might be expensive," Sue had said.

On the other side, Buddy the Pyrenes stood right behind the groom, his friend, Oswald K. Underfoot, who was trying to smile with big tears running down his face. Nobody had told him that some people always cry at weddings, and he had never been to a wedding. Buddy was panting, but he had never been to a wedding either.

Oh great, Leon thought. I'll be third in line behind Buddy. I hope nobody says anything about that. He needn't have worried. Everybody just thought it was wonderful that a dog was included in the wedding. Leon's only trouble was matching pace with Susie who put a heavy drag on his arm when he tried to go faster down the aisle to get it over with.

It seemed that everything moved very quickly then. Oswald K. Underfoot and Susie repeated their vows. Leon had refused to hang the ring around Buddy's neck for him, so it was there in his own pocket to produce at the correct time.

Then "Maawaahsmooch-pop," there was that terrible popping kiss again after the pastor told Oswald K. Underfoot he could kiss his bride.

"Kiss the bride, kiss the bride, I give my permission!" an exultant Oswald K. Underfoot shouted to the guests.

When nobody moved forward, Leon saw to his terror that Susie was looking him in the eye. She began moving around Buddy's nose to get to him, but Buddy stepped forward one step blocking her move. When she moved the other way to go around Buddy's rear to go to Leon, Buddy turned around to block her path once more. She smiled, and shook her head at Leon then before moving off down the aisle on Oswald K. Underfoot's arm to throw her bouquet to the girls.

Leon Gambel breathed a tremendous sigh of relief. It was over.

You can't beat owning a good guard dog.

Cowtime Ritual

Only an ear turned
to catch the whispers
from the hill
above the creek
shows you are ready
for the evening cattle drive,
old horse.
Gently tuned by time
and practice you stand
while the old man
steadies himself
at your rump,
conserving his strength
for the climb to the saddle,

First he raises
one trembling knee
and then the other,
slowly unwinding
his ancient body,
to crawl
into the wooden feed bunk.

The cows are on the hillside
feeling the time for milking approach,
knowing that you will come,
grasping with last-chance greed
for more grass
while their broken-horned leader
edges them
contrarily further from home.

You shiver in your soul,
but you wait
on the struggling man
pushing his gnarly work-worn hands
on your back
to gather himself
to stand
from the weathered bunk floor.

They're the familiar old hands
that charmed and chastened you
from wobbly legs
to galloping prime
to the sturdy knees
of nearly thirty years
that could almost creak
in response to his.

Such faith that he stands there now,
one leg across the saddle,
the other leg precariously
standing in the bunk,
while he gasps
and mumbles to you.
Twenty minutes
you have stood
when he finally
fits himself
into the saddle.

Broken horn has moved
her sisters another
thousand feet up the ridge,
and your forward ears show
that you know that.
But still,
you walk with measured tread
while the man rides
in loose-reined swaying ease,
as in a front-porch rocker,
taking his pleasure in the day.

Anna Marie, You'll Be With Me

Anna Marie woke up from her nodding nap in the easy chair with a start as though someone had whispered in her ear.

She tilted her head to the right and downward so she could look up at the wall to her left around the clouded vision of the cataracts over her eyes. Then, cocking her head the other way to struggle for sight, she looked to the person in the chair to her right as though to question whether that person was seeing something too.

When the other persons showed no obvious response, Anna Marie quickly turned her head again in the awkward posture to look at the wall.

Slowly her chin came down to a normal looking position. Anna Marie's eyes came into sharp, forward focus as she began to smile with a radiance that seemed to take years off the wrinkled, lined pattern of her face. She smiled, smiled and smiled, nodding her head from time to time at the wall.

Then she turned her head to look down the hallway toward the bathroom, still focusing forward with the radiant smile that slowly turned to grinning wonder.

"Anna Marie, what is it, what are you looking at? Are you OK?" asked the other person.

"Yes, yes, I'm very fine, better than I have been for years. He has brought her to see me, my Glenda LouAnn. I have cried for her. Nothing is worse than having one of your children die before you do. And now, she is coming. Just look at the swirls of beautiful, beautiful flowers, all colors, red, yellow, pink, my, I have never seen so many colors. They're indescribable."

"What do you mean, she is coming. Are you trying to say you see a spirit?"

"That was my father on the wall. Usually when he comes, we just smile at each other, and I try to get up close to the wall to look into his eyes. We just smile and smile, it's so happy, so beautiful.

"But this time he spoke. He told me he is bringing Glenda just for me. She hasn't been there long enough to come under her own power. He had to help her. And, I can't really see her, just the flowers, the beautiful flowers. They are magnificent, so spectacular. But I know she's there. She's doing it for me."

Anna Marie looked back toward the wall. "He's laughing, he's so pleased that I can see. He's been gone since the 1930's , you know. We always had a special relationship, me and my Dad. I was his tomboy. Oh, the flowers swirling and swirling all around the room, great big spirals of them."

The sounds in the kitchen where Glenda's widower husband worked ceased.

The person in the next chair was concerned for the husband, but began questioning anyway, "Anna Marie, excuse me, but I want to ask some questions. Are they still here?"

Anna Marie paused for a few moments more in raptured silence, but then answered, "They are beginning to go. There go the last of the flowers back down the hallway. Oh, he is gone, too."

"Anna Marie, do you feel like you are well? Have you begun some new drugs, or is something happening that you are hallucinating?"

"No, I am very well. These things are very real to me, perhaps more real than you and this chair."

"You focused, almost as though you could see with greater clarity than normal."

"Oh yes, I could see them with absolute clarity, like having the vision of a child again. The colors were so bright, his face so vivid, every line of it his but without pain and aging, almost as though he had become younger."

"You said, usually when your father comes. Do you mean he has come before? How long has this been going on?"

"Yes, he comes often, more often all the time. Sometimes at night, I'll nod off watching television, and wake up. There he'll be, watching over me.

"I am 93, old enough and close enough to my own death that I figure I have been allowed to step over into the next world a little bit. It all started about a year ago. You remember? We were in Southwestern Iowa to get nursery stock. We stopped at a restaurant for lunch.

"We were starting into the door when this woman went in right ahead of us. It startled me she was so different, and I couldn't explain to myself the way she moved."

"What do you mean? Different how?"

"Well, she was dressed all in black like a woman of the 1800's, with a black hat on like a proper widow. And she seemed to float as she walked, about a foot off the floor. And, that's not all. When we got in the door, she kept right on going across the floor instead of waiting to be seated. I couldn't believe it, but she floated on up higher at a slant, and went right out the ceiling. It was amazing.

"I didn't have the time to keep thinking about it because there were others, some of them trying to talk to the people who were at the tables, but they couldn't hear them. The strangest ones were a group of children in the aisle who kept trying to talk, and take hold of the people coming through. But the people didn't seem to hear them at all, and worse yet, would walk right through them as though they weren't even there. I was shaken. But when we left the restaurant, there were no more of them. Everything was back to normal although I became a little hungry later because I hadn't eaten much."

"But you are saying that wasn't the end of it."

"No, about a month later in the living room, I looked up, and there was the full profile silhouette of a man. I was terrified, and immediately filled with grief. I was sure it was my son, Robert, and he had been killed in some accident, and was there to say goodbye. But I called him, and he was OK. At that moment, I knew who it had been, my husband, my Bud, there to look over me. He and Robert looked a lot alike in profile, same nose, forehead and chin shapes.

"A few nights later, his shadow came back on the wall. I felt the warmth, the tenderness. I whispered to him how good it felt to have him there. I longed to be near him, and started to the wall to put my hand on him. But he withdrew, disappeared, and I was left with a sense that he was afraid it could hurt me if I touched him. He only came back a couple more times, but I couldn't bear not trying to be near him. He never came back again, but I know he's here somewhere watching.

"You are a person who loves me, and knows me well. Whatever else you might think, you know that I would always tell you the truth."

"Anna Marie, I know you would always tell me the truth of what you see. You could even be crazy, but I don't believe you are. I will always believe that you see what you tell me you see, and you are telling me the truth."

"Good then. I will tell you the rest. It was about a month after that when our Glenda died. I cried, and I cried, and I cried. We all miss her so much. I would sit alone at night, and hold her picture. When I saw her children, I cried inside for their sakes.

"That's when my Dad came. I was sitting holding her picture, and his face appeared on the wall, so clear, so wonderful. I haven't been able to see anybody that clearly for a long, long time. His eyes were so full of compassion. He understood how I felt as though he could see into my thoughts. He was there to comfort me, telling me that it wouldn't be that terribly long before I was with him, not that long before I would hug Glenda again. I guess it was as though I could see into his thoughts a little, too, although I don't think as clearly as he could see. It's like these cataracts. The thoughts were obscured, only partly there.

"Now my Dad comes often, maybe once a week. He brings her and the flowers often for me."

"Have you told anybody else about this, Anna Marie."

"Only, my brother, but he tells me not to tell it to anyone else, or people will think I am insane. It might make him look bad too, you know."

"Anna Marie, I love you, and I believe you."

"I know you do, I know you would, or I wouldn't have told you."

That was March. Anna Marie died later, in the fall, after suffering terribly from chronic heart failure. But her corpse had a slight smile on it that the undertaker hadn't erased.

The person still believes her. He was with Glenda's husband 25 years later shortly before he died.

"Glenda has been to see me," her husband said.

"Yes," said the person not sure whether it was really him or the influence of the morphine that spoke. "How did you know it was her?"

"Why, the flowers. It was the flowers. They just came swirling in big spirals down the hallway."

Sometimes the person now sits alone at night looking through a glass darkly wondering what he might see some day. He hopes it includes flowers, great swirls of flowers.

Vagabond Heart

Soliloquy by evening
under the chilling purple
of the darkening mist
settling in the treetops
that frosts in place
the freezing uncertainty
of the vagabond heart
that flows over the space
where this person
once lived a life,
Steadily it encircles,
entwining in its branches,
the unbelieving mind
telling it without mercy
that no longer is there home,
no longer is there care.
There is only the space
of a wide, unquestioning world
that really doesn't care
if this soul
was meant to be,
leaving it rootless
and falling.

Call out over the tumult,
you who would believe,
through the icing deep
of this consuming forest
lest this vagabond heart
fails to set its
latest victim free.
Pierce through
 the enshrouding fogs
of confusion and grief
that before the
foundations of time,
this person was meant to be,
and will return with me.

Harlan Medlam
Milks A Mudhole

June had been a wet month, and despite the fact that water made the crops grow fast in the humid, heavy air of hot summer, it made Harlan Medlam cross.

He heard the little boys calling to each other from the neighboring pasture as they walked the timbered trail along the creek that would take them up to the grassy hillside where Paul's milk cows grazed.

It only made him grumble more because it was time for him to get cows, too. Florence would be scolding him if they were late getting the cows milked, no excuses for the fact that they both were in their 80's.

The knowledge only made it tougher for him to raise one bony leg over the edge of the wooden feed bunk.

"Hold still, gul darn ya," he snapped at his old mare, Molly, who stood saddled and bridled along the bunk, and who hadn't moved a muscle. "Hold still, doggone ya, I said ya ol' hussy," Harlan Medlam hollered as he paused on hands and knees in the feed bunk after getting his legs over the side.

The old red bay mare with the long black stockings wasn't about to move because deep in the recesses of her horse mind, she knew the secret. Harlan Medlam loved horses.

He was the same old man that held her in his arms as a foal when she imprinted on him. Now, as a 20-year-old horse, she took care of him, somehow instinctively knowing that the frail body of the old man shouldn't be able to take a hit if she moved from him while he crawled from the feed bunk to her back.

Harlan Medlam only took hits that paid off. "There goes Harlan Medlam to the field," neighbors would say when they heard the high-pitched squeals of iron on iron from his ungreased machinery. Harlan Medlam didn't like to grease machinery—too much expense.

But he took good care of horses, even if it took him half a day to get a hoof raised over his knee to pick it out. The big, black workhorse and the big, white workhorse, which worked as a team to pull him through the fields on the days when he couldn't bear to take a tractor out again, watched him silently over the corral fence as he raised a hand, puffing for wind, to grasp the base of the mane on the blood-red mare with the black feet.

"Mind yer own business," Harlan snarled at all the horse adoration as he peeked over the back of the mare at the distant hillside.

"Old biddy, old biddy," he said gazing through the distance at the broken-horn Texas Hereford leading the herd of Jerseys, Guernseys and

Holsteins further up the hill. She knew it was time for him to come, and she would make the journey home as long as possible through contrariness.

He hardly remembered why Florence had steered the low-yielding wild Hereford into the milk barn to join the dairy herd, but it was because the woman noted the cow's freshened udder after having a calf, and she seized the chance to get a bigger milk check.

"Quit yer gul darn prancing around, darn yer heavy thick-skulled stupid soul, ya big dummy," Harlan said as he stood with one leg over the saddle, one foot still planted in the bunk, his hands grasping the saddle horn where his rope was looped, gasping "woo, whish, woo," for more air.

Harlan Medlam couldn't rope like a cowboy. He only carried the rope like a braided tool to pull something.

The mare had her ears forward, turning her eyes toward the hill where the cows moved. "Look at the old biddy moving farther away," Harlan said as he finally sat his seat in the saddle, and rested a moment. "Well, what are ya still standing here for, horse? Ya gonna rest all day? Chic, chic, Molly."

The mare moved purposefully in a long walking stride. Harlan barely gripped the reins as they set off down the slope to the creek, the sweet scents of dense greenery wafting on the updraft coming up to them.

Molly's hooves sunk slightly, so wet was the earth, occasionally turning up a slice of grass clump or beads of mud. She waded through the creek at the stone-bottomed crossing point.

Harlan grumbled, "Easy now, easy now," as splashes of the swollen white-water soaked his trouser cuffs."

"Sss-Boss, Sss-Boss," came the cattle call from Paul's boys, Jesse and Ben, who had already crossed the creek in the neighboring pasture.

The little toads moved pretty fast, walking on short legs, Harlan thought. God bless himself that he had a horse to ride instead of trying to walk after cows every morning and night to satisfy the perpetual need he and Florence had for more money. Some people might think walking was good for health, but Harlan Medlam was sure walking a mile each morning and evening to get cows was only that much more work.

Taking naps in between was what made a man's health. He already was dozing to the rhythmic sway of the horse, and Molly flicked her ears at a couple of his more drawn-out snores. Yes, Harlan Medlam could ride a horse in his sleep so accustomed to it was he.

"Ya watch where yer goin', ya knucklehead," Harlan said as he snapped out of his slumber when a tree twig brushed his face. Molly had stuck to the path, and they were moving out of the timber to the grassy hillsides.

Harlan pulled a cigar stub out of his pocket to chew as they made their way to the back fence line. Yes, there was old broken horn, crowded with the rest of the herd as far away from them as she could get. "The old biddy," he said, spitting out some tobacco and the invective.

The ride back behind the cows went like usual, the mare stepping out slightly faster, her ears moving forward and backward in needed threat to the cows who knew the path home to the milk barn very well. Back across the creek, and up the slope, Harlan Medlam heard the boy's call. "Haalp! Help me, Jesse, Haalp!"

Harlan turned Molly toward the neighboring fence line while the mare inclined slightly sideways from time to time trying to watch the cows walking on up the path in case one of them made a break to back to the hill.

"HELP ME!" came the call more strongly. Harlan looked over the fence, mumbling to himself at the sight of the situation, and thinking maybe he just ought to go on. There was a seep out of a hillside on Paul's pasture just above the pathway. In rainy times it turned a 30-foot-wide swath of earth into a water-covered mudhole where the cows stomped through with their hooves to create a mud-sucking quagmire.

There was brown-haired Ben in the middle of the mud, sunk to above his knees. His older blonde brother, Jesse, was extending a stick to him to take hold of to try to pull him out.

"What's the matter with you? Why are you hollering help?" Harlan Medlam called to the boys.

"It's Ben," said Jesse, the 9-year-old. "He's stuck in the mud, and he can't get out."

Ben, the 6-year-old, was standing in the gooshy mess, big tears running down his cheeks. The boys were flushed hot and tired, and occasionally swatted at gnats and biting green flies swarming around their ears.

The gnats and flies were beginning to buzz at Harlan Medlam, too, and Molly wiggled her ears, and swished her tail at them.

"Well, just pull your feet up, and walk out of it. You can do it," said Harlan Medlam. "You don't need help. Hold still, Molly, gul darn ya."

"He can't pull his feet up, or he'll lose his shoes. They're near-new shoes," said Jesse as Ben rubbed a finger across his nose, pausing his tears to look hopefully at Harlan.

"Get in there, and help him, can't you? Feel down there where his shoes are, and when he pulls his feet out, you grab his shoes. Can't you do that?"

"I tried, and I get stuck, too. I barely was able to get out with my shoes. I'm just not strong enough. What are you going to do?"

"What am I going to do? You think I got all day to watch your troubles? I tell you, just pull your feet out of the shoes. Feel where they are, and pull them up. Walk out of there!"

The little boy struggled, balancing with his arms out to his sides while he tried to pull one leg up. It seemed held solidly until it finally gave way in a slow "whoosh" that ended in a jerk that plopped him over head-first into the water.

Ben pushed himself up, gasping, then wailing, his tears hidden by the green-brown slime that covered his face.

The cows on both sides of the dividing pasture fence stood at the gates that would open to send them to their milk barns. They turned to stare with cow curiosity at the human drama.

"Oh, darn, darn, darn," said Harlan Medlam. "Is your shoe there? Can you find your shoe?"

"It's here, it's here," sobbed Ben, squatting his small body to feel in the mud. "It's here Harlan Medlam, but I can't get it out. Please get my Daddy."

"What are we going to do? What are we going to do?" wailed Jesse, beginning to cry too. "We can't leave him here while we get Daddy. The mud might suck him clear down. What if it's quicksand?"

"It ain't quicksand. It's just plain old mud. Quit your silly talk, you'll scare the little fella. Calm down. I'm coming. I'm coming. Darn, darn, darn, see what's happenin' to us, ya big, dumb horse. Let me get the cows through the gates, and I'll ride my horse around there. You two boys just stand there. Don't do anything. And quit your squalling. Doggone, I can't take that. Just quit crying. You're big boys. It will take me a while. Have some nerve. I'll be there. Come on, Molly, chic, chic, chic.

"Doggone it, Florence Medlam will be fit to be tied if the milkin's late. I can't wait on Paul to get here. Gonna have cows moanin' with full bags," Harlan Medlam said, fuming so much at the situation that he threw a leg over the mare, and slid to the ground at the gates like a young man.

He left the mare, drop-reined in the path where old broken horn might try to turn back, and opened the gates for both his and Paul's cows. He watched them go through for the rest of the walk to their barns, and closed the gates behind them, but not before leading the mare back through into Paul's pasture.

Harlan Medlam knotted the reins over the saddle horn, and walked stiff-legged down the slope, the mare following him like a big dog, to where Ben stood in the mudhole. Both boys stared at him somberly, their tears dried up, waiting expectantly for his next move.

"This is a fine mess you boys have gotten us into. Florence will be furious with me. And what am I going to do if I wade out there after

you, and I flop over in the mud at my age? Are you going to get me out?"
he pointed at Jesse.

"No, sir," Jesse said. "I don't think I can pull you out if I can't pull
Ben out."

"Well, it seems the only one here to help you is me, since your Daddy
hasn't come to help you. Jesse, you walk clear around this mudhole.
Don't try to go through it. I don't want two of you stuck. I'll get my rope
out. I'll loop it on the saddle horn, and square-knot it around my waist.
You just stand there near Molly. Give you something to think about.
Harlan Medlam toed his own boots and socks off. "No use getting
them muddy too," he said as he gripped the soft earth tentatively with
his toes. "Now hold still, gul darned yer hide, ya old hussy. Quit yer
movin' around," he hollered at the stock-still mare whose only response
was to turn her ears forward at him. Now ya hold still, too, gul durn ya
boy. I'm comin', I'm comin'."

The fondness he held for horses came out in like language when talking to the boy. Harlan Medlam held onto the rope like it was a walking
stick, him wobbling stiffly from side to side as he splashed slowly into
the sticky mud. "Darned flies," he snorted through his nose as he waved
a hand at his ears. "Boy they're pesky when a man's got trouble. If they
don't eat me alive, Florence Medlam is a'goin' to. You don't slack off
around that woman."

When he came to the boy, the mud sucking up over his own ankles, he
got down on his knees. Harlan Medlam shook his head, muttering as he
felt the water soak through the seat of his overalls, and reached down to
probe with his fingers around the little boy's feet.

"OK, I got your shoes. Step out of them, Ben. God, how did I get into
this situation," Harlan said as Ben struggled to get his feet free by putting his arms around Harlan's neck to nearly pull his face to the water.

"Hang on, hang on ya little bugger—I got yer shoes. I'm going to sit
down here in the mud, and you just hang on me because I got your shoes
to hold, and I can't carry you out. We'll let old Molly do the work now.

"Back, Molly. Back up. I say back slow there, you old dummy. Molly
back up."

Harlan Medlam felt the rope tighten, and involuntarily said,
"ooomph" as he began to be towed backward through the slick mud
with the boy adding a drag to his neck and shoulders.

As his seat hit solid ground, Harlan hollered, "Hold still there, gul
darned ya! Whoa! Gul darned ya old dummy quit yer movin' around.
Whoa there, gul darned ya."

Molly had held still when she heard the first "hold still" order.

"Here, you boys, help me to my feet. Careful now, careful how hard
you pull on my arms. I just hurt all over. That was miserable for an old
man coming to the rescue. I'm just wore out now, you boys with your

mud and all. Doggone it, Florence Medlam's going to make my life miserable tonight with all her...Hey, wait a minuteÖ"

Harlan Medlam smiled. He looked at the mud that covered most of his body. "I might as well make something of this."

"Jesse, you run home. Get your Daddy. Tell him Harlan Medlam has rescued your little brother from the sucking mud that was about to pull him under."

This was near as serious as a drowning, Harlan smiled. "Tell him Harlan Medlam is just played out, not well at all himself from the strain that nearly killed him getting your little brother out. Tell your Daddy, he needs to get up here quick to help Florence Medlam milk her cows before he milks his own because Harlan Medlam is laid up.

"Then you run to Florence Medlam. Tell her the same thing. Tell her your Daddy is coming to help get the milking done fast, and not to worry because Harlan Medlam and Ben are coming on the horse. They're'just strained, and wore out is all. Tell Florence to get Harlan Medlam's ' pillow out on the bench because he needs it bad, the rescue strained him bad. You got all this, Jesse? You need me to tell you again?"

Harlan Medlam watched with satisfaction at Jesse running away fast, then led Molly to a fallen log. He gave Ben a boost to his seat as the boy climbed first onto the log, and then onto the front of the saddle.

"Hold still there gul darn ya," Harlan Medlam said, grinning in satisfaction as he struggled onto the log to slowly get a leg over the saddle himself.

"Ben, you know what pathetic means? Well, we need to look pathetic, real sorry-like when we ride old Molly into the driveway at my place. That's right, great big frown like you might cry. Good, good.

"Chic, chic, chic, Molly, let's get home. I'm late for my nap, ya old hussy."

When Dark Chaos Overcomes Me

When dark chaos overcomes me,
tearing deeply to open my breast,
then He caresses my weak soul,
and peace overflows me,
like a river in the flood
washing away the debris,
the overwhelming frustrations
of black entangling clutter.

And when the flood subsides,
the channel cleared revealed,
great springs of purest water
well up from the depths
of the whirling spirit,
and there is joy overwhelming,
like lightning over the tumult
that bids the beast decease.

Creation released abundantly,
the happiness is rushing
In bountiful streams within,
of safety and security,
the deep water's great
and caring Friend.

A Flower Girl Sister Surprise

The flowers of youth are fresh and fragrant.

But with age, they can whither to become stale burdens upon the shoulders of those they once blessed.

The Fauntweth sisters were consumed in flowers.

Their flower-patterned bonnets bobbed nearly in unison as the sisters knelt together pulling young weeds from among the profusion of small self-seeded petunias. They were the flowers that would later tumble in copious vines to cover their portion of the banks with white and lavender flowers.

Flowers always cascaded in abundance down the black-earth banks below where their white stucco bungalow with the wide front porch stood. The house was roofed with blue-gray shingles so it was like a third bonnet-covered sister.

Alva and Elsa Fauntweth resembled their bonnet-covered mother who decades earlier had worked with hoe and pruning shears in her yard on the upper crest of the valley road, back during the Eisenhower presidency. They preserved some of her bonnets, and still hand-sewed themselves new bonnets just as she had shown them to do. Their mother herself had preserved the bonnet habit from her own mother from before the Hoover presidency along with the long sleeves and low dress hems that protected them from the sun.

The sisters worked with trowel and hoe, planting and weeding dozens of kinds of clematis, honeysuckle, red cardinal, trumpet and other vines they trained over a variety of trellises. New marigolds, zinnias, cosmos, bachelor's buttons, portulacas and sedums always graced the slopes alongside the beds of iris and lilies, a continual kaleidoscope picture of yellows, oranges, pinks, reds and blues.

Yet, the Fauntweth sisters never seemed to really sweat as they worked, pausing from time to time to sponge a thin bead of moisture from their pink-blushed pale faces with the flower-patterned handkerchiefs they carried in their pockets. To actually sweat might have caused one them to open a perpetually non-smiling, but still happy thin-lipped mouth, to declare in all propriety that it was time for a glass of water in the shade.

Elsa had once married an older fifth cousin, also named Fauntweth, recommended to her by a second cousin, and had had a son, Elmo, who seldom visited the sisters because he had other things to do. She had always admired the Roosevelt presidency, and the fact that Eleanor had married her cousin, Franklin, both also named Roosevelt before.

Alva, 77, had never married although from time to time her stern blue eyes could show twinkles that might attract attention. One could surmise that once upon a time they had attracted attention. But that was a faded flower of long ago.

The week that surprised Elsa began here, in the flowers with the sisters on their knees, when she said to Alva, "You know, I believe it is our turn to provide some flower bouquets for church next Sunday."

"Yes, Dear," replied Alva, "and I do believe we will be required to do a number of extra bouquets. You will recall that there will be a celebration of Cyrus Wethberger's 100th birthday immediately following the service."

"That's right. It will be a special time for the old fellow. He must be very lonely living there all alone, his mother gone now for what, 30 years? How does he manage? He never married, but at 100 years old, he would have had a fair chance of being alone at this time even if he had. He is a little like us. He lost his only sister and her husband many years ago. He has great nieces and nephews, but I suppose they are remote from his life. It's always been said they have other things to do."

"Yes, I suppose they do. But, never say never, Sister. And, I suppose he manages because he has to."

"Well, you call me sister, and there's been no tiff."

"I add it only for emphasis because of the importance of this moment."

And why might it be more important than the last moment or the next moment?"

"Well, you recall that Cyrus Wethberger and his mother were always kind to us as children, have been good to us as friends, and they always were good neighbors."

"Certainly, certainly, they would fall under every admonition the good Lord gave to be good neighbors, and they were always fun too. Mrs. Wethberger was outstanding with her dahlias."

"Yes, she was. So, after the celebration of his birthday next Sunday, I shall marry Cyrus Wethberger."

"That shall be interesting Sister, and I must emphasize that I too only say sister in the importance of the moment. And what do you think Cyrus Wethberger's great nieces and great nephews will say to this union? Why, Sister, they could accuse you of being a gold digger since you are a much younger woman, and, I might add, still very attractive."

"Thank you, Sister, but I think they will say very little because Cyrus Wethberger has already deeded his home and farm to them. I will have no hand in his accounts. He shall come to our house after service, and the three of us shall dine in the front room as usual. Naturally, I will help wipe his mouth off, and see to his needs, so you will have little care."

"I shall appreciate that since although I still see his good looks and kindliness, old age isn't always the most pleasing thing if you are the

hand attempting to average the attention to infirmities for the apprecia-
tion of those who also eat. I assume he has asked you to marry him, and
you have no difficulty concerning the possible attitudes of others?"

"As for our fellow Congregationalists, Sister, I would wager they will
say it was worth waiting for, and only a small leap from being trans-
formed from a Fauntweth to a Wethberger."

"Sister, do I recall correctly that not only were the Wethbergers good
neighbors, but that Cyrus Wethberger showed a great deal of interest in
visiting with you when you were perhaps, say 16 or 17, a most delicate
age for a girl although an age when the interests of other persons in her
are heightened."

"Yes, I suppose we did visit a great deal. I always enjoyed the company of Cyrus Wethberger."

"But, Sister, at the time didn't our mother determine that you were
indeed at a delicate age when it might not behoove everybody for the
attentions of an older man like Cyrus Wethberger to be diverted visiting with a younger girl such as yourself?"

"Yes, Sister, I suppose our mother did determine some such injunc-
tion."

"Well, Sister, I believe our mother might have even extended such
concern to visiting with Cyrus Wethberger and his mother about it."

"Yes, Sister, I suppose that might have been true . But I don't want to
dwell in the past now. Let's just say that I have always regretted that I
didn't get to visit a great deal more throughout the years with Cyrus
Wethberger. I always found his intellect bountiful. His knowledge of
gardening was very thorough. Indeed, he and his mother have always
seemed as though they might have been family."

"What will you do after all these years, Alva, if Cyrus Wethberger, to
try to put this delicately, desires to be intimate?"

"You were as delicate as the petals of a rose, dear Elsa. I hardly think
I need to concern myself about that, but in case consideration of such a
situation occurs, I will determine my attitude at that moment, and you
will hardly need to concern yourself about it either."

Sunday was a beautiful day with Elsa and Alva providing no fewer
than 30 flower bouquets dominated by sweet smelling purple lilacs
throughout the broad, brown plank-board sanctuary with its great
stained-glass window showing Christ leading lambs.

Cyrus Wethberger was led like a lamb himself by two younger men,
so he wouldn't stumble, to a front pew where half-way through the service, his great pale, round, bald head sunk to his chest, and he slept.

But, before he slept he smiled through half-folded eyes upon his stunning bride-to-be, Alva, in a white gown her mother had left with pink-
flowered blue shawl and a white bonnet with pink flowers sewn in it,
her own white hair tightly coiffured to look like part of the decoration.

The bouquets, fresh and fragrant like the joy of youth, were spread around again in the fellowship hall as the congregation sang happy birthday to Cyrus Wethberger who stood to hold himself against the back of a chair, beaming even though breathing shallowly.

"I must thank you all," Cyrus struggled to speak softly, "for being my family in fellowship today after a century of life." He looked at Alva and Elsa, "There is nothing more important in life than to love, and to be loved."

The two young men supported him as Cyrus held Alva's hand during a brief ceremony marrying them in the sight of God. Everybody ate cake, and drank punch.

Afterwards, Alva drove the car home while Cyrus sat beside her, sleeping with his chin against his chest as he breathed very slowly, and Elsa rode in the back seat.

Elsa had prepared roast beef and vegetables which she and Alva ate heartily while Cyrus mostly sat at the table occasionally turning to look at each of them smiling.

"You know," he said, "my mother loved you two. She always said you were the prettiest, most well-behaved little girls she had ever seen. I'm only sorry it took me growing to 100 to admit that I loved you both too. And now we're family."

Elsa couldn't help but bat her eyes a few extra times as her sister used a napkin to wipe Cyrus Wethberger's mouth while the two of them stared into each other's eyes. She thought to herself more than once that it would require her attention to adjust to the presence that had always been down the road being in her home instead.

After dinner, she helped Alva move Cyrus to a front porch chair, and said, "You sit out here together while I clean up. After all, this is an evening you should celebrate."

The sun began its descent to finally disappear as a red ball shining through wispy clouds as Elsa occasionally peaked through a window at the two people sitting side by side on the porch. At times, she saw them holding hands.

Finally as the stars shined to pinpoints of light in the sky, and the night sounds of intensifying frog song and occasional owl hoots grew, Elsa opened the door. "Would you like some hot tea?" she asked.

"I will have a cup, thank you," Alva answered.

"What about Cyrus? Isn't he beginning to chill?"

"Cyrus Wethberger passed away about an hour ago, Sister. I heard his last breath while he was sleeping."

"Oh, Alva, I'm so sorry, your wedding night and everything," said Elsa glancing over at Cyrus who in the dark only appeared to be sleeping.

"No, you don't understand, Elsa. It only goes to show what a fine person you are that you didn't need to ask more questions. This is what Cyrus wanted. He knew he would be dying, and told me he would hold it off until this moment if I was willing. Cyrus said he knew he was going on to be with the Lord, but he wanted to be with family when he did it. He didn't want to die lonely, Sister.

"We'll wait another half-hour before we call anyone. Just give us a moment more to be together. Then we'll need a good night's sleep because I want us to dig a dahlia bed tomorrow to remember Cyrus."

Chopper Ride

Entering the helicopter
the metal's slick,
no handholds
for the maiden voyage
that leaves knuckles
gripping white
on rifles in row.

Eyes roll
under steel pots
over sandpaper tongues,
salt streaked white
on backs of olive drab
from hours of running
on low water.

Trees of sparkling
summer green dance
in life and death below,
no drinkers of blood
despite what the Captain says.

Four hours of sleep
is never enough,
patriotism's a game
that's tough to play
for my brothers
who share my pain.

Hovering over the edge
for the final plunge,
count out the paces
to the woods,

I hope I never have to kill.

Yes, Even A Horse Trader
Can Have A Soul

There was a time not so many years ago when Charmin' Carmen the horse trader began to feel regret about some of the ways he had treated his friend, Will the rancher.

It was for real. It wasn't a story of middle earth, a Grimm's fairy tale, a Tolkien story or something where Tarzan or Superman was offended by misdeeds. Yes, even horse traders began to have souls when some of their sneak-thievery was passed on to car salesmen and politicians.

Charmin' Carmen was just feeling really, sincerely regretful about the time he helped Will out by buying a good saddle horse from him, having it die right there on the ranch before he could haul it away, and making a tremendous profit from it by putting raffle jars on the horse in convenience stores with a picture on each one showing it in good condition. Participants could put their names and addresses in the jar with a dollar attached to each entry. True, he had given the winner his dollar back. But, deep down, he felt Will should have gotten more out of it, too.

As for the participants in the raffle, Carmen wasn't advanced enough in the soul business to feel very badly about them. As he told his wife,Frances, "Well gamblers is sinners, ain't they? Nothin' can be wrong in taking advantage of their natural proclivities. They was created for the whickerin', weren't they? Poor old Carmen was just there to provide it for them. I got to make a living, don't I?"

He would have done the same for somebody moving out from the city who wanted a "gentle horse."

"They want to be close to nature don't they, sweetheart? Well, old Carmen is part of nature. I'm here to meet their needs. They're only going to pay attention to it for a little while anyway. Then they'll put it out on a small acreage to graze, and they'll half starve it because they don't understand grazing rates, how many acres of grass it takes to feed a horse.

"When it gets really thin, I'll come along to tell them it's sick, buy it back for a fraction of what they paid me for it, fatten it back up, and sell it again. I love them people and their money. If I see them getting serious about horses, I'll come back to tell them we made a mistake with that one, and make it right with them, upsell them on the first horse and the next one too. See, Hon, I really do meet their needs."

Will deserved his best. Way back, he sold Will a horse that was too green, and bragged about what a good cow pony it already was. Then there was the time he sold Will's wife a pet goat that got to nibbling their fruit trees until it stripped them off. No use yapping at them about the lead rope training and pet training that went into that goat. They'd paid a premium for it, and then had the good sense to serve it at a barbeque.

Gosh, for every two times he had done right by Will, he had skinned him a little on the trade in between—too many horses sold Will that were either too young or too old. What if Will wouldn't deal with him anymore? Or, worse yet, what if he considered him a crook instead of a friend. Carmen couldn't bear the thought. What if Will actually considered him a liar? Well, no use dwelling on his own natural proclivities.

So, there was the situation. He had to do something good for Will, and Carmen decided he had to do it right away before it was too late.

He and Frances had bought a dozen prime young Quarter Horse geldings from Clarklin Blarklin, one of the better Quarter Horse breeders in the region, a no-nonsense kind of an old boy who put out the kind of cow-sense horses needed on real ranches. Carmen had noticed one young sorrel right away with a special combination of energy and intelligence in the lustrous, large brown eyes.

"Look at him, just look at that one, Frances," he said, nodding at the sorrel. "That's one special young Quarter Horse there, ain't he though?

"Look at the way he's started prancing around the corral, knows we're talking about you don't you fellow. Lookee there, Frances, he's broke into a gallop. I tell you that's one smart colt. When he slows down, look at the way he still dances sideways on his toes.

"That's a lot of spirit. He dances like a flamingo. That's what I'ma gonna do. I'm going to name that cow pony Flamingo, and I'll make a special deal on him to old Will just cuz Will deserves it after all his dealings with me in the past.. Only, don't tell any of the Quarter Horse men that I called one of their own a pony."

"Well, that's commendable, Carmen, giving Will a special deal," said Frances. "I like it that you have that in you, to do someone right after all of these years. But don't you know it's bad luck to name a horse you're raising to sell? At least, that's what you always tell me."

"I know, I know, but it's special for Will. He'll know that I know that horse is really special since I gave him a name. Have you been workin' him in the round pen?"

"Oh, yes, and you're right he's a special one. He caught on right away to come to me. I've even been up on him a couple of time. He never offered a buck or sideways flinch. And Ernest has had him out riding across the pasture two or three times."

"Is that right? How did he do for Ernest?"

" About the same, except he wanted to dance or shy when something didn't look right or he wasn't familiar with it. Ernest said he jumped hard when he went past the windmill, and it turned in a fresh wind."

"That settles it then. It's only two miles over to Will's house. I'll ride Flamingo over there tomorrow. It's far enough just to take the beginning edge off him. Will can notice what an addition young Flamingo can be when even I trust my hide to him when he's just green-broke."

"There, you said it right there, Carmen, trusting your hide to him when he's just green-broke. Do you think that's very wise for you to ride him over there like that? What if he spooks, and you take a spill. You're no spring chicken any more. You can get head banged or break a bone."

Carmen clenched his long white teeth together in a big open smile on his broad Siouxian face, and let his big brown eyes sparkle in their best practiced trader light. "Now, Honey Bunch, you know old Carmen is always careful. No young horse like this here Flamingo is gonna get the best of me.

"I'll take it easy, and just enjoy the ride. It can be so relaxin' to get up early in the morning, ride in the cool of the day's first sunshine while your head throbs cookin' up deals. It'll just be a special time for me. And, I'll really be lookin' for that smile on old Will's face when he realizes what I'm doin' just for him."

So it was the next morning that Frances helped Carmen saddle and bridle the young Flamingo after the horse had been around a few times in the round pen to take any edge off him. Carmen even tied a canteen of water to the saddle horn. No sense being dry.

Frances held Flamingo's bridle while Carmen put one foot in the stirrup, and grabbed the saddle horn to swing the other leg over the horse, mounting rather gracefully for a heavy man. Flamingo exuded a heavy breathing sigh as Carmen settled into the saddle.

"He's saying you're a little heavy, I think, Carmen," Frances said. She opened the gate. "Now you be careful, old man."

"You know I'm always careful, gotta be," Carmen replied as the colt stepped out to walk down the driveway. "Hey, old Flamingo's good ain't he, a swell colt, got a long stride to him."

The young horse seemed to pick it up right away to walk down the gravel road on the paths worn smooth by car tires. Carmen was pleased. Flamingo tried to turn around twice whinnying so loudly his body shook to call back to the other colts he was leaving behind. But Carmen just used the reins to keep him turning until he was facing the right direction to go again.

Flamingo finally just put his ears forward in curiosity as he stretched into a long ground-eating walk, waiting to see what that next tree was blowing in the wind. Three times he tried to break into a trot, but Carmen easily held him in.

The man easily petted Flamingo once above the shoulder murmuring, "Yes, you're a good old colt, ain't you, Flamingo. You're smart, and you're going to make a good old cow pony for Will."

Off down the road, Will was too busy to have been thinking about Carmen because he, a veterinarian and a couple of cowhands were busy running cattle through a squeeze chute, giving them shots and working them over. He had been thinking about Carmen lately, but the weathered old straight-shooting rancher was thinking about his horse trading friend in ways that might have confirmed Carmen's fears.

Will was feeling badly because he decided he'd done something wrong by taking money from Carmen for a horse he'd known was already dead. He felt more than doubly bad when he thought about how Carmen had raffled off the dead horse, and made a big bunch of money from unsuspecting people, even if he had given the winner his dollar back. The whole experience was beginning to turn into a chronic guilt burden that sometimes woke Will up at night, leaving him running his fingers through his red hair, and shaking his head.

To compound Will's troubles, he was beginning to wonder if Carmen really might be a crafty crook instead of a relatively good natured old horse trader, and he might be pausing to hook his thumbs in his belt loops somewhere, and chuckle to a group of listeners how Will had out-traded him—the dreaded credibility of a crook labeling him a crook.

So, when he saw Carmen riding a young sorrel gelding toward the working pens, he felt a sense of fatigue over trying to get his work done, and now here was this trader to try to stress him further with his presence. He tried to ignore that Carmen was there, keeping his back to him at first, but then decided to acknowledge him, and find a way to send him away.

"Hi Carmen, what is it? I'm awfully busy here right now. Don't have time to talk," he said, looking up at the big, broad man in the saddle.

"That's OK, Will, but first look at him, just look at him, this Quarter Horse colt I brought over for you to see. Look at that smart head, Will, don't it just say cow sense all over it? I tell you this here horse, Flamingo that I named myself is prime, one of best you or I will ever see. I saw you look. Didn't you notice the way he was striding out with me, eager, beautiful. "

"I'm not looking to buy a cow horse today, Carmen."

"But, Will, I tell you from the bottom of my heart," Carmen said leaning out over the saddle horn to try to look Will in the face as intently as he could for emphasis, "he's already yours. It's time for me to make up to you the times whenever I might have gotten the best of you in a deal. You can pay me what you think is fair for him, or you can just have him free, what ever you think is right. You ain't gonna hear this often from old Carmen in this life, Will, but you're my friend. And, this is your chance to feel right about me and you.

"Ain't you gonna say anything, Will? You're just standing there lookin' at me like someone run a knife through your gizzard. I'm tellin' you this here horse is yours. Surprised you too much, I reckon, didn't I?"

71

"Look, Carmen," Will said looking into the other man's huge grin, "I am not saying right now that I am or I am not taking this horse. I'm just too busy right now. You've caught me off-balance. I'll talk to you later though. I really will talk to you about it. Maybe you could do me a favor while we're getting this done if you were planning to spend some time here anyway."

"Sure, Will. You just name it. Ol' Carmen is here for you today, gonna make any bad times go away."

"Well, you better hear me first. What I want, since you're already mounted up on a good horse, if you're up to it, is to ride up into the hills on my north quarter to look at a bunch of new calves we just dumped on grass there yesterday. You know, just make sure they're still there, and didn't get to running, and go through a fence or anything."

Will smiled a little despite himself. He knew that he was sending Carmen on quite a ride when the man, not used to being a cowhand himself, probably already was beginning to tire.

"That's quite a ride, ain't it Will?" asked Carmen, therefore confirming the other man's thoughts.

"Yeah, but that's the deal here. You know I don't have time to talk this minute."

"Well, hey, I'm just glad to be able to help you out."

Once he got started, Carmen found the additional riding began to add immensely to the pleasure of the day on such a fine young horse. The pathway to the north took him almost immediately over a small hill where Flamingo had to wade belly-deep through a tall stand of prairie cordgrass brushing his sides. It was a wet slough area where the muddy water came up through the grass around the horse's hooves.

It began to excite Flamingo, and he tried to dance sideways, Carmen reassuring him, "Hoa, ho," and tightening on the reins to hold him in a bit.

Again the colt straightened out as though confident of the support of his rider, and Carmen petted his neck reassuringly. "Lord, but you're a fine young horse. I almost wish I wasn't born to be a trader, and could keep you myself."

Carmen became so confident, he began to trot Flamingo even though he sensed the horse was excited by this trip into the open grasslands. He alternated trotting and then walking, Carmen relaxing in the seat balance that treated sitting a horse like a rocking chair. Flamingo shied once when a covey of quail flew up from an adjoining plum thicket. "You'll get over that though, won't you old Flamingo. Yes, you're a good, level-headed horse, and you'll soon have the experience for things like that not to surprise you," Carmen spoke again in his most gentle low murmur.

They came to one of those climax points in the hills where a high incline of loose shale, algae-covered outcrops and grass interspersed with low herbs climbs to give a view of the surrounding countryside. Carmen turned the colt to look up the hill. "See here, Flamingo, I know it can be kind of spooky for a young horse going up a hill like this for the first time with a rider on his back, but we got to go up there to take a look around so we don't just ride all over the place looking for those calves. So, come on now, chick, chick, chick."

Carmen tapped Flamingo's sides lightly with his boots to urge him on, but wasn't too surprised when the colt began to leap forward to climb the grade. "Whoa, whoa, easy now. Ain't no hurry tryin' to jump your way up there like any lame-brained new horse," he said, gathering back on the reins to hold Flamingo in.

The colt gradually slowed his pace to go at a quick, climbing walk again. "That's better, that's better, shoooh."

Carmen pulled the horse to a stop, and looked off to the north. He saw the calves way off, grazing together only slightly dispersed in a way that showed they were calm——a part of the great vista of broad, green prairie. "That's good, that's good, ain't it, Flamingo. Come on now, we'll go on out there for a ways to have a closer look if we can do it without spooking them. Easy now, easy goin' down."

Carmen thought for a moment of getting off to lead Flamingo down the hill, but no. No, he was getting tired, and he didn't want to have to try to mount the colt at the bottom without someone like Frances there to give him a little shove into the saddle. He felt too tired to do it on his own.

"We'll get down there just fine, old Flamingo. Easy now, easy, just step out slow, and find your way."

Carmen knew Flamingo was sure-footed, probably had gone up and down such hills a thousand times on his own. But it would be different to do it with the unfamiliar weight and balance of a man in the saddle when combined with the natural excitement of youth.

Carmen gripped the saddle horn, and loosened the reins a little to allow the colt to find his way down through the rocks. "Easy boy, we'll go on a little bit of an angle here to help you find your way."

They were doing fine for a ways, but then Carmen hollered in surprise, "Huaagh!" as the colt pivoted downhill, and tried to leap through it as he had done uphill. It was one of those mistakes of youth that even a good horse will make.

Flamingo began to slide as his front feet hit the loose shale hard from the leap, and he tried to turn sideways to regain balance as he went. Carmen was thrown sideways in the saddle, and instinctively trying to rein the colt in just when he needed his head for balance. Flamingo hit a rock outcrop hard with his front feet, and Carmen gripped the saddle horn as he went down.

Carmen's mouth worked back and forth for a moment in an interrupted yowl, but the wind was out of him now. He was stunned from the impact where the base of his neck had hit the ground. Flamingo was on his side with Carmen's right leg under him, the left leg stretched out at nearly a right angle to it.

Then Flamingo rolled himself back away from Carmen with his feet under him, scrambling and struggling back on his hooves to stand. The big colt shook himself like a dog fresh out of the water. He began walking away on down the hill behind Carmen until he was out of his sight.

Carmen's consciousness began to creep back in as the horse moved away, and the next time his mouth opened it was to a long howl of agony, "aaaughwl. Geeze, Louise! Lord, Lord, what have I done?" His entire body was pinpoints of pain, and the back of his head felt like he had been cracking walnuts with it, a dull ache of haze that seemed to envelope him.

Then there was one agonizing overwhelming pain that overshadowed everything, putting his guts into knots that threatened to tear him apart. It was from his right leg. Carmen knew the leg had to be broken, probably in more than one place.

"My God, what have I done to myself?" he cried, big tears beginning to roll down his cheeks. He felt the world receding before his eyes, and began to panic against losing consciousness. It might be hours before Will decided to come looking for him, or before Frances began to think he had been gone from home too long.

Carmen had never been religious, but he thought there might come a day when he would make amends with God before he died. He just hadn't expected it all to have to happen in one afternoon. He remembered vaguely some bible quotation that "it is appointed man once to die, and then the judgment."

Then he hollered loudly, "Oh crap, the judgment! Gawd almighty help Carmen out of this one!

"Jesus, I know you ain't a horse trader, but please help old Carmen today, right away, and maybe I can do some of those things back for you I always been thinkin' of."

He almost immediately felt a big "whuff" of warm air sound against the side of his head. It came from Flamingo's nostrils which were nearly touching him. The colt was standing alongside him, a bright red welt of blood showing on his foreleg that Carmen couldn't quite focus his eyes on.

"Lord, Lord if only Flamingo would hold still for me. You ain't been trained to do that have you boy? If I try to get a hold on you, are you going to move, and maybe hurt old Carmen some more? On the other hand, what if I just die here? What if there's more wrong than I know?

74

Jesus, give Flamingo a thought to hold still for me, an I promise I'll be better. You'll hold still for me, won't you Flamingo?"

Carmen rolled himself to grab a saddle stirrup with his left hand. The colt stood still. In a supreme effort, he pulled the top half of his body up to grab the stirrup with his right hand too. Then hand over hand, he pulled, and tried to turn to get his left leg under him while the right leg stretched out still, uselessly.

He suddenly realized that he was hearing a voice that was going "aaagh, aaagh," and it was him. Flamingo still stood still, so he decided the sound must not make any difference. He kept doing it. But he could still die here.

As if to confirm his thought, Carmen felt drops of light rain beginning to hit his face. He hadn't even seen the clouds move in. It gave him a heavy surge of fear, and a heavy shot of adrenaline kicked in. It was just the stuff to give him strength as he pulled hand over hand with the left leg suddenly under him. Carmen's "aagh" turned into a scream as he pulled on the saddle horn to raise the left leg over Flamingo's back while the right leg dangled.

Where were the reins? Carmen didn't know. He loosened his belt to loop it around the saddle horn, and tightened it back as much as he could. Would that help hold him in the saddle? He didn't know. He only knew he didn't think he could take falling out of the saddle again.

He gripped the horn then with his hands, breathing heavily, saying, "OK, Flamingo. Let's go. Please, God, help Ol' Flamingo not jump forward any more, and just walk. Please keep Ol' Carmen staying on him, and have somebody find us."

And, that's what the young horse did, carefully went up the hill to go down the other side, keeping his footing sure, and moving deliberately as if he somehow understood the fragility of the burden he carried."

Some time later, Carmen slowly regained consciousness. He was wet, very wet, and he was on Flamingo's back numb from his waist down. The rain fell lightly on the top of his head. He was looking at Will's cattle pens where the squeeze chute still stood in place in the dimming light. He realized that Flamingo's head was down, and he was holding one front hoof in the air.

He heard an engine, and there was a truck stopping by him with Will and the veterinarian getting out. When he came to again, he knew he was laying flat on his back while the veterinarian tied his broken leg into place with a temporary splint made with a straight tree branch.

"Bear with us, Carmen," Will said seeing his friend's eyes focus on him. "You're with us now, and we'll get you to a hospital."

"Will," Carmen said, "Please listen close to me."

"Sure, Carmen, just take it easy."

"You see that your veterinarian takes care of that colt really good. I don't care if it costs me $5,000. He's never to be put down, or sent to a meat wagon. He's fine, Will. He's really fine. He's a gift from God Almighty. He's proof that a horse trader can keep his promises. I guess I had me a religious experience out there, Will."

"Carmen, you're a little out of it right now. Just stay still. We'll take care of the horse. You take it easy like I said. Quit trying to talk."

"Why would Gawd Almighty have to help someone when they ain't a little out of it, Will?"

Then Will smiled. And he and Carmen both began to feel good."

In the future, Carmen liked to tell his friends, "That Flamingo is the best cow pony on Will's ranch, I mean cow horse. And, it was me that got him for Will. That horse has quite a head on him, Ima' tellin' you by the Lord Gawd Almighty."

From Such As I

Little brother,
you stand looking at me
in your soft, new,
dun puppy coat
from along the road,
your pink tongue lolling
over youthful, long sharp teeth.

Innocent brother,
learn to run
from such as I
who might kill you
as a rival for meat,
or for the cruel joy
of looking over the hood
at you looking over your shoulder
back at me
in the typical style
of your kind
as you run from
the wheels of death.

Such as I
would put a bullet
through your lungs,
and hang your limp remains
over a barbed wire fence
as a savage warning
to your family.

Such as I
would train the dogs
to seize you by the throat,
to shake you to a bloody pulp,
while hollering get him,
get him, by heck.

But such as I
would also listen with
half-closed eyes,
when your family comes

out at night,
to yip and yap
the familiar calls of the wild,
and explain to visitors
the banshee's voice
in that wild,
unconquered sound.

For such as I
would make you romantic
for your tireless, galloping lope,
for your God-given wisdom and abilities
to survive where
your relatives fail.
You're smart,
you're cunning,
you know how to organize
the hunt,
your den,
the avoidance of
one such as I.

I admire you, little brother.
So, just once,
one such as I,
will honk my horn
to help you live one day.
But it will never fail,
that another day,
such as I
will hear a coyote wail,
then come to find your trail,
to kill you, little brother,
crush you broken to the earth,
wish all your kind
in my bloody grip.

Remember one such as I,
little brother as you chew
a bleeding lamb.
We're really kind of alike.

Eddy Burnt By Harlan Medlam's Lucky Happy Birthday

"**H**appy birthday to ya, happy birthday to ya, happy, happy birthday, Harlan Medlam," the old man said, smiling at his wrinkled nut-brown face in the rear-view mirror of the old black pickup truck.

Ah, the luckiest day of the year. Ah, to be alive at 86 on the luckiest day of the year, and to have lived long enough with enough experiences to be sure that your birthday was the luckiest day of the year.

You could call it what you wanted, Harlan Medlam's expectations or the excitement of birthdays going clear back to boyhood. But Harlan Medlam knew it was just the correct alignment of everything on his birthday, faith, lucky stars, craftiness, the years of one beautiful spring day after another. Yes, the world always just lined up to give him opportunity on his birthday.

Even when his father had given him a whipping for selling his mother's broom to a neighbor years ago on his birthday, he had found where the old man had dropped a nickel on the ground afterwards, hadn't he?

Plus that, the neighbor had felt so badly that she told him to keep a penny. Then he sold it 40 years later for $5.00 to someone collecting Indianhead pennies—not bad, not bad at all. You just couldn't beat Harlan Medlam luck when it gathered all its force on a birthday.

He laid his teeth on the truck dash in front of him, and popped the cigar stub into his mouth to chew with the moist spring breeze blowing through the open wing vent into his face while he grinned.

Even Florence Medlam was happy to send him away from home to while away the day on his birthday. She could hardly hide the eagerness in her pale blue eyes to send him down the road. No point keeping Harlan Medlam home to work on his birthday while all the luck in the world was waiting on him for some kind of treasure that he could bring home. He even had an extra nickel in his pocket for another cigar at the co-op oil store.

Why, Florence even figured to have most of the milk cows bred, and dried up, so they didn't freshen until right after his birthday. That was done even if she had to milk a few by herself, or get someone in for a day to help with the milking. There could be no interference with the happy, lucky birthday.

Last year's birthday he had made a great swap for a deep freeze that seemed like it might work forever, then got a crippled hog free to fill it.

Yes, Florence Medlam would make him a yellow cake with white cream and sugar frosting, but only heaven knew what kind of spoils Harlan Medlam might bring home on such a day.

The new green leaves were shooting out on the tree branches, the redwing blackbirds were trilling spring song from tree-filled gullies, and it was Harlan Medlam's lucky, lucky birthday. "Happy birthday to ya, happy birthday to ya," he sang lifting his red greasy ball cap from his full head of gray-black hair.

By the time Harlan Medlam drove onto the farmers cooperative oil store lot, he was nearly jubilant with a tight smile and the cigar stub chew wadded up in one cheek, but his eyes were already set in careful study looking at all the trucks and other vehicles to see who else might be inside.

You didn't necessarily have to make your luck or seek it out, but you had to be able to recognize it. Luck was a God-given fact of life that you needed the perspective to seize on to when it came. He knew that such luck comes to everybody. But, he figured nobody was better at seizing God-given luck than Harlan Medlam.

There was a small group of men pulled in a circle under the big slow-moving over-head fan that blew a mild draft of new spring air down on them. They were laughing boisterously in great community, "hee, yahay , ahaw," so somebody must have told a joke.

Judging by his posture, it must have been Dick Heineckan because he stood with one hand at hip, and the other in the air holding his smoking pipe. It must have been a hum dinger too because Deacon Cozno , called Deacon precisely because he was the opposite, was slapping the knee of his striped coveralls one more time.

Even that new smoothie in the community, Eddy Jones, had a widespread, thin-lipped grin on his face, sitting there stolidly with a hand on each leg.

"Well, Harlan Medlam, you old coyote," said Dick, and Harlan smiled because everybody liked Dick, and being noticed by him.

"How'd you get away from the poor farm? Florence sick or dead? Or, did you just run away from home at naptime."

"It's my birthday, Dick. I don't even get sleepy on my birthday, but then, I don't work much that day. I just get lucky."

"Oh, sweet lord, stay away from me you old devil. I remember horse trading with you on your birthday. How is that team of mares anyway? What are they—30 years old now. They probably can't even die when you own them, you're so darn lucky."

"Why, they're fine, Dick. They still pull real good, but we use a tractor a lot of the time these days. Guess they was kind of a bargain."

"Bargain you bet. You about stole them you old devil, and if I remember right, I even threw in some fryin' chickens besides."

"Guess I was kind of lucky, but it was my birthday."

"Well, you've probably met your match here today, Harlan. Doesn't anybody get much luckier than Eddy here. He just got back from Vegas with enough winnings to pay for the trip plus give him a thousand dollars to boot."

Harlan looked at the younger man, smoothly olive tanned with slicked down brown hair touched with blonde highlights, looking as though he had just left a beauty parlor.

Aah, it was as though a light was coming on in the room. This was the guy, the God-given moment, his lucky, lucky birthday coming true before his eyes in the person of Eddy Jones. He grinned as broadly as he could exposing his bare gums because his teeth were out when he chewed cigars.

"Lucky, huh?" asked Harlan Medlam. "Well, I guess a thousand dollars is powerful lucky. It's just that you can't be as lucky as me when it's my birthday."

"You probably got that right you old coyote. So, Harlan give me some of your old man's wisdom here before I have to go back to work," Dick said. "Tell us where the price of wheat is gonna go this year? Eddy here's always lucky, ain't you, Eddy. So, Eddy planted more wheat last fall on the land he got from his Great Aunt. Does that mean the price will be up, Harlan?"

"Why, God bless, Dick, it don't mean anything who planted it. The price of wheat is up now, and it will be down by the time you cut it. Everybody knows that. It's always up to get us to plant it, then down when it's time to sell it. That's the way the world wants it, and that's the way it's gonna be, just like I'm always lucky on my birthday," said Harlan looking deliberately at Eddy with a smile.

Eddy tried to smile thinly back at Harlan, but a narrowing of his dark eyes that sparkled with inward arrogance was almost all he could accomplish. This was such a dirty, nasty old man. Look at him there with a drool of cigar tobacco beginning at a corner of the mouth before he licked it away. Detestable, that contemptuous, nasty smile. What a pleasure it would be if he could somehow bet a thousand dollars off this old man.

"I tell you what, Harlan Medlam," said Eddy, his smile deliberately widening in a challenge, "why don't you come spend the rest of the day with me on the farm? I'm mostly puttering around today with the wet weather we've had. I'm going to be burning some brush I had pushed out around the farm buildings.

"Maybe we can stand around, watch it burn, and some of that birthday luck can rub off on me. I can always use a little more luck."

"Well, I never knew of it to rub off on anyone else, but I do like to see fires burn while I smoke a good cigar, and enjoy a little talk. Guess'n this would be real neighborly fun with'ya."

"I don't know if you realize what you're getting into here, Eddy," said Dick as they walked to their trucks. "Harlan Medlam's a dangerous man to be around on his birthday."

"Don't you worry about me, Dick," said Eddy. "You just come on old Harlan. Climb in that old black truck of yours, and follow me."

Harlan Medlam broke out in jubilant song once more as the two trucks turned down the last gravel road slinging chunks of brown mud from the tires, "Happy birthday to ya, happy birthday to ya, happy birthday to ya old coyote best friend Lucky Eddy will ever have."

But then, Harlan Medlam became a little somber as they pulled into the driveway of the old farmstead Eddy had inherited that had been familiar to Harlan since he was a boy.

He called out to Eddy as they climbed from the trucks, "Eddy, what's happened? Where are the spirea rows, the lilacs, the fruit trees, all the big trees that used to between here and the house. And, there was a long hedgerow over there."

Then he saw it himself, a huge pile of wilted leaved branches and logs shoved tightly together southwest of the barn."

"I had them all shoved out with a bulldozer. Sure makes the place clean, doesn't it? It's a lot easier to mow. I'll probably hire someone to mow it. I hate doing it, and I can afford the help. No sense doing everything yourself, right Harlan?"

"Wouldn't know about that. I always did everything for myself, and if I didn't think of doin' it that way, it's for sure Florence Medlam would. Why, you don't have any good shade left, no fruit, and where's the rabbits and birds gonna go with all your shrubs gone. This place is darn near naked. And, now, you're gonna burn your barn down."

"Burn my barn down? What are you talking about, old man. I have no intention of burning my barn down."

"Yer lighten' a brush pile southwest of the barn. Anybody'd know yer gonna burn the barn down with a fire southwest of it. That's the way things are in this part of the world."

"Look, Harlan. I'm just going to throw a couple of cans of diesel fuel on this brush pile, and light it up with some old paper feed sacks to get it going good. It's more than a thousand feet away from the barn, there's no wind today, and even if there were, the ground's bare and muddy between here and the barn."

"Well, I'm tellin' you for your own good, all luck aside, that yer about to burn your own barn down."

"You are a pain in the behind, Harlan Medlam. No wonder Dick doesn't want you around on your birthday, or maybe for any other day for that matter. We've only been here 10 minutes, and all you can talk about is how I'm going to burn my barn down. No, 'my how you've cleaned the place up,' or, 'you must enjoy living here.' What a dirty old bore you are. I don't know why I asked you to come along."

"Well, ya don't have any horses in the barn, do ya? I'm not one to stand around with horses in a fire."

"No, I don't have any horses in there. It's mainly full of hay. There might be 2,000 bales in there. I guess there might be a few pieces of old harness if you're interested in horses."

Harlan Medlam pursed his lips to blow some air through them in disapproval. "Ya know, 2,000 bales is worth a lot of money. That's going to be a powerful loss in a fire."

"That barn isn't going to burn, old man. See, we're southwest of the barn. With the spring cool front that came through giving us this pleasant weather, the slight breeze we do have is northerly. Even the sparks will go away from the barn to the south if they could travel a whole thousand feet."

"Yer gonna burn your barn down. Care if I look at the harness?"

"Sure, go ahead. Look at the harness."

"Why, that's good harness, still pliable. And look at the sets of reins, no rot or breaks in them. All you'd need to do is soak them all for a while in some neatsfoot oil, and they're good leather. What a waste to see them all burn."

"There isn't anything going to burn in the barn here, Harlan."

Harlan Medlam narrowed his shining black eyes to look at Eddy, who was brushing back the blonde-brown hair with a carefully manicured hand, very unlike Harlan's big, boney hands with the dirt under the nails. "Well then, do ya care if I rescue all this horse stuff from the fire in advance? Supposin' there's a fire, can I just keep it then."

"You're not going to set my barn on fire, Harlan."

"No, no, no, I'd never do a thing like that, Eddy. I might be lucky, but I'm honest. I'll tell you straight forward that I've been dealin' with you, no gimmicks."

"OK, I'll tell you what then. You can take anything you might want out of this barn then, and put it in your truck except for the hay. You can keep it if the barn burns down.

"But, if there's no fire, you have to put it all back in the barn just the way it was, and I'm not going to help you even if you're falling down dead from the strain. I don't want any hay pulled out because I don't think I want to wait on you to get it all put back."

"Deal then, I'll do that," said Harlan Medlam, ah the God-given moment of birthday luck. A fire southwest of a barn was sure to burn a barn down. It was a rule of life.

"There's one condition though," said Eddy, narrowing his eyes a little in his turn.

"What might that be?" asked Harlan.

"I have $1,000 cash in my pocket from Vegas right now. See, here it is all neatly stacked in $20's. Let's have a cash side bet. I'll bet $1,000 cash against $1,000 cash from you that this barn doesn't burn down. I'm betting you are wrong."

"And I still get to rescue anything from the barn for myself that I want?"

"That's right. But where's your thousand dollars?"

"Turn yer back."

"What?"

"Turn yer back gul durn it, Eddy. I ain'ta gonna show anybody where I might keep a thousand bucks."

Eddy slowly turned his back as Harlan watched him on the way to his truck. He reached up under the seat on the passenger side, and twisted an oil can down out of the springs. Then he took the rubber bands off a roll of cash in the can, counted $1,000 from the roll, and returned the rest up under the seat where he'd found it.

"Now, ya ain't gonna knock me in the head for my money or anything are you, Eddy?"

"No, no, no, I'd never do a thing like that, Harlan. I might be lucky, but I'm honest. I'll tell you straight forward that I've been dealing with you, no gimmicks. I'm just surprised you had that kind of money with you."

"Well, Eddy, the government doesn't mess much with cows, and I don't mess much with banks. We each do what we do best. It keeps us happy."

"I see, I think."

"Ok then, if yer abound to, get your fire going while I get stuff from the barn."

Eddy was splashing the first five-gallon can of diesel over the brush to spread its effect when Harlan called from the barn, "Criminy, but isn't this a motor boat on a trailer back here in a stall, Eddy?"

"Yes it is, and it's fair game on the deal if an old coot like you wants a motor boat."

"Can you help me hook it up to my truck?"

"No deal, Harlan. Just back your truck in there, and hook it up yourself. I don't help you. That's the deal.. And, remember, you have to put it all back by yourself too when there's no fire."

Eddy could hear the old man grunting, and the sounds of items being put into the truck bed as he put the second can of diesel on the brush pile. "What are you finding, old man?" he called out.

"Well, there's hay hooks, lots of buckets, a near full sack of oats, a couple of corn shucking gloves, log chains, wrenches, a couple of old milk cans, a mirror that ain't even broke, three corn knives, the hood of I'd say about a '35 Chevrolet--why, the place is a treasure chest."

"I'm about to light the fire, Harlan. And, the breeze is just the same."

"That's alright. The truck and the boat are clear full. I'll be out to watch her burn. Ah, here's some near full buckets of red paint. Paint's expensive, Eddy. There's some brown bottles of stuff with it."

"Come on, Harlan, if you want to see the pile burn. I'd say you just about have everything in there anyway."

"I'ma comin', I'ma comin', but it does seem a terrible waste to leave all that hay. It's bad enough just to lose the barn."

"The barn and the hay are going to be fine, you greedy old man. Just come on so we can watch me win my bet together. It's going to take a lot of work for you to get all that stuff back in there. It will take time for the pile to burn, and then for you to do that."

There was a jumbling sound of junk jumping and falling into place as Harlan drove the old black truck pulling the shining red motorboat past Eddy and a little ways up the exit driveway. Then Harlan came shuffling back carrying one of the brown bottles.

"Why did you park way up there?"

"I wanted to be out of the way when the barn starts burning."

"That barn isn't going to burn, Harlan."

"Whatever you say, Eddy. Let me see what's in this bottle while you strike your match."

Harlan Medlam used his pocket knife to pull a cork from the bottle while Eddy lit the feed sacks on one side, and then lit them on the other side of the pile as the diesel began to burn. Harlan Medlam was drinking a long draw from the bottle as he came back around the 30-foot radius.

"What is it, Harlan?"

"Tastes like peach brandy to me."

Eddy hesitated for a moment as he watched Harlan Medlam lick his repulsive pink lips. Then he decided a drink might be too good to pass up.

"Here, give me a swig of that. Must be the last of Auntie's peach brandy. There never will be any more of it since I shoved her peach trees into this pile, no more trees, no more Auntie. You can bet I'm not going to buy peaches or make brandy myself, either one."

Eddy took a long draw from the bottle. Harlan took a long draw from the bottle. Then Eddy drank again, and Harlan drank again. They smiled at each other as they backed away with the flames roaring over their heads, the wood popping as it caught fire from the tremendous heat.

The two men were already beginning to wobble when Harlan saw him. A cottontail rabbit was running circles bobbing around here and there out on the bare ground where the spirea bushes once had been.

"Look there, Eddy, see there. The poor rabbit's lost because you shoved his brush out."

"Let him find someplace else, just let him find someplace else," Eddy nearly gurgled as his face turned brandy-singed red.

It was then the rabbit made a straight-a-way fast hopping run right into the brush pile that was burning.

"He's committing suicide," said Eddy.

"He's confused," said Harlan.

Then the rabbit burst from the brushpile, a running, burning ball of fire going straight for the barn."

"No, he can't," said Eddy.

"Yes, he can," said Harlan, "runnin' right in to burrow into that hay to try to get away from the fire. Poor little bunny. He had to try to go home on my lucky, lucky birthday."

As the flames went up through the roof of the barn, Eddy handed Harlan his thousand dollars, his mouth gaping in shocked amazement as Harlan sang, "Happy birthday ta ya, happy birthday ta ya, happy, happy lucky birthday ta ya, Harlan Medlam!"

The truck and boat did a little weaving as they came into Harlan Medlam's driveway.

Florence Medlam looked through the open window, and sniffed. "Why, you've been drinking, Harlan Medlam. Never knew you to take part in the expense of alcoholic beverage before," she said looking at his silly attempt to grin.

"Look here, Florence, we got a boat."

"I know, let me go in, and get an ad into the newspaper for the silly thing before they close for tomorrow's issue. Here, lean on me while we try to decide what it's worth. Then you can show me the rest of the stuff.

"I swear, Harlan Medlam, it's like fishing in a barrel for 20-pound catfish sending you out on your lucky, lucky birthday. Where'd you put the money. I know you must have gotten a little cash, too, if you got this much other stuff.

"Then we'll get your cake, and we'll eat it too."

Meandering Creek Language

Bolder trees break the banks
while willows wind with the stream
whispering in the westerly wind,
their gentler tender sighs,
the language common of the creek,
replied across the
gurgling waves of water
by bees buzzing in
languorous insect lingo,
laboring from oak to elm to ash
as always bees have on this brook
echoed only in
scolding outbursts of chatter
from scattered querolous
scurrying squirrels,
all running on
and on and on and on,
the sentence of life immortal.

Getting Married
Is A Matter Of Faiths

Brandon Brigstone came from the bright autumn day of a college campus, with red oak leaves drifting across the sidewalks, and into the fluorescent-lit rows of tables where graduate engineering students drew their plans.

The brown, blonde and red-haired young men concentrated their efforts on fine line drawings that showed everything from auger settings to electrical hookups to conveyor systems.

Brigstone was here to meet his roommate, Charlie, who was amid the dozen young faces that looked up in greeting as he walked in.

One face shone with unusual intensity and curiosity from the middle of the group—white teeth shining from nut-brown complexion that contrasted with the other pink faces. It belonged to a man a half-head shorter than the rest of them who was introduced to Brigstone by Charlie as Shuklah.

"I am very, very pleased to meet you, Brandon," said Shuklah, grasping Brandon's hand. "I like your roommate, Charlie, very much, and I enjoy all these fellows, even Ed over there." Shuklah gestured at a blonde smiling from the corner.

"You just say my name like Shoo Claw, OK?"

"That's all the name you have?"

"It's enough name for you. I don't try to get Americans to say the rest of it, OK?"

"Shuklah is a new grad student who just came this summer from India, Brandon," Charlie said. "We've been having a good time helping him get familiar with everything."

"Yes," said Shuklah. "Right now I am helping plan a feedlot so someone can raise more cattle to eat. It even has its own miniature railroad. Some setup, eh?"

"So, Brandon," said Charlie, smiling with an even more knowing look at his roommate, "do you want to eat lunch with us, or are you seeing Sue for the noon hour? How are things going with her anyway?"

"Ah, you have a girlfriend do you, Brandon?" asked Shuklah. "I am going to be married soon, too."

"You are?" asked Charlie, turning to Shuklah.

"You didn't tell us," said Ed, getting to his feet with a half-dozen other young men to gather around Shuklah. "Well, tell us. Who is she, Shuklah? Somebody here, or is she back home."

"Oh, I don't know her yet."

"Then how can you be getting married soon?"

"My parents are finding somebody for me. They are advertising in the Delhi and Bombay newspapers for somebody of my caste who will have gone to some college like me. We will have a Hindu wedding next summer."

"But you don't know her. You won't be in love with her. Why would you want to do that in this age?"

"Sounds like a recipe for disaster to me, eh, Brandon," said Charlie with a wink.

"Of course I will love her," said Shuklah. "She will be my wife."

"But you won't know her," said Ed shaking his head. "Sounds like preparations for a divorce to me."

"I think I will get to know her very well, and I will love her," replied Shuklah. "She will love me. By the time I come back here next fall, we will be very much in love."

"You come back. Won't she come back with you?" asked Brandon."I would hate to have just gotten married and then not bring her back with me, if I was in your situation."

"That will depend on how much money our families have. If she doesn't, we will write to each other," said Shuklah.

The young American men looked at Shuklah, and at each other smiling, a couple of them with tongues in cheeks.

Charlie said, "Shuklah, don't you have any id, any pizzazz to pursue a woman on your own? How about this, Brandon? Do you have so little drive you want your parents to go pick a woman for you? Would they have chosen Sue?"

"Well, Charlie," said Brandon, "they have met Sue, and they do like her. But she also has obvious attributes that had something to do with my interest that at least my mother might have missed. Besides, Sue might have missed seeing it if we advertised—wouldn't even have thought to look."

"Hey, I have id. I have pizzazzes, or whatever you called it. I am, as you say in your movies, a red-blooded man too. As a matter of fact," said Shuklah, "I can hardly wait to be in love.

"Doesn't your Jesus tell you to love your wives? Hey, tell Joseph John to come in here. He is a Jesus man. Joseph John, come in here."

The door swung open, and a small black man in suit and tie walked in.

"Brandon, this is Joseph John. He comes from Zambia. Joseph John, you are a Jesus man aren't you? Tell us about your marriage. You must explain to Brandon how old you really are, too."

"Yes," said Joseph John, who looked to be in his 20s like the other men around him. "I became a Christian many years ago. You see I am 55 even though most people here seem to think I am younger.

"Well," added Joseph John, rolling his eyes in his smooth, youthful looking face, "you see, I already had three wives when I became a Christian. One of them became a Christian, too. But the other ones still keep little figures of their gods.

"I must not turn any of my wives out because I made covenant with them. Now I must love them forever, because what would happen to them if I didn't?"

"Where are your wives, Joseph John?" asked Ed.

"They are in Zambia."

"In your house?"

"No, they each have their own home. I don't have a house. I just go to their houses when I am there."

"You see, you see?" said Shuklah. "That is even more different than me. I think I might like to study more about your Jesus and his love. I especially am intrigued by the story of how Jesus the Vishnu defeated Shiva the destroyer by rising from the dead in your history. Is Manu the monkey god in your bible, too? What kind of a Christian are you, Charlie?"

"I'm a Baptist with a wife I chose myself, although I could credit Jesus with a job well-done in sending her my way. How about it, Brandon, did Jesus and God the Father do a construction job with Sue to your liking?"

"That I guess they did," said Brandon, turning pink for the first time.

"Very good, that's higher than Methodist isn't it?" asked Shuklah. "I mean you, Charlie, being a Baptist. I am Brahmin, warrior caste, to you. I must remain enlightened. I will help your people study Vishnu, too, if you like?"

"No, Shuklah," said Charlie, "being Baptist isn't higher up than being a Methodist or a Catholic or a Presbyterian or any other kind of a Christian. We're all washed in the blood if we ask to be—it's just different traditions."

"So," said Shuklah, "you can bring a Hindu in for a blood wash, I suppose?"

"You might have to make a choice to be Christian," said Joseph John. "You can't follow Jesus and Hinduism both."

"Who wants hamburgers for lunch?" said Ed. "I'm going for hamburgers. How many, Brandon, Charlie, two each?"

"I will also take two hamburgers," Shuklah said. "I love American hamburgers."

"Shuklah," said Charlie, "I thought you were a good Hindu."

"Oh, I am."

"I thought Hindus wouldn't hurt cows. How can you eat beef?"

"Oh, this is American beef. This is your ancestors we're eating, not my ancestors. I especially love to have one of those 16-ounce steaks—talk about a pedigree."

"I don't think I saw anything about Gandhi eating beef in his campaign to make India an independent nation from the British Empire," said Ed.

"Gandhi once said he could almost become a Christian, too, if it weren't for the Christians. But, it's true , he was mostly talking about the British," said Shuklah.

"You Americans have been kinder. Gandhi didn't eat beef, but some day I will go to England, and eat beef. That will taste very good since we Indians have a little bit of the English soul already in us.

"Hey, these are feedlots we're planning. We're stepping up the process."

"Hey, yourself," said Ed. "I really feel a little more like eating fried chicken now. How about it guys? Can we forget the hamburgers today, and I'll go for a bucket of fried chicken?"

"Chicken is good, Ed," said Shuklah. "I apologize in great sincerity if I bothered you. I can be a good Hindu full of id with a great curiosity of Jesus, and eat fried chicken, too.

"I find American chicken quite good. I will try not to explain why, except to say we are what we eat, but you know this."

Soft Eyes

Soft Eyes,
you with the curls,
behind the coffee cup
over in the corner,
being your own best friend
is a first rule of life.

Lips trembling,
you with the loss of heart
sighing over the table,
losing a love
is like losing
a part of yourself.

Get straight,
Soft Eyes,
looking to the future,
you have to love
yourself first,
you're God's
greatest gift to you,
you with those soft eyes.

Find contentment
in the solitude
of the great alone of life,
no diversions,
no noise,
no chatter,
only you
as a companion
shining soul
from those soft eyes.

Then you're ready for love.

One Of Our Own

Cyrus didn't exactly look like the classic plains Indian that day—no eagle-feather bonnet blowing in a prairie wind—but he still looked Native American.

There's always been a problem with recognition of American Indians anyway. Society has usually had them portrayed as strictly groups with a few outstanding villains or heroes in the movies when actually many of them turned out to be individuals with the blessings and problems common to humankind.

Cyrus was an individual. There were even Pottawatomies hesitant to claim him at a given moment, which only goes to show that many among them were intelligent individuals.

His face was rounded, but he had the almond-brown eyes sunk into 60 years of wrinkles and a full shock of medium-cut black hair with a little white running in it.

His lips were set in a quiet, amused smile as he watched his friends, Horace and Lindsay, who had just arrived from the city, step up the sunken limestone walkway to his house.

"Have you heard the big news today?" he called to them.

"No, nothing out of the ordinary," replied Horace.

"Well, we got you white boys now, we got you now. We got you where it's really going to hurt. You are gonna be twistin' in the wind."

"How's that?" asked Lindsay, brushing back his mop of light-brown medium length Beatles-cut hair and playing uncomfortably with the corner of his glasses because he didn't like the cat rubbing against his leg.

"They gave final approval to the Pottawatomie casino. And now it's payback time.

"You white boys got us drunk, and stole our land down at Happy Hollow. But now your people are going to be spending all their money for years and years in our casinos. Us Potts are gonna be the fat cats."

He paused to wave one finger in the air at them— "Got ya."

"I'm glad I'll know at least one rich guy to stay with when the system collapses," Horace said.

"Ah, yes, Horace Richmond, I'll take care of you and your poor bleeding fingers from playing our one-armed bandits. I like your curly short hair and your little spectacles and your little goatee. You can help me with my investments while I take care of you. It will be almost as fine as hanging your scalp in my living room.

"I would take care of you before I take care of my brother-in-law, Joseph. Joseph has just enough white-boy blood in him to make him sneaky, so you can't fully trust him. While you, you are a really nasty

93

white boy that takes care of paperwork for other people, but you take your fiduciary ethic seriously so you can be a parasite—you do right by people so you suck their blood only a little at a time. I can see exactly what you are.

"But you're going to pay now by the holy spirit of God almighty—we got our casino.

"Sometimes I like to play like I could be a rich lying white boy, too. I go down to where the new Mexicans are working in the nursery fields, and say hola to them so they think I might just be a different looking one of them.

"But when they try to talk to me, I fire back with Pottawatomie with a few French words in it, just like you talk business off those papers so I can't understand you. The Mexicans want to be white boys like you so bad that it's good to have somebody making them wary."

Lindsay was trying to keep the cat off his lap, but Horace was smiling as he said, "I thought you might like to ride with Lindsay and me up to Alice Beau's place. I think she likes to see you come in with us. I'm helping with the federal loan on her cattle."

"You think Alice Beau likes to see me, huh? I don't know why you think so, and I don't even know why you come by for me, Horace Richmond.

"I know you were best friends through high school with my son, Tom. He got enough white blood from my wife to be like you, too, only he's a banker instead of an investment counselor, or whatever it is you call yourself now. But you don't have to come by here because you miss him."

"Why, Cyrus. I come by here because I enjoy you taking rides with us and getting your viewpoint on the world. We're friends. I think you'll enjoy this ride, too."

"Maybe so, maybe so. But ouch, ouch, ouch, Horace Richmond LeClerc. Don't you know you poor white boys got your black boys you have to learn to get along with? But us poor, poor Indians, we got our Kickapoos.

"The big crooked white father in Washington couldn't have twisted the knife in us Pottawatomies better than to put us next to those Kickapoos. Most of them left, and now they're coming back from all over the country to live next to us because the money's coming here.

"God, how oh how am I going to learn to live with these Kickapoos, even when I'm rich from robbin' the white boys like they ought to be robbed. Thank God the Sac and the Fox are here to moderate them a little.

"Don't you know that Alice Beau is part Kickapoo? Plus that, she's got a little white boy blood in her and a little black boy blood in her— just enough to stir around down there in her hell pit. She says her other part is Cherokee and Pottawatomie twisted together, but I don't know. I was in Oklahoma once, and some of those Cherokees are lookers, so that could be why she don't look half bad.

"But I don't know at all if you ought to be rubbin' me next to somethin' that's got Kickapoo, white boy blood and black boy blood all throwed into it. Shall we leave right away? She might be frying chicken today."

"Sure, Cy. Lindsay and I are ready to head right out. Just thought you might want to have a drink or comb your hair or something before we go to Alice Beau's."

"No, no I'm fine the way I am for the likes of Alice Beau being visited with an about-to-be-rich, good lookin' Pott fellow. Just a minute while I put a little more shine on my hair."

They took the highway north through the loess hills past fields of corn, sorghum and soybeans that were bright-green in the hot sun from the effect of timely rain.

Lindsay sat in the back seat, picking cat hair and stick-tights from his double-knit trousers while Horace and Cyrus sat in the front seat of the small station wagon with Cyrus rubbing his hands together in front of the air-conditioning vent.

"You got good air in this little red car, Horace," said Cyrus. "I like red. Now, tell me, how many acres does Alice Beau own now?"

"She has an entire section, 640 acres, Cyrus, and it's 80 percent tillable. It has good dairy barns on it and a modern three-bedroom house. Plus that, she has 50 good Holstein dairy cows."

"Good night, I only have 40 acres. I knew she had some ground, but all of this? It must be her blood, uncommonly sneaky to get this rich on nothin'."

"I helped her, Cyrus. I have paperwork for her to get another 160 acres in my briefcase today. It's all federal loans with no down payment except what little ground she had to start with for equity. She's a woman and a minority in the farming business, and that's good enough for the government."

"My God, so the white boys are so sneaky that when they run out of other people to rob, they rob themselves to keep the game going. Is that what you're telling me, Horace Richmond?"

"Something like that, Cyrus."

"Does she still have that old man, Jasper, living with her?"

"I hope so. He's some kind of relative to her. She's got another old fellow there sometimes, too. But I'm concerned about Jasper. Last winter when I was there he was out sitting against a building in the snow shaking like a leaf. I asked him if he didn't want to go in to get warm, but he said Alice Beau told him he couldn't come in anymore because he wasn't any good."

"Heck of a woman, that Alice Beau," Cyrus nodded approvingly. "She has the nerve to make sure her relatives work. Maybe she isn't so bad as I think."

"Anyway, I took Jasper in the house with me, and Alice Beau asked what he's doing there—that he's no good. I made sure Jasper got something to eat, Cyrus. But if we don't see him here today, I'm afraid I might find his body sometime out in Alice's grain fields while I'm pheasant hunting in the fall."

"No, don't worry about that, Horace Richmond. The animals would carry most of him off, and I don't think it would be any worse than finding a cow skull in a pasture. Besides, she was probably just disciplining him. Even Kickapoos with white-boy blood and black-boy blood honor the dead. She must be a tough woman."

As they pulled into the long driveway with its equally long row of white, chipped-paint dairy buildings with weeds growing around them, Horace looked out with puzzled raised eyebrows. "Look, Lindsay, do you see any Holstein cows, any black and whites?"

"No I don't, Horace. The only cows I see out there look like black white faces and straight Herefords—grade range cows, wouldn't you say?"

To Horace's relief, Jasper was sitting on the front porch, looking well in blue jeans and a plaid, cotton shirt, his thick white hair shorn close on his brown scalp in a crew cut.

"Good to see you, Jasper," Horace said.

"It looks like you're staying healthy," Lindsay noted while stamping his foot at an orange and white cat that was beginning to make its way toward him.

"I am staying as well as a man of 90 can, Horace Richmond LeClerc and Lindsay Loden. Who is the poor, old, feeble man with you? Would that be that old Pottawatomie, Cyrus Bonair?

"Good Lord, why do you put us poor Kickapoos next to such people as the Pottawatomies with all of that French blood in them that they don't remember—too much white blood. But it's good to see you anyway if that's you, Cyrus, and not some vision come to lie to me.

"Or, maybe you've come to lie to me anyway, to tell me how the casinos and throwing in with those Easterners could be good for us?"

"Of course I think the casinos will be good for us. And it's good to see you again anyway, Jasper, although I know for a fact that you probably have enough white-boy blood and black-boy blood in you to be afraid of all the money you will lose sneaking around a casino."

A stern-faced woman with lips set tightly threw open the door to look at all of them.

"Jasper," she said, reaching back to check the knot of the red scarf tying back her bun of white streaked black hair. "Go kill another chicken. We will have company for dinner."

"Yes, Alice Beau," said Jasper.

"Alice," said Horace. "Where are your good Holstein cows I helped you get? All we could see driving in was that beef herd."

"Yes, Horace," she replied, smiling and narrowing her eyes so they gleamed and glittered at him. "They were good, high-producing registered cows. They gave more milk than Jasper and I could contend with. They were worth a lot of money, so I sold them, and got these old common cows out here. Not a bad deal—eh?"

"But Alice, you had close to a 100 percent loan on those cows with the federal government. I don't know that you paid them anything when you sold them, and I have no record of you buying these other cows."

"Horace, what the government don't know won't hurt them. I haven't cheated them any. They carry a note on 50 cows, and I still have 50 cows.

"I am still a good Native American woman, so I suit their purpose. You will figure something out. Now come inside, we will talk about you getting me some more land, and we will eat together.

"Even Cyrus can eat with us because he's not too bad a man, most of the time, for a registered Pottawatomie. Hah, that's a good joke. Maybe the government thinks he's worth more money, too."

"Hah, Alice Beau," said Cyrus. "You are some person, even with all that bad blood in you, standing up to the government like that. I don't think you are common or grade maybe, eh?"

Horace, Lindsay and Alice did her paperwork around the kitchen table while Cyrus sat in the next room pretending to watch a soap opera called "The Young and the Restless" on television while keeping an ear tuned to the tidbits of business he could hear.

When Jasper had the chicken cut up, Alice added it to the other one there, breaded it, and threw it in an iron skillet to fry in deep grease. She gave Cyrus a knife and a bowl to cut up potatoes at the other end of the table.

As they ate, Cyrus said, "You are a good cook, Alice Beau. Plus that, you are very sharp and almost rich even before the casinos come in. You shame me that I didn't find a way to have so much before we got the white boys to gamble their lives away. But we got 'em. We have them now, and all of us will be taken care of. You were just forward thinking."

"I don't know about that, Cyrus," said Horace. "Alice has to quit this kind of stuff. She could be in trouble here. Nobody fools with Uncle Sam forever and gets away with it. Even though I want to try to get all I can get for her, she has to remember that there are those people who are trying to help her as one of our own. It isn't war anymore."

"Hmm, those would be good ideas, Horace," said Cyrus. "I am trying to figure what the white boy lie could be in it. But I'm not worried for

Alice either, because now that you have her in the money channel, you will work to keep her there. You are an excellent white boy, Horace Richmond.

"Now, I will have some private advice for Alice Beau, too, if she will step into the next room with me."

"I think that would be safe for you, Cyrus," said Alice.

"As soon as Cyrus and Alice are done in there, I think we better get him home, and us get back to the office, Horace," said Lindsay, kicking at the cat that chewed a drumstick bone between his feet. "It's going to be a longer day than we planned on with this. I think we need to get started right away."

"I know what you mean, Lindsay. Cyrus, are you folks going to be much longer in there? Lindsay and I need to get back."

"You guys go on ahead," said Cyrus, raising a finger at them from the next room where he and Alice Beau had turned off the television, and sat down in chairs opposite each other.

"Alice Beau will drive me to the city this evening to see a Barbra Streisand movie, and then take me home. We like it when Streisand hits the high notes. She sings pretty good for a white girl, you know.

"Then we're going to sit down over ice cream to discuss getting a Small Business Administration loan together to put a tax-free cigarette store near the casinos before the government turns tough again.

"Alice Beau knows a full-blood Kaw from Oklahoma—we might get her to run it as a compromise.

"Maybe a Kaw could feel at home north of the Kaw River. What do you think, white boys?"

Sister Silence

Silence, my sister
companion of the night,
surrounds me with
her loving solitude,
so still, so still,
carrying me back
to her big eyes crying
in the dark,
alone no more
with nothing else
but her.

Maxwell Fabian's Rhubarbs Create Commonality

The welcoming smells of rich, baking foods carried through the dining hall doors on the slow breeze of the building's cold air return to where Maxwell Fabian stood in line with hundreds of others waiting to enter.

He was content with the way the conference had gone so far, all meaningful and informing. He was tired from sitting, and ready to stuff himself with whatever was being served for the annual conference dinner.

At least, Maxwell told himself, he wouldn't have to put up with his friend, Bird, today with all of his left-wing sounding off-the-wall ideas. Maxwell knew what was right in the world, and the main place Bird had it right was in their mutual love of rhubarb pie.

As they passed through the doors, he strained to look through his graduated lenses at whatever they had on the serving tables. Ah, buffet style. That would be nice. There also were hundreds of round dining tables seating a half-dozen each to choose from.

Chicken breasts smothered in something like a mushroom sauce, potatoes and gravy, green beans, rolls—ah, and there was the salad bar down on the other end.

He'd start from the hot-food end following his number one rule of buffet eating—salads and sauces are strictly packing materials meant to keep you from eating more of the really good stuff so they come last.

Maxwell quickly chose a table not that far from the food. He didn't know there wouldn't be seconds, but the habits of youth die hard. Then he went back for a heaping plate of salad stuff out of respect for his wife because she said he should despite buffet rules. Ah, cole slaw, he did like that.

Other people were taking seats around his table, too. On his left was a portly woman in her 40's with blond frosted hair and wire-rimmed glasses.

The woman across the table looked like a diminutive wrinkled grandmother with kindly sweet face smiling at everyone.

The man between her and Frosted Hair was tall, brown-haired, in his 30's, and wearing a powder-blue suit.

The couple to his right just looked too pleased to see everybody—him with bushy white hair and a goatee and her with mousey brown hair returning Grandmother's smiles, both of them sitting quietly with hands in laps.

After introductions, Maxwell concentrated on the food, listening and replying to chit chat around him. They all seemed like pleasant people, but he loved to eat.

What was this? People were coming back with slices of pie from somewhere. Frosted Hair had gotten up a moment before, and here she was back with pie. And, it was rhubarb pie.

My goodness, he would kill for good rhubarb pie. There would be no need to fight poor old Frosted Hair for a piece of rhubarb when there was probably plenty for everybody, Maxwell smiled at himself. My goodness, Frosted Hair looked severe and sour, just like good rhubarb. At least his friend, Bird, wasn't sour.

"I thought I would go back for dessert early before all the pie selection was gone," said Frosted Hair. "Look what I got, rhubarb. I haven't had rhubarb for years."

"We both got banana cream," said Mousey Brown, glancing lovingly at Goatee.

"I got chocolate cream," said Powder Blue.

"And, there are fruit flavors of all kinds," said Wrinkled Grandmothr, holding up her saucer of peach pie.

"I love rhubarb more than anything," said Maxwell. "Where's that pie table? I don't know how I missed it."

After the others pointed it out, he hurried over only to return moments later with a face as sour as the sourest rhubarb.

"Peanut butter cream, that was all that was left. I got peanut butter cream. I got peanut butter cream when they had rhubarb.

"I don't suppose you'd care to swap that old rhubarb for some really yummy peanut butter cream, would you?" asked Maxwell, bending with a cheerful, full-cocked smile toward Frosted Hair.

"No, I wouldn't. I like rhubarb just fine myself."

"Well, you see," said Maxwell, "I don't just like rhubarb fine. I need rhubarb. You know, I can just hardly stand to see you with rhubarb next to me when I can't have any. I don't suppose you could see your way to trade me that rhubarb just to make me happy? I would really appreciate it," he added, smiling with all his square white teeth showing.

"No, I don't suppose I would trade it," Frosted Hair said, smiling back at him. I'm really looking forward to eating it, too."

"That's Ok, I understand," said Maxwell as he licked his upper lip. "You are very kind, and I'm embarrassed to have been so insistent on really wishing you would swap pie because I couldn't get rhubarb, and now I have to have this really, really sweet, kind of yucky peanut butter cream."

"You don't have to eat it."

"But I will because I took it. I don't suppose we could swap bites? You could give me a bite of your rhubarb, and I could give you a bite of this really yummy peanut butter cream? Maybe we could even trade more than once? We could use our own forks. You don't have to eat after me."

"No. I want my pie. It's not a matter of eating after you. I love rhubarb."

"I know what let's do," said Wrinkled Grandmother. "I have a good riddle for you all. I just heard it the other day."

"Yes, ask us your riddle," said Mousey Brown with her mouth half-stuffed with banana cream.

"I'd like to hear it," added Powder Blue.

Maxwell just twiddled his fork at the peanut butter cream watching Frosted Hair chew her first bite of rhubarb.

"OK," said Wrinkled Grandmother. "Think of the 12 disciples of Jesus. Then tell me: Which disciple was the liberal?"

Everyone around the table looked thoughtful except Maxwell, who was wiping his mouth with a napkin trying to suppress disgust with his first bite of peanut butter cream with its roasted peanut flavor combined with sweet-smooth richness. He began to work his fork across the table toward Frosted Hair's rhubarb while pretending to concentrate on the peanut butter.

But Frosted Hair noticed his move. She gripped her fork a little higher meaningfully as though she might stab him in the hand.

"Perhaps Peter, the rock of the church," said Powder Blue thoughtfully, raising his eyebrows toward the ceiling.

"James or John, or even better maybe Doubting Thomas. They all had hearts for helping all of mankind," injected Goatee.

Silence reigned for a moment.

"No, no, that's easy. It's obvious which disciple was the liberal," said Maxwell. "It had to be Judas, the betrayer of Christ."

"Judas? Why would you say Judas?" asked Wrinkled Grandmother, trouble knitting her brow. "I don't know that you ought to say Judas."

"Judas was just misguided," added Mousey Brown.

"Yes that's what I thought I was saying," said Maxwell. "Judas was misguided. That's a liberal. Misguided, liberal—liberal, misguided. Fits, doesn't it?" Maxwell asked while he stared longingly at the half of rhubarb slice left on Frosted Hair's plate.

"Well," said Frosted Hair. "I don't think I like that. I'm a liberal. I've considered myself a liberal for a long time. The liberals have done great things in this country—civil rights, education, taking care of the poor. I'm proud to call myself a liberal."

"Baby killing, gay marriage, spend, spend, spend—I'm proud of them too," said Maxwell.

"I resent those remarks," said Frosted Hair.

"Good, I've always resented them, too," said Maxwell.

"Now see here. I'm proud to be a liberal. I'm proud to be a Democrat."

"I'm sorry," said Maxwell."

"What do you mean, you're sorry. Sorry that I'm a liberal Democrat, or are you apologizing?"

"I guess it fits either way, doesn't it? A real liberal would have shared the rhubarb pie." said Maxwell.

"Maybe we should forget my riddle," said Wrinkled Grandmother.

"This is getting interesting though," said Goatee.

"You have to understand," said Maxwell, "that I grew up Republican with real values. We grew our own rhubarb. Why, I was 25 before I knew that a Democrat was something other than a box elder bug. In our house, we had Saint Lincoln, Saint Eisenhower and Saint Reagan, let alone the 12 disciples."

"Dole, you left out Dole," said Mousey Brown. "What about Saint Bob Dole? I didn't hear you say that?"

"No, I guess you didn't hear me say that," said Maxwell. "He wasn't president, you know, just seemed more presidential than his opponent. I guess it's fair if the liberals don't want to mention Clinton, then I shouldn't mention Dole. After all, Clinton was far removed from the party of Harry Truman."

"Just like you're far removed from this piece of rhubarb pie. Besides, I liked Bill Clinton," said Frosted Hair.

"That figures," said Maxwell.

"Dole is like a plastic soda straw," said Goatee. "Laid out all straight, but he bends, he bends."

"Just the thought of him," said Mousey Brown, "I jut can't stand him in those Viagra advertisements."

"Speaking of soda straws," said Maxwell with a vicious grin, "there's a lot of people who say Clinton just......"

"Don't you say that. Don't you say that at all you, you, you," said Frosted Hair. "I suppose you are going to say you're proud you've given us George W. too?"

"It seems to me," said Powdered Blue, "that the whole country is too divided right now. We ought to try to find common ground. We ought to realize we are one people even if there are differences of opinion."

"How can we have common ground if half the country has no values anymore? Imagine, serving peanut butter in a pie. That's disgusting. Just try to buy rhubarb at a fast food," said Maxwell.

"No values? How can you say that?" sputtered Frosted Hair. "You wouldn't take care of anyone. You'd let the poor rot."

"And you'd let them never aspire to anything," said Maxwell. "Freedom and liberty were the great gifts from our forefathers. Remember, they said we're endowed by the creator with certain inalienable rights. How can a person follow his own dreams, the things he was meant to be, if the government is interfering in everything he does? You even ate my rhubarb pie."

"Your rhubarb pie? I'm the one who went back, and got it."

"Yes, but anybody who knows me at all would know that I can't hack peanut butter cream. Rhubarb is my flavor. How can a soft-hearted liberal not give me her rhubarb pie—or at least reach across the table to steal some without severe penalty?"

"It seems that rhubarb pie is the only common ground here," sighed Wrinkled Grandmother.

"I'm willing to go with that," said Maxwell. "Madam," he continued turning to Frosted Hair, who was glaring at him with something approaching real hatred as she chewed her last bite of rhubarb pie. "I love rhubarb. It's apparent that you could develop a relationship with rhubarb, too.

"Out on the highway, there's an all-night cafe where the waitress keeps pure rhubarb pie in the freezer to microwave for me if I come through—not adulterated with raisins or strawberries or anything else.

"My friend, Bird, put me onto her, and we might do this together after a really good argument. I would consider it an honor when we blow this joint if you would join me there for a midnight cap of rhubarb pie."

"I guess I could do that although it's difficult to feel inclined to," said Frosted Hair. "After all, it's a nice spur of the moment suggestion, not really too conservative. Maybe you'd be nicer with rhubarb in you instead of rhubarbs coming out of you. After all, didn't Jesus also say something about it's not what goes into a man that offends him, but what comes out?"

"Why don't we all go," said Goatee. "I like rhubarb, too."

"Rhubarb pie," said Maxwell, smacking his lips. "the great common ground of the little man. If they don't promise us the liberty of rhubarb pie, let's throw them all out of office."

"Now there's a fine rhubarb for all of us," said Frosted Hair.

Lovelight

Lovelight of my life,
the clouds of evening
parted pink-orange
luminescence bright
to reveal in
the blue-black depths
pinpoints gold-white,
sparkling god-fire
of a moonlit starry night.

Moonlit starry night,
dreams of you
that won't let me go,
dreams of you
from so long ago
on a moonlit starry, starry night .

The haunting coo
of the night dove,
the stirring cool of dark,
the dwelling ache of heart,
the draw of your arms,
brings back your face,
surreal in the dim
reflected white
of a moonlit starry night.

The love of your smile
coming back to me
on a moonlit starry night,
it won't let me go,
no, it won't let me go,
whether restless sleep,
or warmth in the glow
of a moonlit starry night,
lovelight of my life.

Bob-A-Long
Sings A Different Song

I see the color yellow. You see the color yellow.

Although we can agree we are both seeing yellow, inside your brain is the interpretation of yellow really the same vision that my brain interprets as yellow? What if everyone's mental interpretation of the world is a little different, and some are so different, the others can't tell those people are seeing the same world?

The school bus roared in down-gear, gleaming yellow in morning sunlight with great roiling clouds of dust around it.

It came down the curve from the plateau of big open pastures above the tree-studded chasm that broke to the creek.

The cottonwoods, bur oaks and walnuts grew right out to the narrow road shoulder, so like most drivers, Dan Dillingham steered the bus to the middle of the road. It was just in time to avoid the small man in gray overalls wearing a gray-striped engineer's cap who stood there looking at a crack in the road.

At sight of him, the high school girls in the back of the bus broke into song, clapping hands in rhythm like a cheer at a game, "Baw, baw, baw, baw-bawb along, baw baw baw-bawb along. We sing your so-o-ong, baw-bawb along."

Then the grade school kids and the pair of older boys joined in, half of them sticking their heads through the tops of the windows where the balmy air flowed in, singing, "baw, baw, baw, baw-bawb along."

Dillingham slowed the bus, glaring back at the children from the rear-view mirror. "Alright, you kids, pipe down. Stop the singing. Get down in your seats. I know you saw Bob Longfellow there, but control yourselves. He's OK, just different, wounded as a veteran and all that, you know. You kids should be showing him some respect instead of singing at him."

"Ah, he didn't even notice us," said Peggy from the back of the bus. "Old Bob-a-Long was just bob-a-longing around, and he don't know any world went by. Baw, baw, baw-bawb along," she sang, and the rows of young people broke into smiles and singing as they joined her.

Peggy was right. Robert Wallace Longfellow had barely noticed the bus go around him despite it flinging dust and gravel. He was comfortable in the still, cool air of a late fall day, and concentrating on a trail of ants that disappeared into the crack in the road. He hadn't been concious of Dan Dillingham steering further to the middle of the road to avoid his own four-wheel drive Subaru wagon.

For the next two hours, Bob Longfellow would change position only to sit alongside the ants while he dragged a finger back and forth in the shoulder road dust letting the tactile sensation remind him that he was living. Only when he became aware that he might have to go to the bathroom, and that his stomach was growling for food did he finally get up to go to his car. Even then, he paused for 15 minutes with his face tilted up, sniffing from widened nostrils on his long nose in the soft wind that was shifting to northerly, heralding a great, moist cold front.

When he got to the car, Bob dug through an assortment of tools on the floor, from wrenches to nylon come-alongs with toothed jack handles attached, to get to a pile of notebooks where he pulled out a yellow one to record ant travel data in it along with a drawing of a particularly nice oak leaf.

After eating a sandwich in town, Bob Longfellow spent time on his hands and knees on Main Street with a tape measure appearing to carefully measure the street while recording information in a red notebook he had dug from the floor of his car.

Deputy Owen Reuben, who had just eaten a steak at the Deerhead, stood working a toothpick in his teeth for a while watching Longfellow work. Pedestrians along the sidewalk only looked briefly at Bob Longfellow with his gray hair sticking out raggedly from the engineer's flat-topped cap. They were used to seeing him.

Cars carefully steered around the thin, little man who occasionally looked up at them from a still youthful, but lined and wizened face, as though half surprised to see them there, but still not fully aware they were even there.

Satisfied that the entire town was taking care of Robert Wallace Longfellow, as usual, and that he wasn't risking getting hurt, Owen Reuben sauntered away in a cocky cop's walk to the county jail.

Bob Longfellow noticed another crack, this time in the sidewalk in front of the Deerhead. He stood there in the early afternoon as the breeze picked up into a soft moan, and gray clouds came scudding across the sky. When customers began coming into the Deerhead for afternoon coffee with half-frozen spits of rain coming from the sky, Bob was standing stock-still with the red notebook under his arm watching the crack.

"Ain't that Bob Longfellow a piece of work," said black-haired Johnny Beauregard looking out the window of the Deerhead from where he sat at the long table sipping his steaming coffee. "Looks like he'd be getting cold standin' there like that. Guess you got to work hard stayin' crazy for everybody, keepin' your veteran's benefits and disability and all that."

"Lordy, lordy, watch your tongue, Johnny Beauregard," said Charmin' Carmen the horse trader. "His mama over there in the corner will hear you. I knowed most of the people around here all my life including Bob Longfellow, and I can tell you. That kid ain't fakin' anything. He's nuttier than a fruitcake, got a steel plate in his head. Done got shot in the head, I hear. Look at that, the rain's changin' to ice, gettin' heavier."

"I figure," said Johnny Beauregard, "that he was nuts anyway, and saw a good chance to get a pension out of being nuts. He's nuts like a fox."

"No use you just talkin' about a fellow," said Charmin'. "It ain't becomin' to anybody who makes deals or has a life just to gossip about poor shot guys who are nuts. Go ask his mama. Go ask Martha Longfellow over there if Bob was nuts before he went to the army, and if he's more nuts now. Martha's a straight shooter, she'll tell you, then you can shut your mouth about it."

Johnny Beauregard stood, rubbing his palms on his hips, and smiling. "I'll just do that, Charmin' Carmen. I'll ask her." Then he walked to the women's smoking table in the far corner where the puffy-faced Martha Longfellow with long jowls sat with a cigarette dangling from her lip while empty-headed Mary chatted at her.

"Martha Longfellow," said Johnny Beauregard. "Me and Charmin' Carmen were talkin' over there, and I was wonderin'. Was your boy, Bob, nuts before he went to the army, or just nuts afterwards? Matter of fact, no offense, I even wonder if he could have been certifiably crazy without ever gettin' shot in the head?"

Martha Longfellow sat with her forehead wrinkled looking at Johnny Beauregard for the longest time. Most of the room full of tables across the great expanse of the Deerhead's main room had gone silent as people realized the woman had the perfect right to slug Johnny Beauregard for the inappropriateness of his remarks.

Finally Martha Longfellow puffed a great plume of smoke into Johnny Beauregard's face making him choke a little. Then she spoke, "Naah, Bobby was always nuts. Always claimed he heard voices. There you have it straight from his mama. But the army took him just like they'll take most warm bodies if the time is right. And it was them that got him shot in the head. So he's entitled.

"Now is he any more crazy than he used to be? I can't say for sure. He was nuts when he was a baby staring up at me with those big eyes. But, I'll tell you a couple of things. He's entitled to anything he can get, and he's actually smarter than the whole bunch in here put together. Bobby is a genius. Now, do you feel satisfied, or do you still feel a great need to show everybody here what a butt you can be, Johnny Beuregard."

"No, I'm satisfied, Mam."

Johnny Beauregard walked back to the table trying to show composure just as Doc Frenchie the veterinarian walked through the front doors with his arm around Bob Longfellow listening to him read from the red notebook. "Here, you sit right down here, and have a cup of coffee with me, Bob," said Doc. "No sense you just freezing out there."

Bob Longfellow drank his coffee slowly looking at Johnny Beauregard and Charmin' Carmen across the table. Then he announced in a high voice, "I have the final figure. The area of our Main Street is 158,363 square feet, which does not include, of course, parking spaces and turn-in spaces for side streets."

"And, who cares if it is 158,363 square feet besides maybe some planning engineer somewhere," said Johnny Beauregard.

"Why, I didn't think we knew, so I found out," replied Bob Longfellow looking puzzled. "I think we have to know."

"Know what, Bob?" asked Doc.

"Why, everything we don't know yet."

"Look here," said Johnny Beauregard winking at the others. "I see in your future six feet on a side. It's important for you to know."

"What is it? A square?"

"Naah, it's something else, like a force."

Bob Longfellow jumped to his feet, "Isosceles triangle then, all sides equal pull with the triangle leg a vector of force. It's for me to find out what it means?"

"Yeah, something like that is what I see, like a riddle," said Johnny. "I think it's important for you."

"What kind of nonsense are you talking?" asked Doc as Bob Longfellow rushed out the door.

"I just thought I'd say something with numbers like I knew what I was talking about to see what he did. Got him excited didn't I?"

"You hadn't ought to bait poor Bob-a-Long with anything. Every body ought to just help take a little care of someone like him," said Charmin' Carmen.

"Even meaningless garbage can get him to going. Look at that ice out there. It's really covering everything. Can't hardly believe it started out a nice day."

Bob Longfellow headed up the creek road to where it broke out of the prairie pastures all excited. Something about being told six feet was destiny had gotten into his mind like a real intellectual breakthrough. He had measured the trees near the curve, and there were three big trees exactly six feet apart. A coffee bean tree and a cottonwood tree across the road also were six feet apart. Some of his nylon come-alongs were six feet long when fully extended in double loop. What was important about this?

The big yellow school bus, encrusted now with a coat of ice over the top and most of the windows came slowly down the curve. Dan Dillingham was nearly alone on the bus now with most of the children returned to their homes leaving him bending over the steering wheel to see through the ice that accumulated a little faster than defroster and windshield wipers could work. He geared down to a crawl as he came with the bus still trying to fishtail on the incline. He was just hoping to have it made when the last high school girl in the back, staring out the window began to sing by herself very softly, "baw, baw, baw, ba-bawb along."

The bus was trying to slide, and one wheel dropped barely over the side of the timbered chasm, skinning softly up against an oak before coming to a stop. Dan Dillingham sighed tiredly. Better see how bad it is, and radio in for a wrecker. Thank god there was only himself and the girl still on board. The wrecker could take her home if need be.

He opened the door to climb out when a face turned ruddy red by the cold under an engineering cap covered with ice came through the mist in front of him.

"I knew it was important if I could connect it. I knew if I would build it, someone would come to need it. They told me to listen to Johnny." said Bob Longfellow. "Sit still now so you don't upset the balance, and I'll have you right out. Still, you hear me, sit still."

Dan Dillingham paused at the sound of straps being winched around the bus, and metal hooks on come-alongs being shoved into place. Then he could see Bob Longfellow hurrying to where his come-alongs were hooked to trees in triangular patterns to work jack handles here and there, then running across the road to do the same. Slowly the bus moved in sideways small jerks, its weight offset by the lack of resistance sliding on the ice, until it was pulled over the road shoulder back into place.

Nobody's going to believe this even when I tell them, thought Dan Dillingham.

There came the sound of clips coming loose, and straps pulled away. Bob Longfellow stuck his head in the door. "You better get to town now. Sorry I can't visit, but I want to try to see what the ants did in this weather.

"That Bob-a-Long is nuts," Dan Dillingham later told Doc Frenchie.

"Yeah, but he's a nice boy, probably nicer than his mama if the truth be known," said Doc. "Sometimes I wonder if it's us that lives in the real world, or if it's him."

Memorial Sleep

Wild roses grip the muddy shoulders
of the Six-Mile Road on Decoration Day,
and despite the sparkling May sun,
the sky is practically dying to descend
in bursting little showers
from dewey clouds that grow to surprise
from the damp, sappy spring of the morning.

The road rises through the stone-arch bridge
where the car passes packed with
peonies and spring dresses and suits
and the living who go to the graves,
full of roast beef dinner to look
at the stones where
great grandma and great grandpa lay,
the same who once knew those pink roses
on the Six-Mile too.
You wonder what their lives knew.

So, play tag with cousins, catch fireflies,
then slide into slumber.
Lightning slices the horizon promising
the easy yawning day is growing to a stormy night.
You sleep the depth of childhood,
and your time is passing along.

Jezebel And
The Sale Barn Solution

O.B. Goodfellow took an extra minute to yawn, and stretch his legs under his big mahogany desk.

The next cowboy novel he had to read looked good from what he could see in the table of contents—lots of action and lots of shooting. Good, good, very good that probably the villain would get what was coming to him in the end. O.B. hated soupy, sentimental or socially correct books.

"There's enough correctness in the real law," he told his wife at times. "What I like is justice at the end—either at the end of a six-gun or a rope."

He could read nearly all day today—after he took a few minutes to be what he was supposed to be, an attorney. But at 70 years old, it would be a shame if he let too much of what he was supposed to be get in the way of what he wanted to do.

That was for the young—the young jezebel in the next room, the barracuda he was turning loose in the community fish tank, the blonde in the beige suit the firm of Banghor, Baker and Burger had sent him from the city to learn from him for a few weeks.

Where had she found such a suit, he wondered—tweeded like a carpet and so pale it was almost white, cut off above the knees to give maximum exposure to sheer white hosiery. He supposed he was supposed to be attracted to that, but he knew the cold, green-eyed look of a tiger. The woman was mean.

Plus, she whistled through her partially parted front teeth, and it irritated him. It probably wasn't her fault unless she'd parted them with a crow-bar to make her noticeable in the legal world. He could picture that, her rolling around on the floor with the bar between her teeth. It was a better amusement to picture than one of her as possibly a somewhat neglected child who had become tough enough to fend for herself.

O.B. stuck his bald dome of a head through the door, "Miss Jeze—oh I mean, Miss Jerney, would you please come in here?"

"Yess," she said, hissing the last letter of the word into a double.

She was actually a little taller than him, even if it weren't for the black high heels, O.B. decided. How did she walk holding her knees together like that? It gave her a mincing short gait—well, no concern of his.

Her hypnotic eyes seemed to hold his. "Ahem, Miss Jerney."

"Yess."

"We have a situation down at the sale barn—that is, the cattle auction barn—which I would like you to make an investigation of today. The barn is a client of ours, and whenever an accident occurs there, we do a short investigation to see where their interests might lie should the incident cause concern."

"Yess. Get the information. Ssue the persson who had the accident for negligence before they act. Sseize everything they have even as they recuperate. Yess, hss."

Good night, she actually hissed an extra time. Get out of here fast if her tongue begins to flitter. "No, we don't necessarily want to carry things that far, Miss Jerney.

"We just want our client protected. They want their employees taken care of if they're hurt. They'll put out collection jars that everyone can contribute to for expenses beyond medical coverage. They usually send them gifts both from the company and from the other employees. It's like a big family."

"Hss, how gushy, gushy nice. I recommend we get a stop put to those practicess. It's an admission of guilt."

"No, Miss Jerney. We can't do that. Out here in this little community, it wouldn't be in their interest. They need the community to consider them as part of one big family, too. Why, Jackson Juxton, the sale barn owner, wouldn't feel right if he didn't call the family, too, and put out collection jars in a few more spots in town.

"The farm and ranch families who take cattle to them expect that kind of behavior from them right along with free calendars, pencils and ball caps. They wouldn't even need us except they've had the problem of the state or a trouble-making lawyer coming along before."

"Yess. We at Banghor, Baker and Burger like to watch for such tush-tush situations."

"Tush-tush? Well, never mind. You need to know the situation. Thaghor Branhart was working the ring that night when they turned these range cows in—you know, old broken-horned, broken-mouthed Texas Herefords with a fly under the tail for never having been penned up so tight before."

"Yess, I know, faulty corporate equipment."

"Well, maybe, you don't know. But you just write up the report best you can and I'll take care of it from there. You see, old Thaghor was just being his usual self out there, cock of the walk. He was popping his whip in front of the cows, and pointing his finger at the bidders to holler, 'Yeah.' Then he'd wiggle his hand at the next guy or point at him to get a counter bid just like a good ring man ought to."

"Yess, professional to a point just before his own negligence."

"Well, he probably got a little exuberant with the bidding, and popped his whip down a little hard on the hip bones of an old biddy, and she let him have it. One of the cows kicked poor old Thaghor right in the...well, she kicked him between his legs. I guess proper language, Miss Jerney, would be that she kicked him in the...well, the groin."

"Yess, she gave him a good smack in the privates. Serves him right for negligence. We got him, Ssir. He can't claim sterility for something he did to himself."

"No, no, no, we don't have him. Good night, the man is in agony, all swollen up black and blue. He can't walk. He's going to have at least a three-day hospital stay as I understand it. And that's not to mention the hunk of hide taken out of his back when the fellows dragged him out of the ring all doubled up like that before the cows could run over him again.

"No, we're on the same side as Thaghor because he's a member of our community. We want him to get well, and come back to the barn where he belongs."

"Yess, hss, I understand. Don't worry, Mr. Goodfellow, I'll nail him."

"Well, just bring me the report, and at least you'll have a bit of experience from it. And, not to tell you how to dress, Miss Jerney...."

"Actually it's Mss. Jerney."

"Yes, but you ought to at least wear rubber boots down at the sale barn instead of high heels. You'd sink out of sight in those. The soils are rather soft-textured. You can use the pair I have in the closet. My wife keeps a pair of tennis shoes there you can use with them to keep you steady."

She was a peculiar figure walking between the livestock trailers on the broad mud lot between the puddles of water, wobbling as though trying to stay stable in several pairs of shoes while holding her knees together. Jackson Juxton couldn't decide what kind of a person this was—in a beige dress with hair dyed blonde, and frosted in a frizz out to the edges.

"Let me get the door for you, Ma'am," he said.

"Hsss. Would you direct me to Jackson Juxton, please?"

"Why, you got him, Ma'am. I'm Jackson Juxton," he said, tucking his hands in his pockets and leaning backward as though to show her regard from an extra space away. "Auctioneer at your service, whether you're dealing in horses, hogs, cows or antiquities, Jackson Juxton is your man."

The laugh in his pale blue eyes above the high-boned pink cheeks was stopped short by the cold glare of the green eyes.

"I'm here for the Goodfellow Firm, Mr. Juxton," she said, "in the case against Mr. Branhart."

"Just call me Jackson, Ma'am. And, actually, this ain't against old Thaghor or nobody for that matter. We just try to cut ourselves a little slack in case. And what would your name be?"

114

"Mss Jerney, hss. Let's look around. You might consider paving your front lot."

"Well, you could have parked closer. Tomorrow's sale day, and the trailers just brought in some stock. They're getting them penned out back. You didn't have to park where they do."

"Hss, show me the ring. Has Mr. Branhart been careless or had accidents before his negligence in this one?"

"Oh, I think he went nose to nose with a horse once, and got his broken with a couple of teeth knocked out, but he ain't never been negligent, Miss Jerney, just taken a few knocks is all. Heck, if I don't have an extra groove in my back from a Simmental bull myself. You just always got to think what you're seein' come into the ring next, and jump behind the steel barriers there if it's somethin' that's a little perky."

"Hss, oh, look at that—I have mud all over my boots, and there's even a few little bits on my stockings. I would like to have a wet paper towel before I leave."

"Certainly. You can go the lady's room before you leave. The women in the office keep it real clean so it's never like where all the fellas go.... Well, never mind, you can use it."

"Yess, and this would be the ring you speak of, this round, fenced-in area."

"Yes, Miss Jerney, let me get the gate here for you. You see it's all fenced with high, heavy steel pipe railing so the buyers and sellers can sit back in the theater chairs there in comfort. The auctioneer and bookkeeper are up there. And, the ring men are the old boys down here lettin' the stock in and out, and keepin' them movin' so the buyers can get a look at what they're biddin' on."

"Oooh, hss, this green substance on the floor, and on my boots, it wouldn't be?"

"Yes, it would be Miss Jerney."

"Animal droppings?"

"Actually manure, we call it, Ma'am. The cattle just came in off grass so it's kind of...."

"Hss, don't explain the droppings to me, Mr. Jexton."

"Jackson, Miss Jerney. You can just call me Jackson because if you're going to be here any time at all, everybody in town is just like one big family. Heck, we don't know a stranger."

"Hss, you should get to, Mr. Jexton. You should really get to. But then, I suppose it helps coming from a strange place yourself."

"Uh, Miss Jerney, I really wouldn't recommend you lean against the arena fence in that dress. You see...." He paused as she walked across the ring with the parallel stripes of green manure across the back of her dress, wondering if he should say anything about it."

"So, I suppose, Mr. Jexton, that this entryway would be where the cows come into the ring?"

"Sure would be, Miss Jerney."

"And our Mr. Branhart would have been standing here, looking into the gate to await their arrival."

"Heck, Ma'am. I suppose old Thaghor was lookin' at a bunch of things. He was probably standin' closer to where I'm at, grinnin' kind of happy-like with a chew in his mouth if he was like usual. He'd have been sportin' with the boys outside the ring to keep it all cordial. He woulda' had one eye on the price and weight flashing up above on the last bunch to keep the figures in his head. He'da had one eye on this gate and another eye on the gate on the other side where the other ring man was closing it behind the last bunch of cattle.

"You can reckon on a good ring man going like he had four sets of eyes in his head no matter where he's standin' or lookin' for the moment. Plus, I know the poor devil'd had to go to the bathroom for an hour before it all happened—bladders an' bungs of iron is what a good ring man's got cuz the hours are long."

"You can't know that."

"I sure can cuz I was one of the fella's that helped cut his britches off him for the doctor to have a look."

"Hss, bad, an employer should have adequate toilet facilities. But he was negligent, too, trying to look too many ways at once while fraternizing unnecessarily with the customers."

"But that's his job!"

"Were the cattle unusually wild? Were they any wilder than what he was accustomed to?"

"Ma'am, those cows was right rank."

"Yess, hss, I can believe that. The whole place stinks. But were they wild?"

"Rank is wild, Ma'am. Miss Jerney, a rank cow means a wild cow."

"Hss, not good, not good. You may be responsible for keeping animals that haven't been adequately gentled for the work. So, this hallway through the pens goes back to where the wild cattle are kept?"

"We call it an alleyway, Miss Jerney. And all kinds of cattle come down it from your old cows that have been handled all their lives in a dairy, to your ones fresh off grass, to stockers, to baby calves, and some of the randiest old bulls you'll see anywhere. Ma'am, I don't think you better be walkin' back down there today. Like I said, they're workin' the cattle into the pens for tomorrow. Or, at least stick close by me if you have to go look."

"Yess, well these little cows are rather innocent looking."

"Ma'am, those are baby calves, little Holsteins from a dairy."

"And, why is the man trotting his horse down your hallway?"

"Oh, fer gawd's sake, jump in here with me, lady, into this pen behind this gate. Old Cyrus has doodled himself a bull on the other end of that rope, and his horse ain't got much else place to go until Frank has a rope on him from the other end."

"Aaah, hss, hss."

"Don't worry, Ma'am. I know he's a powerful big old black bull hittin' the sides of the pen that way, but he ain't going to get in. See, Cyrus has his rope tightened, and Frank's on a capable old cow-horse tighten'n up on him from the other end. See, they're startin' to pull him away."

"Ooh, ooh, hss, hss."

"I'm sorry, Miss Jerney. It looks like the horse splashed up stuff on your legs, oh, my gosh, under your dress, and on it. You sure are a'goin' to need that restroom."

"That won't be necessary. I just need to get back, write up my report, and talk to O.B. Goodfellow. I doubt you've ever had an OSHA inspection here. This place is a mess. I'll be writing recommendations all week just from what little I've seen."

"I see, Ma'am. Well, at least let me or one of the other fellows take you back in the truck so you don't mess your car up with all the mess you picked up here."

"I didn't bring my car. I drove O.B. Goodfellow's new car."

"In that case, Miss Jerney, I guess you don't need our help. You just drive old O.B.'s car back, and give him our thanks for sending you down here so we could get some real professional help. You have been more than a help. You've been an inspiration for us to do better. Is that the car he got with the white, velvet seat covers?"

"Yess, hss."

"Good, good, that's real good. He won't mind if you dirty it up a little, Ma'am. O.B. is a real country boy—grew up here you know."

She drove away with the same ivory, cold lip-tuck she drove in with.

O.B. was on Chapter 15 already when his secretary told him he had a phone call from Jackson Jexton.

"Yes, Jackson, this is O.B. You must be calling because my girl's made it down there?"

"She sure has been, O.B. She's on her way back, OK, but a little dirtied up. I guess you won't care if I say you are quite the old coyote. I see what you mean. We don't need any lawyer checkin' up on us all of the time. Guess she brought it home to me just fine. These are cattlemen working down here just like you said, and they know the ways of what they're doing."

"I tried to tell you that, Jackson. Things are tight enough without you pouring money down a rat hole. Now, if you ever do really need an attorney, you call me. If you ever suspect you need an attorney, you call me, and I'll let you know whether I think you really do. Maybe next time you'll listen to me."

"I hear you, O.B., and I'll do that next time without needin' a lesson like that. Don't know what you'll be doing with that young lady though?"

"Oh, she'll put her time in here, write her report, maybe do a couple of things for the banker and the school board before I send her back. I might use her on some real estate research. She'll have an experience.

"I like to do right by the young people. A young lady lawyer could never have a better friend in learning the ways of the world than O.B. Goodfellow."

Click.

"Miss Zimmerman, can you can come in here. Jackson has hung up now."

"Yes, sir?"

"Ms. Jerney is on her way back in. Jackson was quite pleased with the work she did for him. You know that bill I told you to make to him for our services. Wasn't that for $500?"

"Yes, sir."

"Well, knock it up to a full $1,000. He learned so much from it that I want to make sure he values the full experience."

Set Free

A quiet-time shadows the earth
as a moist spring fog rolls
over the Flint Hills,
so still in the new light
of the red rising sun
that a cow lowing her voice
from two miles away
to call her small calf
can be heard as if she
were next to you.
The booming ground soft coo
coaxes from mating prairie chickens
call you to your home
in the center of being.

To fill the lungs
in such a setting,
to feel the chill from
the dew-laden sweet growth
of the new green prairie grasses
seeping down inside the swelling chest,
to smell the breath of creation,
is to invigorate the spirit
with the touch of life's hand.

You mount your pony,
her own ears turning expectantly,
and she steps out gingerly
over the ancient stone outcrops
that have been a part of you
and those who came before you,
and your heart is set free.

Mrs. Macon's Cemetery

The magic of big, soft late-winter Missouri snowflakes falling on a broad vista of still-green fescue pasture and interspersed trees leading to heavy stands of timber wasn't lost on Jonathan Stetler.

Everything here was magic to him, and different than his growing-up time on the western high plains. He and Julie were newly married, which was a magic in itself. They had been fortunate to find this old farmhouse to rent south of work in the city in Central Missouri.

"Look at this, Julie, look at this snow and the trees down there. Isn't this incredible?"

"Beautiful, beautiful," she replied, smiling at him.

The flakes were so large, he could see the geometric designs of their crystalline structures just looking out the window. They stood there together, looking through the glass at Merideth Macon's two-story, white home across the road and up a quarter-mile driveway.

The Macon farm was lined along the road and up both sides of the driveway by white-board fence. Huge red-oak trees were evenly spaced along the driveway.

"The snow's so heavy you can barely see Mrs. Macon's house now," Jonathan said. "It's building up on the tree limbs already."

"Oh, Jonathan," Julie said, "isn't it wonderful just being here together? I hope we get snowed in. Wouldn't it be nice?"

"Yes, that would be nice, like magic, like a Camelot, just being here together, and not having to go in to work. You know, Julie, I would like to ask Mrs. Macon just one more time if she would allow us to walk on her land, too. I would love to explore that timber."

They both stood there, contemplating their move into this neighborhood.

Harlan and Betty Freiley—tall, sandy-haired, pink-faced people, up the road to the west, with the big horned Hereford cows and robust new spring calves—had greeted them as a welcome addition to the area. They showed them their poultry hobby, their guineas, ducks, geese and bantams.

Jonathan and Julie liked to hike, and the Freileys assured them they were welcome to go from their landlord's farm through the fence to roam the Freiley land at will.

"Just check with us ahead to see where the bull is," they had cautioned.

The people in the nearby small town had been nice, too. Julie took clothes to wash at the laundromat while Jonathan was at work. The very first time she had been there, a lively 6-year-old black boy ran through the door to watch her rubbing a spot from a shirt.

As his mother, a young golden-brown woman only a few years older than Julie, came through the door carrying a baby and a basket of clothes with two other small children following, he asked, "What's your name?"

"I'm Julie. What's your name?"

"I'm Eddy Johnson, and that's my Mama, Elaine, and my baby sister, Echo, and my big sister, Elen, and my brother, Freddy. You got any kids?"

"No, I don't yet. You're a bright boy," she had said, smiling at the mother. Afterward, they spoke to each other a little every time they met. Mr. Johnson apparently was a house painter who did very well because the Johnsons lived in a very large, two-story, well-kept home on the edge of town.

Julie determined that she would get to know Elaine Johnson better.

Mrs. Macon had been different than any of the others. "She's really different, don't you think?" Jonathan asked.

"Yes, I'd call her different, nice maybe...pleasant enough, I think. You know, Jonathan, she was almost strange, like maybe she liked us but wasn't sure she wanted us here. I don't think she liked it when you asked if we could walk on her place, too."

White-haired, ruddy-cheeked, square-built Meredith Macon, in her pink and white homey apron, hadn't seemed immediately different. She smiled at the sight of the tall, thin almond-eyed newlyweds standing with arms wrapped around each other in matching red sock hats in her doorway—smiled like nearly any older woman will at the magic of young love.

She brought them into her front parlor, and served them homemade oatmeal cookies.

But her expression grew more somber as the young Stetler lovers talked about walking across the land and their first sighting of ground-hogs in the rain in the Freiley's most remote back pasture.

"We just love the big maples and oaks here," Julie said.

"And that reminds me," Jonathan added. "Would you mind if we walked on your land, too? We'd be careful not to bother anything."

Meredith Macon had narrowed her eyes pausing for a moment looking at him.

"No," she said, "I don't think that would be possible. I don't think I would want anybody to walk on my land. No, definitely not. I don't want you walking on my land."

"Well, if you say so," Jonathan said, unaccustomed as he was to being turned down. Most people were fine with it as long as their permission was asked to show respect for private property. "If you want to think it over at all, the Freileys can tell you we've been OK on their place."

"No, I don't think so. Just stay off my place. Thank you for coming over to see me. You do seem like a nice young couple, and I'm happy to know you. Stop back at the house sometime. Now, if you don't mind, I have things in the oven, and I need to get back to my baking."

Meredith Macon had brought them over a plate of cookies for Christmas.

When Jonathan asked Harlan Freiley about Meredith Macon, Freiley replied, "Well, she's lived there a long time by herself, and that can make people set in their ways, you know. Meredith is the last of her family. She never married. Her brother died in the war. Her folks have been gone probably 40 years.

"They once had a couple thousand acres, but Meredith sold most of it. She's got plenty of money to take care of herself without doing anything on what's left. I'd guess she must have 200 acres left there with the house and outbuildings and the cemetery."

"Cemetery?"

"Yeah, Jonathan, there's an old cemetery of some sort back down in those woods. Saw a little of it once myself. But even though I've lived here most of my life, I've never really been down in there to look around. Meredith doesn't like anybody even asking about it."

"Why not?"

"Folks say it's a slave cemetery, left from the people the Macon family once owned. I figure Meredith just doesn't want anybody poking around down there—wants to keep it just her business."

But Jonathan was only made more curious by the revelation. He tried to focus his eyes through the snow at the timber to see if he could see anything.

When he got the binoculars out to look some more, Julie said, "I've looked, too, but I don't see anything down there."

The snow began melting quickly the following day in intense sunshine with birds singing spring songs that promised a quick change in season. Jonathan again was at the window staring in satisfaction at hunks of watery snow falling from the trees.

"We really ought to get out for a walk this afternoon, Julie," he said. "It's going to be warm."

Jonathan stared back through the timber as splotches of white made way for the black of bark and wood on the trees. He saw a squirrel far away through the binoculars. Then came the moment he noticed an aberration, a white against the black that wasn't irregular like the snow, but instead squared off.

"Julie, I'm seeing something I couldn't see before. It's something squared off...ah, a board, I think. Yes, it's held up by another board. Julie, it's a cross. I think I'm seeing that cemetery."

"You really think so, Jonathan? There wouldn't be any board cross left on something that old would there? Don't you think it would be all rotted away, and overgrown with vines and trees and grass and stuff? Here, let me look."

That's when they decided. They would drive the car down to the next road south of Meredith Macon's, and walk back in to her land from the other end. They would see the cemetery, and Mrs. Macon would never have to know they had been there.

Their Mustang spun out hunks of mud behind it, and all but bottomed out twice as they went up the cross-country road. The timber lined the road so thickly on the north side of the road that they couldn't see Meredith Macon's home even though they knew it was less than a mile away.

"I guess this is about it, Julie. I would guess we're about straight through from the cross I saw if we can walk it through the trees. What do you say? I think we'll get wet and muddy. Are you still up for this?"

"Oh brother, you know I am. I'm as curious about this slave cemetery now as you are. Just hold the barbed wire apart for me, so I don't rip my sweats climbing over. We'll be so hidden by the trees I don't think anybody will ever know we've been in here. By the way, what do you want to say if we do get caught?"

"I don't know. How about we came in from the south, and didn't even know we were on her place until we came to the cemetery."

"That's OK, but don't even mention the cemetery. Just say we came in from the south, and didn't know where we were. I don't think it would be good to let her know that we knew the cemetery was on her place."

To their delight, they walked on leaf-pack instead of mud, with moisture seeping up under their footsteps. They came out of the trees onto an expanse of fescue grass that also provided the same solid footing. It was only when they tried to jump across a small slow-flowing stream that they slid in mud going up the short bank on the other side. At least they had saplings to hold onto.

Away through the next fringe of trees they came to, they could see through the branches the broken outline of Meredith Macon's big box-structured house with its large front porch. Much further to the west was the suggestion of a dip where the road should be and a faint patch of white that might be their own home.

"I don't see anything of a cemetery, Jonathan, do you? Don't you think we should be there?"

"I'd say let's bear left, and don't go much further ahead. I'm afraid if we get too close to those trees, somebody might be able to see us from a ways off. Watch these thorns. Hey, I think these are blackberries. Maybe we could come back here in the summer. Maybe Mrs. Macon will soften up on us walking here if we get to know her better."

"Oh, Jonathan, look through the trees over there—white crosses! Why there must be more than 30 of them all freshly painted white. Somebody is keeping this up. Look, boards—they're building a new fence around it."

"Sssh. Try to talk more softly. I'm beginning to feel like we could be a little exposed here."

They stopped at the edge of white-board fence, looking at broken pieces of old native stone roughly in lines with new wooden crosses marking more clearly where graves would have been.

"There are a lot of people buried here, Jonathan. This place easily could have been used for 50 years."

"As a matter of fact, we think it was," said a voice out to the side of them. Jonathan and Julie were frozen in place by the sight of a tall black man in tan coveralls walking out from among the nearest trees.

"Who are you kids? What are you doing anyway? Oh, don't worry. You're OK. I'm Josh Johnson. I've been doing some fence-building, cross-building and painting for Mrs. Macon down here. Finding these graves, and putting a cross on each one of them is an extra we like to do. I trade work with her all the time for our place in town. You might even have seen my house, big white one on the edge of town. Now I've let you know who I am, so, you don't think you stumbled onto a bugga-boo out here in the woods. Why don't you tell me who you are?"

"I'm Jonathan Stetler and this is my wife, Julie. We live over that way. We were walking around from that road back that way, and kind of lost track of where we were at. I guess we just kind of stumbled in here. Are there people really buried here?"

"Yes, there are people buried here. I was about to go up to the house to have some cookies with Mrs. Macon and my family. Why don't you walk on up there with me? Mrs. Macon can tell you more about this place if she wants to, and you can meet my family."

They emerged from the trees walking across the large expanse of green fescue together, Johnson asking them what part of Kansas they grew up in, and telling them a little of his own youth in St. Louis, long before he had come out to school and met his future wife, Elaine. "This is the first time in my life I ever really had anything," he said.

Meredith Macon's eyes narrowed as they came in the front door. The wrinkles in her face sunk into a frown as Johnson explained how they were lost, and he met them at the cemetery.

"We lost track coming in from the other way," Julie said.

Meredith Macon wiped her hands on her apron as her frown softened into a grim smile. "Well, I guess you are from Kansas, nosey yankees. My Daddy said his Grand-dad would tell how the Jayhawkers would ride in unexpectedly. You might as well have some cookies with us. Do you drink coffee? I will offer you courtesies and friendship even if I don't believe you just stumbled in here lost.

"You'll have to excuse the papers on the table until I get them cleared off. We were going through some business. This is my last living relative, Elaine, and her children.

"Since you seem to have been so curious about our history as to have accidentally stumbled into the cemetery, I'll tell you that when I die this will be her place, or her children's if she goes first. She can even choose Josh for her heir as long as her children follow him."

Jonathan looked across the table where Elaine nodded her deep brown face at him, and back at Mrs. Macon whose pink cheeks were set in pasty white skin.

Mrs. Macon observed his glance, and added, "I suppose you think it's odd that a white woman is leaving her land to a black woman? You yankees never have understood our peculiar family institutions."

"Oh no, Mrs. Macon, I didn't mean anything by it—I know we're butting in here. Maybe we should be going."

"No, no, it's just that usually I don't like to have anybody coming in here, looking at our cemetery. I've come to look at it as ours. Josh Johnson says he and Elaine may open it to the public when I'm gone. That will be OK if it's our own people who open it, and not a bunch of yankees holding it up like a freak show. It would be nice if they could figure out the name of each person who went in each grave. They say my great grandmother tried to keep track of it if we could find it among all this paper.

"I suppose you think relationships between all slave owners and their Negro people were destroyed by the Civil War. Our old timers told how the blacks helped hide them in the storm cave when the Union cavalry came through so they wouldn't tear the place up too badly.

"It was a peculiar thing that you had relationships with folks who were your property, but they had their own situation here. They were used to it.

"Many of the people who used to be slaves stayed on, and worked for my great grandparents. There got to be fewer of them all the time as their children went off to the cities, and the machinery got more modern. I'll admit that I never thought it was much anything odd for us all to stick together. My Daddy used to raise thunder if any town officials tried to make trouble for our black folk.

"I'll also admit there was a time when I was uncomfortable with black people named Macon in the same community. Both sides of the mix of feelings were there. Then Elaine got married, and she wasn't a Macon anymore. She was a Johnson. She was the only one of the black Macons left.

"She's very pretty, you know. Aren't the children cute? I've come to love Elaine's little family in a very short time, but I had to decide to go out of my way to do it.

"Some of the old-timers got to be really harsh at times. It was the way things made them back then. But we don't have to keep making the same mistakes our parents and grandparents did, do we? Love can overcome everything.

"These are really the last relatives I have left. It's the best of what we were.

"I didn't mean to have folks like you drawn in from the outside to try to understand our strange way. Elaine and I, we go so far back that our families became family.

"I know that there are people who are going to say that Elaine somehow tricked me into willing her property. I tell her to ignore them because they can't understand.

"If you've ever known the magic of a beautiful moment, like the snow when it fell this week in those big flakes—love is like that, isn't it? Except that, where the snow melts, love is what keeps you going for years and years. We delivered their babies, and they delivered ours. They cared for us when we were sick, and we cared for them. The same rhythms went on decade after decade after decade. It took more than a season to change them.

"The love I have realized from it has made me alive again. Love truly is the magical cure for everything. Love is hanging onto what was wonderful about the past, even the ordinary long-lasting day to day things, and letting the ugly slip away.

"You yankees have understood the worst of it. Keep coming over. Maybe you can understand the best of it."

Shunga Nunga

Shunga Nunga,
living pathway of all,
beautiful stream of childhood gone
looping your way between
the green grassy hills of home
down to the very bedrock
of everything that has been before.

Bullheads and bluegill
lived in the shade of
your geat masthead trees
while blue-green dragonflies
added more sheen
above the ripples
on your many bends and curves.

You no longer slowly
make your way below
the high wooden bridge
on the bend by Marilyn's,
or wander by the goat farm
below the ancient hill
named for Chief Burnet
because your way
has been laid straight.

You were stretched to lie
like a giant gut ripped
from the bowels of the earth,
your life left to dry
in the sun
and at night
before the orange-red
glowing embers of
your years of timber growth.

Bulldozers piled the
ruptured piles of black soil
and yellow-white clays until
they could be laid over by the miles
of asphalt and concrete,
houses and stores
to leave you a canal
with the trees slowly growing
as the harbingers of life
try to replace
the hundred thousand years
of vitality green growth
along the promise of
the drainage sewer.

What childhood is it now
to remember the sterility of
your hard-surfaced drainage
and your floating flock
of fast food cups
and plastic bags?

Shunga Nunga,
the tennis courts
are nice,
and the people can get
more than a hundred
channels to look at
instead of looking
at you.

Payback Time
For Mean Dean

Dean was just dozing off in his favorite spot in the back pew when the Rev. Bugbuoy said, "That reminds me of a story."

Right away Dean blinked his eyes to attention because one of the few times he listened was when the preacher told a story or a joke. He glanced sideways to see if his wife, Sharilyn, was glaring at him for going to sleep. Sometimes she even elbowed him in the side. But she was looking forward at the minister, a slight smile already on her face. Good—unusual but good. Better that she hadn't noticed him.

Rev. Bugbuoy was touching the top of his bristly, dark, shaved-off head, looking really sober—which was good. It was one of his mannerisms before a really funny story.

Then he said, "There was this high school teacher giving a mid-term exam, and four boys in the class didn't show up. They hadn't called ahead. The teacher didn't have any excuses for them.

"About two hours later, they did show up—four big old gangly boys standing there in front of the teacher, not looking her or each other in the eye. They all said they were sorry, but they had a good reason for missing the test. They had a flat tire on the car they all came in. Could she give them another chance?

"Now, this teacher was an old, experienced hand. She knew what integrity looked like, and these boys were looking off at the corners of the room, or up at the ceiling, and only occasionally glancing at her face. But, OK, she says, she'll give them a chance at a make-up test, but it will include some extra questions. 'That's fine, that's fine,' all the boys said.

"So, the teacher takes the boys into another room by themselves, and seats them apart from each other at the four corners of the room with a pen and paper for each. The first question, she announces, is, 'Which tire was flat?'"

The congregation was laughing, and Sharilyn was chuckling hard as she looked at him, but Dean could only pretend to laugh. Good Lord, where had Rev. Bugbuoy gotten that story? Could he know? Did he know that Dean had been one of those boys? Oh well, probably this was a happenstance occasion, coincidental—probably some joke book had happened to give the Rev. Bugbuoy a true story.

Dean snuggled back comfortably into the cushions on the wooden pew as Rev. Bugbuoy loudly proclaimed, "Integrity....." to begin his sermon.

Dean's eyes were closed, and he gasped into a snore. He automati-

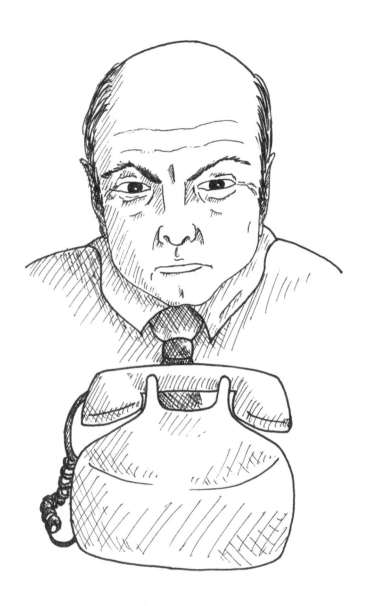

cally woke himself up before Sharilyn could give him the usual elbow in the side. But she wasn't looking at him this time. Her brown eyes were focused forward at the podium, where the Rev. Bugbuoy was saying, "That reminds me of a boy another time.

"He was at an abandoned house with some friends, an old falling-down thing with the plaster lattice showing bare like the ribs of a skeleton from the inside. They were poking with sticks to try to get rats that ran through the walls. They finally brought in firecrackers, and poked them through the holes to explode on the rats. They got more and more enthused pushing wads of firecrackers into the wall. Finally the wall caught fire.

"They sat on a hill a little way away, watching that old house burn in the wee hours of the morning when they all should have been home in bed. None of them ever told who did it. That boy didn't tell his daddy he burned down the house. But it was private property. It belonged to somebody. The boy lacked integrity...."

Good golly, Bugbuoy must know something, Dean thought. This was the second story about him as a young man. He glanced around to see if anyone was looking at him, but even Sharilyn was only brushing at a corner of her brown curls as she looked straight ahead.

It made it tough to sleep again. Before Dean knew it, the service was over, and he'd stayed awake through the rest of it.

The Rev. Bugbuoy just said, "Good morning, good to see you, Dean," as he went through the line to go out the door.

Mrs. Bugbuoy took his hand, too, but then held it a moment longer as she pulled an envelope from the table behind her.

"I almost forgot, Dean. Somebody left something for you here marked 'Personal.'"

Dean took the envelope, turning it over in his hands as he walked out the door into a blustery north wind. He walked quickly to the car without visiting with anybody. Then he tore open the envelope to find a single sheet of lined stationery with three words written in lower case in the center, "It's payback time."

Payback time? What could that mean? It was probably no use worrying about it. But that Bugbuoy and his wife—they did know some things about him, didn't they?

"Why are you in such a hurry?" asked Sharilyn as she got in the car.

"Just tired, and it's Sunday. I'd like to get home, eat dinner and just relax a little—wouldn't you?"

"Sure, but there's a few chores we'll have to do."

"I know, I know," said Dean.

At home, he hurried into the house ahead of her and punched the telephone answering machine as he went by it. Immediately, he heard a funny, low, gravelly voice that could have belonged to a man or a woman.

"It's payback time, Dean," said the voice. "Remember when you stold gasoline out of the tractor? Snuck right into the shed to get it time after time, didn't you? Well, a list has been kept all these years— the payback list. It's payback time, Dean."

Then, "click," the voice was gone.

Old Man Simpson, that's who the voice had to be. Dean used to sneak into the shed where Simpson's tractor was stored, loosen the pet-cock on the gas line to drain some gasoline into his can, tighten it back up, and sneak back out again. Nobody should have known. Nobody could have been the wiser. But somehow Old Man Simpson knew and he was connected with the Rev. Bugbuoy.

Wait. Old Man Simpson was dead—had been for 20 years. Nobody would believe the Rev. Bugbuoy had a connection where he could hear the dead, least of all Dean. But the thought made the hairs on the back of his neck rise.

"Brrring," rang the telephone.

"Hello," said Dean as he picked up the receiver.

"Hi, Dean," said the same low, gravelly voice. "Remember when you and the other boys did a drive-by egging of Sheila and her boyfriend? You ruined her dress and their evening. It's payback time."

"Who is this?" hollered Dean. "Who are you anyway? Say, is this Bugbuoy? OK, Mrs. Bugbuoy?"

But only silence could be heard on the other end. Dean listened a few minutes, then hung up.

Sharilyn came through the door saying, "Dean, do you realize you didn't feed or water the dog when you got up this morning? You better take care of him before we eat. I don't really appreciate it that I had to check on him."

"Yes, dear," said Dean. He felt really tired.

"Dean, do you think you might be able to help me with the dishes after we eat?"

"Yes, Sharilyn."

Later that afternoon, after she had cleared the dishes, and was washing them alone, he was snoring in the reclining chair in front of the football game on television when the phone rang again.

Where was Sharilyn, anyway? He wanted her to answer the annoyance that was waking him up. The last thing he wanted to hear again was that gravelly voice.

He muted the game. "Sharilyn, where are you? Can you answer that phone?"

"Brrring...brrring...click." The answering machine was coming on. He could hear it.

"Are you there, Dean?" asked the low gravelly voice. "Wake up, boy. It's payback time. You're the one who made Russell miserable calling him four-eyes when he got dark-framed glasses, remember? You even slapped him on the back of the head when he was going down the stairs. That was mean, Dean. Now it's payback time."

Click.

Who was that? Russell? Would stupid old Russell come back years later to connive with Bugbuoy? But Russell couldn't know about Old Man Simpson's gas, could he? He'd kept that quiet.

Heck, he didn't even know where Russell was or what had happened to him. Yet, that gravelly voice did have a tone of familiarity to it.

Whoever was behind this gravelly voice, didn't they know he never did pranks or bothered the property of other people like this any more? Heck, he had grown up. He just wanted to do his work, have his peace, and get along. Why bring up the past?

Sharilyn came in. "Good, you're finally awake," she said. "I took a walk with the dog, and I've been playing ball with him. I wish you'd come along, too. It seems like forever since Shellie left for college. All you do is work and sleep."

"Oh, come on, Sharilyn. I get tired, you know. I'm entitled to a little relaxation."

"A little, yes. But you're sleeping away our time at home. It seems like you sleep everywhere we go. Of course, you're worst at church."

"Hey, I can't help it if Bugbuoy's boring and it's warm in there. Anybody ought to be able to go to sleep in there."

"Well, you missed the extra part about remembering our veterans who died in action. I guess the only one from our era was Russell Fontclare. You remember Russell Fontclare, don't you?"

"Old Russell Four Eyes?"

"You might remember him that way. I remember him as Russell Fontclare, a really nice and caring guy. You might have known him better if you hadn't spent all the time making fun of him."

Wow, Russell was dead, too. Maybe old Bugbuoy really got messages from the other side. Who knew what a preacher might do getting into all that spiritual stuff?

It was 3 a.m. when the phone started again. "Brrring, brring."

"Get the phone," said Sharilyn, elbowing him in the backend from the other side of the bed.

"I don't want to get the phone. Let the answering machine get it."

"What if it's an emergency, Dean? Just go get it. You've had more sleep today than I've had."

He heard the answering machine click on to take the message, but the person on the other end didn't speak. Then the phone started in again. "Brrring, brrring, brrring."

"OK, OK, I'm coming," said Dean. "But it hadn't better be this pay-back stuff again.... Hello?"

"Hi, Dean," said the gravelly voice. "Remember when you used to do this to Mrs. Walters late at night? You'd call her, and ask her lame riddles. You nearly scared that woman to death, Dean. Since she's deceased, who knows but what you didn't contribute to her death. It's payback time, Dean."

Man, were the dead after him? No, it had to be somebody alive, some-body who knew him really well. But who knew him that well? Sharilyn was breathing deeply in her sleep. He wished he was asleep. Maybe he could ask her for an idea on who gravelly voice could be.

Dean didn't sleep well the rest of the night. Didn't whoever this was know he was a reformed guy now? Most people said he was even a nice guy. Life might not be terribly exciting, but he had learned to cope with-out excitement, hadn't he?

"You're going to be late for work if you don't get up now," said Sharilyn, shaking him by the shoulder. "Hurry into your clothes. I have some eggs and toast ready for you. Hurry, hurry."

"Sharilyn, can you think of anybody we know with a low, gravelly voice?"

"Your mother when she's giving hints, maybe."

"Let's not start in on Mom."

He was stunned when he went out to the car. Written with shaving cream across the hood in big letters were the words, "PAYBACK TIME." It was written the same way across the windshield, across the trunk lid, and on both sides of the car.

The shaving cream might eat finish off, he thought. Whoever Gravelly Voice was wanted to make sure he got the message. He didn't know whether to feel angry and threatened, or just confused. The past should be the past, shouldn't it?

"There's a funny message slip in your box," said Teresa the secretary as he walked through the door at work. "The guy didn't say who he was. Just called, and said to write it down. He said you'd understand."

The pink slip simply read, "Payback time."

Dean found himself staring at the telephone at times all day Monday and all day Tuesday, but no calls came. There wasn't even anything on the answering machine.

When the phone rang at midnight sharp Wednesday, Dean jumped from the bed as if to attention to a 10-gun flag salute. "What is it?" asked Sharilyn sleepily, but he already was running for the phone.

"Hi, Dean," said the gravelly voice.

"Talk to me," said Dean. "I'll figure out who you are. This stuff better stop. You have to realize, whoever you are, that I'm a respectable man now. I don't do things like I did when I was young."

"Oh, ho," said gravelly voice. "You're a fine one to talk when you get on the receiving end. Remember poor Mrs. Belcher, Dean? You boys all used to belch when you stood in lines to ridicule her name.

"But that wasn't enough, was it? It was you who stuck the M-80 in the exhaust pipe of her car. That's like an eighth of a stick of dynamite, Dean. It really damaged her car when it went off, Dean, and she couldn't afford the repair.

"Now it's payback time. It's time for you, Dean. I'm making a list, and checking it twice, gonna find out who's naughty and nice. And it's you that was naughty, Dean. It's payback time."

"Look, whoever you are, I've made things right in the world," said Dean. "I could pay Mrs. Belcher money if that would help. I don't do anything any more, just live and let live I say."

Sharilyn was almost snoring, so he couldn't tell her about the latest call. But old gravelly voice had almost broken into song, and that tone, that tone.... He knew he knew that voice from somewhere.

It went that way the rest of the week. Thursday morning he thought again of the M-80 in the tailpipe, and went back to check his own tailpipe before starting the car. There was a pink slip wrapped around a stick in the pipe that had "Payback time" written on it.

Every day, the answering machine croaked out two words, "Payback time."

Friday morning, his car wouldn't start because it was out of gasoline. When he raised the fuel lid, the note there said, "Payback time."

Finally, it was church time again. Dean got ready with unusual vigor—even beating Sharilyn to the car.

"My, my, you're eager for once," she said.

He kept an eye on everyone, but especially Bugbuoy and his Mrs., during Sunday school. When church began, he surveyed the room for anyone looking too long at him or for anyone with a suspicious expression.

He watched intently as the Rev. Bugbuoy got up to give the sermon.

"Well, I promised," said the preacher, "to give you a two-part sermon—first on integrity, and then what can happen when you don't have integrity in your values, in yourself as a person. There always comes a payback time, and that's our subject today. It's payback time."

Dean nearly jumped out of his seat. He listened intently the rest of the service, curling and uncurling his fists. This minister had to confess to him about who gravelly voice was so he could tell them both what a decent man he was now.

Why would anybody pick on a guy like himself when there were other people who still did things wrong? What about forgiveness?

Yeah, what about forgiveness? Wasn't church supposed to be partly about forgiveness, just letting people get on with their lives?

He was so obvious in his distress that Sharilyn was glancing back and forth at him. Finally, she was grinning at him, he was looking so stressed and odd during the sermon.

As they got up to go through the minister's handshake line, she said, "Well, you certainly paid attention, and didn't nap through church today."

"First I'm going to get that preacher to tell me if he's gravelly voice, or who it is if he's not," said Dean as he clasped his hands tightly together. "Then I have to explain how I don't bother anybody, and just lay low. Why would they wish payback on me?"

"I don't think our pastor knows you well enough to have come up with any personal incidents about you, Dean," said Sharilyn. "If he said something that got to you, somebody probably tipped him off, probably somebody who knew you well."

Dean glared at Sharilyn for a moment. "I'm going to talk with the pastor because he knows something that I don't," he said.

Sharilyn tilted her head, smiling with a pertly upturned mouth like she was quite pleased with herself, then stepped against him to kiss him full on the mouth. Other parishoners around them quickly looked away.

"For crying out loud," whispered Dean, looking at her stunned. "What are you doing? You've gone and kissed me in church. It isn't right."

"I know I did. It was just like we were living people again, wasn't it? You didn't complain when I kissed you at our wedding in church. You just come with me to the car because I know who gravelly voice is. Pastor doesn't know."

He said "Who?" a couple of times as they walked to the car, but Sharilyn just smiled.

At the car, she sat on her side for a moment, then asked, "What would you say, Dean, if Gravelly Voice has been telling you it's payback time because he's your friend?

"What if he's tired of seeing you sleep your life away, not growing as a person, and not spending any time with your wife like you should?

'What if he only means by payback time that it's time for you to get some real meaning in your life, be what you should have been, get some joy and action and meaning in your life, instead of laying back, and saying, 'Ah, I'm good now, snore?'"

"Well, I don't know, Sharilyn. I guess by getting respectable, I might have settled for not doing much real living at all if that could be what gravelly voice is trying to say?"

"It might be, Dean. You have been a little like the living dead."

"Maybe this last week has shown me he might have a point if he's a friend. But who is it?"

Sharilyn smiled at him. Then she put a handkerchief over her mouth, and one hand on her throat to say, "Hi, Dean, did you know it's payback time?" in a low, gravelly voice.

Dean widened his eyes at her with a stunned, surprised look on his face.

"You see, I know you very well," she said, "and I want you to come alive now to live actively as you should, not all subdued like you're already in hell.

"You used to tell me how you wanted to still go swimming and fishing a lot, read more books, go out more with me, and stay alive even as you aged.

"What happened, Dean? Did getting respectable mean you decided to die? I got you to pay attention, I think, and now we can see what happens from here.

"I know a few tricks, too. It's not hard to punch the call button for a call forward recording on a cellular phone in your hand while you hold it over the side of the bed.

"You slept through it when pastor told us two weeks ago he was going to give a two-part sermon on self-integrity and the payback for it when you didn't have it.

"That's what gave me the idea, and I decided to talk to him about his sermon. He doesn't even know the person in the stories I asked him to tell was a real person. God gave you a wife who wants you to truly be happy, Dean."

Dean's mouth was open in amazement only a moment more before he burst into a loud face-splitting laugh with the tears running down his cheeks.

Sharilyn began to chuckle too as she put the handkerchief over her mouth one more time to talk to her husband in the gravelly voice, "Now give your wife a kiss, Dean."

Creator Fire

Creator fire
capping the crest
of the skull
to hold the blaze within,
humankind dancing ritualistic,
locked in futile struggle,
trapped in vain concerns,
while creation waits
the true and soulful dominion.

All particulate matter,
even unto
the mysterious nature
of eternal light
sings out to the center,
great God Almighty
emanation of divine throughout
bring us to destiny.

Poor Hemingway

(Author's note: I was challenged to write a story using certain words such as Mount Kilimanjaro, ripped bodice, ass and tomcat. This was the result.)

Mount Kilimanjaro, easily the largest pig at more than 800 pounds on the Copperhead Hog Farm, had laid the bulk of his large black body, only the snowy white peak of his patch showing, contentedly into the mass of taffy and chocolate mixed candies.

Understanding that part was easy. Everybody understood how once a hog had developed a taste for candy, it would struggle to get to it. But not even Alfie, who had seen nearly all of the event, knew how the big swine's favorite orange-striped tomcat came to be sitting at the edge of that snow-white patch looking hot, dried-out and panting, eerily licked clean as only a cat can be on this island amidst a candy sea. Whatever the reason the cat was there, Alfie knew it was the direct temptation that also got Charlene Toogle's Mammoth Ass stuck in the sticky pile.

First, he had seen Mount Kilimanjaro raising his head, and sniffing when a rare northerly breeze brought him a heady dose of the candy smell from the next pen. With that strong whiff, Kilimanjaro got down on his knees to crawl to the electric wire squealing all the way. He knew he was going to take a shock, but it was for candy. He got his back under the wire, creeping and shrieking until it snapped at the apex of the white cap.

Darn the hired man. Alfie had told him when he went to the candy factory up north for its surplus never to take the taffy. Hogs got stuck in taffy on hot days he knew from his sad experiences getting them out. Well, Kilimanjaro was uncommonly big and stout. Maybe he'd be OK, so Alfie decided to leave him while he gathered fence repair material.

When he got back the cat was there, and he could see the Ass watching it from the next pen. He'd tried to please her by putting logs and tires in her pen to play with, but an Ass can get uncommonly bored if it chooses to do nothing but stand around snorting hot air. So, Aunt Charlene's Ass, intelligent as any Ass out there, had chosen chasing and biting cats as a way to fill the hours.

Not only was the Ass smart, but sensitive as well. She knew the electric wire had been shorted out. With a savage Ass smile, she had laid back her ears, and bared her teeth to charge through the wire for the tomcat. Unfortunately she had gotten the wire wrapped around herself. Then struggling through the warm taffy-chocolate mix, she had gotten herself laid over backward and stuck trying to reach the tomcat as he cleared the puddle in a couple of lightning bounds.

Doctor Blacklorth, Alfie's usual veterinarian was on vacation, so he had to call old Doc Frenchie from the next community over. As best he could, he tried to tell Doc the situation.

"Well, you see Doc, it started with the orange tomcat there on Mount Kiliminjaro so dried out. He obviously didn't know how to cleanly cross

the candy puddle without the threat of a blow from an Ass."

"You aren't gonna tell me that cat needs treating, are you Alfie?" asked Doc. "I really try not to treat cats. It's not that I don't like cats—it's because I'm allergic to them. When I handle a cat I just swell all up. Heck, my wife and I have cats at home, outside of course. Alright, darn it all, Alfie, I just hate a darned cat. You aren't wanting me to treat a cat are you?"

"No, heck no, you don't have to treat a cat, Doc. The cat was fine once the Ass ran it off. It's Aunt Charlene's Ass that I want you to look at. She's mighty particular about it since it's the first thing she's ever owned that's registered."

"Slow down. What's this about an Ass. I don't treat people."

"You know, a Mammoth Ass, a donkey, a burro. Those people are particular in their history and registry. Oh I know some of them will call it a burro. But the rules say it's a proper, capitalized Ass, and Aunt Charlene is particular. She even wants to call her Ass a jennet instead of a jenny.

"I want you to look at some cuts and swollen places where it got wire wrapped around the joints. And, there's a little hair gone off it too. I don't know why—a darned hog never loses hair if it gets stuck in the candy. It was tougher to wipe an Ass off, and still make it look good.

"It was even tougher wiping Aunt Charlene off...well, well especially her top half, Doc. She's always been so stiff, so tight and upright looking. She was just furious about her Ass. Honest to god, Doc, I had no idea Aunt Charlene still corseted herself up instead of wearing undergarments like them privates that modern women put on.

"Doc, don't tell anybody, but Aunt Charlene got so tangled up trying to drag her Ass out of the candy that she got a ripped bodice. I'm telling you, me and Albert had a terrible time getting her out of there between wondering where to hold her at, and her still trying to hang onto her Ass. She liked to scream her head off at me when I hooked onto her Ass with the tractor cable and ropes to pull it out.

"But at least after we got some tylenol down her, and got her off to her own doctor, we knew she would be fine if we could get her resolved about the health of her Ass. That's why I need you out here, Doc. Please come. I'll even pay you extra on mileage for coming out of your territory if you'll just satisfy that woman that her Ass will recover from everything in time. You can bet, I'll always keep it in a wooden paddock from now on."

"I don't know, Alfie. I got some scars on my own posterior from a time I hung in the barn rafters trying to get away from a jack burro."

"Ah, Doc, this is a jenny, and gentle with people."

"I guess I can try it then. What about the hog, that Mount, what the heck did you call him?"

"Mount Kilimanjaro is what I call him, Doc. He's my best boar. He's a purebred Poland China with a strange color pattern, all black all over with a big white patch on top, like the mountain in Africa. Heck, Doc, I'm a Hemingway fan. I even liked Gregory Peck in the movie—might even call my next Poland China Gregory or Ernest, whichever I fancy. Mount Kilimanjaro doesn't need treatment. When we pulled him out, he was fine, tough as they come."

"I thought you liked Duroc hogs because they're red like the copperhead snakes?"

"I do, Doc, but crossbreeding is the name of the game. Poland China and Duroc is a fine cross."

"Which brings me to my next question, Alfie—I'm taking it for granted you still live up the creek valley, and down amongst all the hog pens in your white two-story house so the pigs eat the snakes, and they can't get to you?"

"Yes."

"Well, I'll come out to treat the Ass if you'll meet me at the top to open the gate. I don't want to be bitten by a poisonous snake."

"I sure can, Doc. Oh, sssh, sssh, hang on a minute, Doc. What's she doin' here...

"Doc, this is Alfie again. I'm talkin' real low because I'm in the next room on the remote, and Aunt Charlene is out there. She's even sweetened the pot if you'll get out here—baked us an apple pie.

"But, Doc, just ignore the big piece gone out of it, would you please when you get here? I told her everything would be OK. She stopped to see her critter, and Aunt Charlene's Ass took a bite out of the pie."

Cultivating Ethel's Bottom

White-yellow hot,
the afternoon sun
paling the bow
of the broad blue sky,
narry a breeze
to carry away
the Johnny popper exhaust
and the deep humid breath
of the black-turned moist earth
between uncurling leafed rows
of knee-high corn,
a pair of red-tailed hawks
rising high in the thermals,
the old brown and white shepherd-collie
stretched to cool his belly
by the water jug at row's end,
panting patiently, smiling up,
brown eyes of love
on the tractor turns,
the fat field mouse,
running back down the row
behind the weed-turning shovel,
hoping that none of them
noticed him,
the short whine of hydraulics,
the jerk of biting tines
lowered back to waiting soil,
that crumbles apart
with a weight of worms,
Mom on the phone back home
saying with a chuckle
that just like my Dad,
I've been cultivating Ethel's bottom,
the pause on the old wooden bridge,
going home,
with the dog barking impatiently
to say "come on let's go,"

looking into the deep green pools
to see the lolling catfish,
the dog bounding joyfully in front
to show the way,
the half-cooked eyes,
the legs that shake from the hours,
Mom and the old dog,
two puns of fun.

Stumping Stump

Lola stood 6-foot-2, with arms and shoulders befitting a weight lifter, and hips as broad-a-beam as the Lusitania.

On the other hand, her husband, Louis, was nearly tiny, slender, wiry muscled and short at 5-feet-5. He was nicknamed "Stump" because his grandfather had said when Louis was a boy that the child would never be taller than a stump.

The nickname "Stump" was retained with the satisfying knowledge that his grandfather had only been 5-feet-4.

Once, when his grandfather saw Louis in one of his terrible angers because his mother had laid out a green shirt for him on a Wednesday instead of a blue shirt, the old man remarked that he should have called him the burning stump.

Stump made up for lack of height with the fury of his focus. In a nearly predictable nightly fit of rage, he arrived home with the cords sticking out on the sides of his thin neck because the world had failed to bend entirely to his will.

"Lola," he would shout, "What time's supper? I swear things better go better tonight than they did during the day. Why can't these people get it right? I show them what to do...."

But before he could go on, she would gently point toward the back-yard. "Go out back, Louis. Take some of that out, and then we'll talk."

She could hear him picking up the sledgehammer to bang away on the old Plymouth wreck they kept out back for that purpose. All of the glass had been knocked out of it long ago, and its green body was a mass of dents and cave-ins. Stump Lapitteo was beating a car to pieces in his rage.

The neighbors didn't mind the car or the noise. Ignoring it was far better than asking Stump what he was doing.

"I swear," Lola said to relatives who listened, "Stump is like a railroad engine when the rest of us are like automobiles. We travel roads that twist here and there with unexpected turns. Stump is focused down a one-way track."

It was true that Stump Lapitteo worked wonders in a factory fabrication welding shop. He ran a tighter, smoother bead than any other man there. That's how he became a foreman, by perfection and persistence— it wasn't just because he insisted on perfection from everyone else there.

Stump seldom took breaks, but stayed in the mask hour in and hour out with the burning blue-white torch applied to glowing red metal. Sometimes the other men under him dreaded the supervisory moments when he came out from under the mask with his deadpan, finely chiseled dark face.

Stump only spoke to give criticisms because perfect work needed no comment—it was expected. Workers with 20 years experience, like Mike and Horace, still shuddered when Stump examined their work, pushing his tongue against his teeth as though it somehow didn't measure up.

They tried to show with a nonchalant attitude that they were accustomed to the routine.

"Better check the angle of that joint there with the printout, Jones," he would say to a man who had seemingly performed a flawless piece of work.

"Looks a little off to me. You may have to grind that bead down a little. Try to do your best," he would add as though everyone listening knew Jones hadn't done his best.

At the end of a day, Stump was tired and grimy with glowing ghost of a white oval, like the shape of the window on his mask, always in his vision. He never waited more than five minutes outside the factory door, going from simmer to boil as he thought about how things should have been.

After all, he not only found a speck of metal out of place on Jones' work that had to be polished away in 30 seconds at the wheel, but Jones had walked up the left side of the work floor speaking to people as he departed work. Anyone should know to walk out the right side, and stay quiet.

It was Lola who bought the Plymouth and the hammer. It was Lola who was able to bring Stump's fits to a standstill by the force of her voice and reason. Sump didn't back off to Lola because she was so much larger than him, but because he dreaded the force of her return anger and the way she could pick apart his reasoning.

Only once in the last two years had Stump failed to go bang the car instead of spending a half-hour tirade hollering at Lola. After he had covered work, he had talked about the stupidity of other drivers on the way home. Then on the domestic front, he brought up the alignment of the white socks with the black socks in his top drawer.

"Plus that, Lola," he said, "supper was five minutes late yesterday. I checked. Then I noticed your shoes weren't lined up. When I go outside, old Jasper Willingsworth next door didn't trim the grass straight next to us. What's wrong with people? Why can't....."

But Lola had quit listening. She was pointing out back at the Plymouth, and gently pushing him out the door. That was the day he busted the taillights out, and he'd never felt so low when she wouldn't speak to him at bedtime.

The result was that to show his care, he bought two big gray side-by-side reclining chairs with no arm between them, the ultimate in romantic togetherness for evenings watching television.

Louis even succumbed to Lola's desire for a house cat, giving her a kitten named Carrie that since had grown into a fat, soft hulk of neutered purring contentment.

In the evenings after supper, Louis and Lola would settle into the recliners to watch television, Louis on his fourth of the chairs—Lola on her three-fourths with Carrie enjoying the expanse of her lap. The cat didn't appreciate Stump's bony little lap, especially since he snuck opportunities to twist ears, hair and tail if she drifted too far onto his side.

Stump controlled the remote, obligingly turning to Lola's favorite sit-coms until she slept. Then he switched to his own favorite reality and violence programs, occasionally reaching over to give Carrie's tail a pull until she left.

Lola sometimes noted to herself that the home routine never seemed to get better. But it wasn't getting worse either, so she and Stump had a comfortable routine.

But one day Stump went to work with a scratchy throat. He had a buildup of fluid, and had to take breaks more frequently for drinks. By noon the throat was red and sore. He could only croak when he tried to speak. His head was burning.

By 2 p.m., Stump Lapitteo couldn't speak at all. For the first time in 25 years, he was so sick he had to go home early. Mike and Horace called an impromptu break on the floor at 2:30, and bought everybody a soda pop. Nobody talked about what they were celebrating, but they all knew.

Stump couldn't stand the bed, so he sat on his side of the recliners, chilling under a blanket while Lola brought him soup. He hadn't even gone out to beat the car, just plopped right down pointing "uh, uhh" at his throat.

Lola left. She came back home while he was watching the evening news, Carrie glaring at him from the side of the television.

"Look what I got for you, Sweet Baby Stump," Lola said with a smile across her big broad face. "It's a whole quart of brandy. It's the best thing for any kind of cold or congestion. It will keep you from coughing tonight, too."

The brandy and Coke was good stuff. By his third serving, Stump was drinking it nearly half and half, and he was glowing a hotter red than he ever had using a welding torch. He suspected Lola might be drinking at about a rate of five servings to his three.

Stump had never seen her more lovely, occasionally grinning at him from her big black-hair surrounded face when somebody on the TV said something funny. His throat was soothed, but he didn't have the energy to sneak a pinch at Carrie.

After a few more drinks, Lola began to snore. Stump switched pro-grams, but his eyes seemed to be drifting in a curly pattern to the ceil-ing. Just before he drifted into deep sleep, he began to glow inside with the added heat of anger. Yes, he was sure of it. One of the ceiling tiles was a quarter-inch out of line.

Somewhere in the dark depths of his alcohol-and-illness-induced dreams, Louis "Stump" Lapitteo realized he was trapped in an unlighted garage with the engines of trucks and cars running around him. Then they weren't just around him, but on him, squeezing him down, down so he began to smother. He had to get out. As he tried to wake up, there was a sensation of hair and weight on his eyes.

Stump sputtered, and tried to shake his face until Carrie finally quit purring, and got up, pushing off with one paw next to his nose to climb out on Lola's bulk. Only Stump couldn't get himself up. Lola had rolled. She laid there belting out loud, sonorous snores against his ear, the larger of the two-dream engines.

Her hip was turned into his pelvis and upper legs crushing them downward into the seat. His arms and shoulders were pinned by the weight of her body above the hip.

His head and neck were clamped sideways and up at the ceiling. Yes, he realized with irritation, that one ceiling tile was a quarter-inch off.

Stump tried to holler, but it only came out a soft "aagh, aagh." He still had laryngitis. He struggled. She didn't move. He tried to bounce the side of his head on her back. The snoring continued unabated. Stump was trapped.

Why hadn't the guy he had hired for the remodeling put that ceiling tile in line with the others? What if the ceiling was warped, and the whole house was out of line? What if he tried to bounce his body? Maybe Lola would wake up then.

That didn't work, and neither did twisting his bare feet from side to side. It only attracted Carrie down on his legs where she began to lick his one small toe. His panic and rage were growing in a black cloud of confusion. The throat thickened more. Forget the Plymouth, Stump tried to holler. I'll take that cat out to the hammer.

But what if Carrie clamped down on his toe with her teeth. What if she tried to eat it like she would a mouse? Got to keep the feet twisting. No, more motion might attract her more. There, twist the feet apart, and down, away from her. Come on, Carrie, go gor it, go for it. Get your head between my feet. Haah, got ya. Nope, she got away, but at least she's off me.

But what to do now, Stump asked himself. Couldn't panic, couldn't afford to get worked up any more now. It was getting difficult to breath with an already swollen throat. Lola's steady snore promised no relief or movement.

There's another pressure, too. It's the bladder. Yes, it would be the bladder after downing so many drinks of Coke and brandy.

Let's see, thought Stump. The telephone is on the nightstand next to my chair. The cord to the floor jack runs close enough that if I could get a foot down between the cushions on my leg rest, maybe I could pull the phone in with my toes.

Oh no, there's another one. That's two ceiling tiles out of line.

He twisted his leg, he gasped, and mentally tried to contort his hip to help the ankle turn. He had to stretch the Achilles tendon the other way briefly to take the cramp out that developed in the left foot he was twisting.

Finally he got the little toe Carrie had licked winched against the side of a cushion. The knee socket felt like it could pop out of joint as he twisted and pulled with the toes and foot.

But finally the whole foot slipped through, and with it the ankle up to the knee which was then was clamped harder into the chair by Lola's weight along with the other leg. The same little toe was the one first to feel the edge of the telephone cord. Thank God Carrie hadn't eaten it.

He grasped the cord with one toe, then with three, pulling it an inch to three inches at a time until the phone fell off the stand. He could hear the dial tone followed by the "beep, beep, beep" of a receiver off the hook, but Lola didn't budge.

Carrie jumped back up on the cushion of the foot rest, and then on to Lola to lay there staring into his face. He tried to spit at her, but he didn't have the moisture or breath left.

Finally, he felt the phone with its comforting touch-tone keys under his toes. But he still had to pull in the coiled receiver cord for the main phone body to push the hang-up, so he could dial. Thank God the phone company knew how to line up the phone keys the same way every time. Save the rage for the tile guy now, he told himself, must be controlled.

The 9 had to be in the third row of keys down on the right just above the "#" sign. One big toe punch, and it was entered. The 1 had to be at the upper left, and he felt a sense of satisfaction as he gave it two toe punches.

Stump tried his best to croak a loud "aaagh" when he heard the 911 operator on the line. It's fortunate that emergency personnel can trace addresses from silent calls for help because just then Lola rolled a little more, leaving only Stump's nose out for air while he sputtered helplessly against her back.

Lola was surprised when the police officers and firefighters woke her to pull her to her feet. But Stump had a hard time not flying into a fit at them when he could breath without the oxygen mask more easily again. Why did they have to kick the front door in? He had supposed they carried skeleton keys.

Stump's voice was coming back just as Lola lost hers. All the brandy hadn't stopped the virus from running its course with a new victim.

Apparently it couldn't bring newly learned control back again either.

"Look what you almost did to me," Stump was saying. "That stupid Carrie almost smothered me, too. My knee feels like it's been dislocated. The ceiling tiles are out of line. Now we have to get the front door fixed."

He sputtered, and began to turn red. Lola gently shoved him to the back door, and pointed at the hammer and the Pontiac out back. That was the day the hammer went through the ceiling of the passenger compartment.

It was also the last day they had a soda pop break down at the fabrication factory.

Abyss

Gray-black and dark
before the beginning of light,
the abyss opens wide,
and the winds
of time and eternity
are pulling to the edge.
The plunge bodily gripping
for newfound plateau end,
all spirit tightening together,
called by the Tongue of Fire
with the knowledge
of all that is
even to the last darkness
of mortal life.
Be still and hear
the power of the Word
oh man who can only hint
at full aspiration.
I Am has spoken.

The Saint Louie Bird Call

Bird was only in his 20's, and not nearly so clever, likely to survive or good looking as he is now. That would be his opinion, not his wife's.

Bird had hair on the top of his head then, all brown and combed nice, and a face that was smooth and round, not squished and lined.

He rode with old John, who told him stories about what it had been like to be one of Merrill's Marauders fighting the Japanese in the South Pacific. These were usually ferocious tales, nearly all true , including atrocities committed by various Asians as well as the Marauders themselves.

John was the driver, and Bird was the attendant, on a bus that picked up children with cerebral palsy for school.

John and his wife had a half-dozen biological children as well as a half-dozen adopted children, 9 of the 12 already grown and out of the home.

"Why do you drive this bus, John?" Bird asked one morning after their first 2 or 3 trips. "I guess you need the money with all your children, huh?"

"No, actually Bird, I don't really need the money although it's nice to have a little pocket change. I just always have to have something to do," replied John. "And besides that, look at these kids. How could you not do something for them after you've seen them. Look at that Kevin back there in his wheel chair grinning at us. He listens to what we say, don't you, Kevin, bright as a light."

In response, Kevin stretched as much as he could in his chair, freckled face tilted up, mouth stretched wide, gurgling a laugh.

"Wipe his mouth there for him, Bird. Kids like Kevin are a relief for me, something that makes me feel better away from my regular work. Hey, what's your first name again? Bird's your last name isn't it? I don't remember what you told me."

"Just Bird's good enough."

"No, really what is it? I want to know."

"OK, it's Luellan. My mother liked it. I don't. So, just call me Bird, OK?"

John grinned, Bird blushed, and Kevin yowled, "Arrgh, arrgh, arrgh."

Old John liked the attendant for his innocent looking embarrassment and for his attentive naivete listening to his stories. Nobody had called Bird "Grump" yet, least of all his wife, who usually knows the truth.

After several weeks of lifting wheelchairs, and assisting children in and out, John leaned toward Bird one day, looking first at Kevin in the rearview mirror, then lowering his voice. "Say, Bird, I've told you I'm a truck driver for Railway Express, haven't I?"

"Sure."

"You realize there's a Teamster's strike going on right now?"

"Well, I saw something about it in the paper, but I don't know anything about it. You aren't short of money being on strike or anything, are you?"

"No, no, nothing like that. But you know a Teamsters' strike can get rough, really rough, almost like a war."

"Sure, sure, I guess it could," said Bird, raising his eyebrows and thinking of John's South Pacific tales, almost like a big movie in technicolor.

"Guys hauling things through the strike lines have had shots fired through the rear of their trucks. A guy I knew was whipped with a lengtrh of steel pipe after he got out of his tractor. It's really rough."

"Kind of out of the trench, and up the hill, eh?"

"Something like that. I have longevity. I've been a union steward, and now I'm a local chief. That means I can still drive my truck if it's marked, but only if I haul critical things like drugs and bodies—things that have to go through no matter what."

"Bodies? You mean dead people? You get a lot of extra money for that?"

"Sure I get paid, but it's not the money. Teamsters have morals and ethics, too. People still die during a strike, don't they? Their bodies still have to go home for services. You wouldn't expect their families to wait around until the strike's over, would you? And people get sick. The pharmaceuticals have to go through."

"Yeah, I see, John."

"Anyway, I have to make a run to St. Louis late tomorrow night, and it gets a little lonely. Want to go with me?"

"Sure, I'd like to take a truck ride."

"We'll be just fine. They know me and my truck."

"OK."

That's how Bird came to be standing on pavement in the dark and beside a rattling big diesel semi-truck with a cold, north wind pinging ice crystals around his ears.

"You got to go to the bathroom or anything?" old John hollered over the engine and the wind. "We won't stop once we start."

All Bird wanted to do was take the high step up into the warm cab, and settle in while John mumbled, incoherently to Bird, on a radio microphone. They throttled up to full power through all the gears on I-70, and the engine was so loud and vibrating that Bird only heard John when he hollered.

"Raise your flaps, Bird. We're taking off. The patrolmen know what

I'm hauling, and where I'm going, so they close their eyes when I go by."

Bird looked at the speedometer from time to time. It held at a steady 90 miles per hour going down the left lane past all the other traffic.

"We got to make time. Don't worry, Bird. We'll be fine. Relax, they'll have a pot of coffee at the docks in St. Louis."

Bird wasn't worried. He knew he had lots of years left, and anywhere in America was the safest place in the world.

It took years for him to get clever and grumpy. He thought maybe the heavy truck could hold the road better than most vehicles running over the ice crystals, and he fatalistically watched distant lights speed by.

Names on signs like Fulton and Wentzville passed in the night, and before he knew it, there was St. Charles and then St. Louis with heavy urban traffic and mile after mile of brightly lighted urban area. He hoped the cars got out of the way before old John's truck swallowed them under the hood like a shark swimming through fish.

The semi went down a ramp into a warehouse landscape spread out like a great plain with occasional street lamps and security lights standing lonely sentinel duty. Ice crystals still danced through the wind past them. His watch said 2 a.m.

In the distance, highlighted by half-dark aisles past the buildings, Bird could see huge orange glows against the sky—just like home when purposely set springtime prairie fires moved through the night.

As they got closer, he saw smoke climbing through the glow, then the huge bonfires by the buildings made with piles of shipping crates and scrap lumber.

Crowds of men stood around the fires, some of them carrying three-foot lengths of lumber like war clubs.

John's truck crept past the crowds at what seemed now to be a very slow rate. Most of the men seemed to be either talking animatedly to each other, or hunkering over, wrapping themselves against the cold. A few of them turned to stare silently at the truck. When the truck stopped, a great crowd of them began to gather around it.

For the first time on the trip, Bird was feeling a little nervous. Staring faces, most of them older and more mature than his own, looked up at him without expression.

"Do all of these guys drive for Railway Express, John?"

" No, kid, but they're all Teamsters. Come on, let's open the doors. It's OK."

As Bird opened his door, some of the men seemed to make way for him, but then he realized they were all trying to get to the other side of the truck toward the swelling sound of conversations. He joined them trying to press his way to John.

John was there on the other side of the truck, a dozen men trying to talk to him, one of them with a hand on his shoulder in supplicant-like gesture.

John gestured Bird to his side, and said, "Come on inside. Just stick right by me kid wherever I go."

Bare light bulbs hung suspended by long cords in the warehouse that spread out like a giant cavern before them. John pulled Bird with him as he and a half-dozen other men went into a glassed-off corner office while a couple-hundred other men stood outside the windows.

John poured a cup of coffee, shoved a steaming styrofoam cup into Bird's hands, and took a second cup for himself.

"This is my friend, Bird. He's OK," John said.

The others shook hands with Bird, and one of them, a short, dark man with black, oiled-back hair and hard brown eyes that looked directly into his kept Bird's hand in his own for a moment.

"My name is Benny," the man said. "And, what would you be to John, a relative?"

"No," said Bird. "I work on a bus with him, taking kids with cerebral palsy to school."

"Part of his hobby then. Good, good, I bet the two of you enjoy that, visiting and everything."

"Yes, John's told me all about his World War II experiences."

"Good, good," said Benny turning his attention back to John who had kept talking with the others, but also had watched Benny with Bird."

"What are they trying to pull here, John?" one of the men was asking. "We specified we'd compromise on the over-the-road rate close to where they were at, and now Brown's stalling. What do we do?"

"We hang in there, John said looking at Benny who was nodding,

"They're stalling, and we can stall longer than they can. They know it. We're hurting them. All the membership's with us. Our men have stayed here on the docks. The companies couldn't even lock us out."

"Can we ask the men to hang on much longer?" another man asked. "They need paychecks, not just promises."

"I'll talk to them," said John swallowing the last of his coffee.

They tipped a heavy crate over on the warehouse floor for John to step up on. He raised his arms to the couple-hundred already there and the others coming in through the doors. Benny and the others from the office stood at the foot of the crate. Bird leaned against the wall by the office door knowing he was very, very tired.

"Men," said John, "we're close, really close. We've made our points, and we're going to get the increases we want and the benefits we want. On article one of our list...."

Bird listened to John outline a contract that meant nothing to him. He hoped it wouldn't last long, so they could go home.

Finally, when his ribs and back began to ache, and he could hardly hold his head up, they were walking back to the truck. It was 4 a.m.

They drove past the smoldering bonfires, out of the city lights to meet the foggy gloom and early-morning diminished traffic to where they started. Bird couldn't sleep thinking of the sights he'd seen.

In the parking lot, old John tapped his forehead to the steering wheel, and looking up, said, "Well, Kid, I made it again. Thanks for going along. It was good having company."

"Glad I could go, John. It was a different experience."

"You know that guy, Benny, you were talking to?"

"Yeah, he seemed a little different."

"He's killed three people that I know of. He's mob," John nodded his head watching Bird who was looking back at him with eyebrows half-furrowed in disbelief. "They have an interest in this too, and he watches what I do."

"Golly, John. Why do you mess with such a thing? You could just work some job like you do with me. Take an early retirement or something."

"I can't shoot Benny or control him or his group without help from somewhere. It's a tough world out there for guys like you and me, Bird. We just want to work and get along.

"I haven't always done what I should have done, and I'm a simple type of a guy. But I decided I didn't want to finish life short.

"So, I decided I have to do it becaus it's there. I'm expected to carry on in life. It's what I am.

"I'm trying to be what I was meant to be. Somebody has to serve, just like I did in the Marines. They expect me to lead them, and who am I not to do it for them?

"I don't mean to be preachy, Bird, but what would life be if you didn't do what you were called to do?"

Our Hows And Whys

It's the hows we know so well,
the hows that put us in control.
It's the whys that we have only nodding acquaintence with,
the whys that make us lose our order.
We know how the atom works with
protons, neutrons, electrons reduced
to quarks and other parts.
We know how grass grows and birds fly,
and many other things,
how to make an engine go,
and how to make a toothache stop.
That's how you and I can sit
in sophisticated pose:
because we know how.

We know a little of the hows of earth,
to cover it with altruisms and greeds,
our mowed lawns, cars and concrete.
We masters of the hows are on a pinnacle
that continues to grow, each person
ever more part of the mass of the hows,
left less to be his own.

It's the whys that bother us,
that cause us
to cling to our mass of hows,
to avoid plunging
into the depths of the whys.
We carry only
the smallest piece of the whys
to justify all our hows.
So, we'll spend our time talking
about how we'll set
the order of the world,
how we'll run ourselves,
not why the atom,
why the grass,
why the birds,
why us.

If anyone ever tries to tell us whys,
let's nail him to a cross,
and spend 2,000 years
explaining how he was.

Uncle Art Is Barely Bearable, Especially When He's Bearly Barable

You might say that Aunt Lydia's fried chicken was barely bearable to eat it was so extremely delicious, with its delicate crisp brown crust and the succulent layers of white and dark meat underneath.

At least that's what Uncle Art said, that it was "barely bearable," some of the best he ever had. "And that's the gospel truth," he added. "It don't get any better for an old single fellow than to be invited over for a spread like this.

"My innards can hardly stand the ecstasy of consuming such a well-singed rooster. Why things don't often get barely bearable like this unless the situation warrants.

"Yes, it takes somethin' special like what I'm rememberin' now. Guess I might as well tell you about it."

"Oh, Art, you aren't going to tell one of your stories when I'm about to bring out hot sour cherry pie with vanilla ice cream are you?" asked Lydia. She was smiling, but she had let him sit at the head of the table where his brother, her husband, used to sit, and she could hear a low moan spreading among the other guests.

"Uncle Art, you aren't going to tell a story when we can have cherry pie, are you?" said Paul.

"Oh, come on everybody," said Paul's sister, Linda. "Let's eat, and listen at the same time. If Uncle Art can't talk fast enough, maybe we'll have some pie he might have eaten."

"That's right, Linda, give me my slice of pie first—I don't have to have seconds, but not having firsts might leave me with the pits," said Uncle Art.

"And, it was nearly the pits. Like I was sayin', we was travelin' through the Rocky Mountains, me and Aunt Gladys and Uncle Ernest and little Jimmy, I believe it was, probably close to where Jimmy built his double deck house when he grew up.

"The mountains were beautiful, all open with grand vistas of black-green pine and fir trees, snow to contrast with it in the gullies on the naked rock parts above you. The air was thin and heady so I felt like singing like I was the gal in 'The Sound of Music,' barely bearable you might guess.

"Actually I probably was oxygen starved cause everything those trees puts out sinks down the draws.

"That's fortunate these days because folks down the slope in places

160

like Denver would smother in their car fumes if oxygen went up. At least that's my theory, and it's probably as good as the next guy's.

"That's why those people are building their houses higher up, too, instead of down on the flatlands where it's easier. They're instinctively

tryin' to nip a share of the oxygen from the trees before it gets to the bottom. Of course, the grass puts out oxygen too, doesn't it?

"I guess that oxygen is driftin' down the slope to Kansas City and St. Louis. God knows what the people in Washington D.C. are going to do with what's left of the oxygen sinking their way, but then, they're the government so confusion is a way of life to them.

"Which, probably you see, explains why the government was doing things so differently in those days, and why they contributed so heavily to the situation I'm tryin' to tell you—I see you lookin' at my pie, Paul. Now I'm going to want it when I run out of jaw here, so keep away.

"You see, the forest service or the park service or maybe some refuse service, they're all government so it don't matter, would put out toilet houses every once in a while along the roadway, or privies if you are acquainted with older English.

"They would put them on the edge of high over-hangs or cliffs, usually stuck there a little ways over the chasm itself supported by bridge beams so the waste would drop maybe a thousand feet before it was forcefully flattened on the ground or some unfortunate far below.

"It was an early attempt by the government to be environmentally successful. They didn't have to dig holes for public sanitation, it fertilized the trees down below, helped fill up gullies, and there was usually pretty little pure water mountain streams flowing down to help spread the benefits.

"It also kept the flat-landers from seeking secure spots for their habits near the picnic table. Oh, I forgot to say the spot usually included a picnic table for the rest of a privy-goer's family to sit at contentedly while he was occupied because, after all, the place was scenic. You might say it was also an early attempt by the government to create convenience stores, too.

"But the government changed its mind about all of this as time went on. They do every time a new crop of meddlers gets in, and there have been a couple of generations of them since then. They get to be barely bearable. Hey, I want ice cream on my pie too.

"Yes, let's see here. Oh, we had to stop at one of these privy overhangs because of me. I tell you the pressure inside me was something fierce in that thin mountain air because my innards was used to being down lower. The others didn't help any because they all wanted to come in to look down the thousands of feet through the privy holes before they left me to my privacy to sit around the picnic table and wait. I wanted to strangle Jimmy when he remarked that his toothpick was spinning end over end as it went through the hole.

"Now you see, these mountain roads frequently wrap round and round the mountain you're on, so way up above us, there was more road. Away up there, the rest of the family told me they heard a car horn honking several times. The flat-landers who drove down the slope later on to admire my situation later admitted they started it.

"Big old boy with silver hair and a shameless smile named Roy Dean, now what kind of mother would combine names like Roy Dean, said he was drivin' when they came around the curve, and surprised this big brown bear in the middle of the road.

"The bear stood up on his hind legs, so Roy Dean figured from everything he'd heard that it was going to charge his car, maybe scratch it up, and who knew whether an animal with such big paws could break a car window? Anyway, Roy Dean just laid on the horn as hard as he could, and it startled the nerve clear out of that bear. He hadn't heard such a thing before because tourists were newly invented.

"I guess you could say it was barely bearable for that bear, get it Paul, barely bearable. You got ice cream still on your mouth.

"Anyway, that bear did something that even most experts don't know a Rocky Mountain bear will do. He turned his head down, and wrapped his big body into a somersault ball to start rolling down the steep slope at high speed.

"He must have hit 70 miles an hour rolling down that mountainside, until 'kerboom,' all 600 pounds of him crunched into that toilet to knock it off its beams with me in it.

"How do I know he was 600 pounds going 70 miles an hour, Paul? Well I guess I don't rightly know for sure because I was otherwise occupied than to get precise instrumentation. Maybe it was 599 pounds at 69 miles an hour. At least it knocked the government's good intentions right from their foundation.

"Fortunately, the force of that big of a fur ball saved me. I'd just fastened my belt, and when he hit, the force knocked my rear back to lock into that privy hole, kind of like vacuum sealing a Mason jar.

"You see, I could have been throwed out of that privy to my doom. The government types took note of it, and a couple of generations later came out with vehicle safety belts.

"Me and the privy and the bear went sailin' over the edge of that mountain arching like a basketball on its way to swish through the hoop. The family said it was an awesome sight, barely bearable.

"I got knocked into the hole even tighter, and the whole toilet broke in parts when we hit the big tree about two thirds the way up it, maybe a hundred feet up it.

"No, Paul, I never did go back to measure it. But it was big enough to hold a big bear with a privy roof stuck over his head like a party hat and a young man hanging upside down by virtue of being puckered through a privy hole.

"I was light-headed, and getting more so by the minute swinging back and forth like that. No, Paul, I wasn't going to say it was barely bearable. What's barely bearable is the disappearance of my pie when I got up to circle the table for the climax.

"Oh, Lydia, you say you did put it in the refrigerator for me? That's good. Thank you. Well, why'd you let Paul eat the ice cream off it just cause it was meltin'. No, Paul, I ain't going to say that it's barely bearable.

"Now for those of you who want to hear the end of this story. The bear did hit the ground first, and the party hat broke off him. He just shook his head, moaned as he got up, and then walked off.

"I was grateful I was severely suctioned, and not down there for his leave taking, although he was so quiet I don't think I ever met a more bearable victim.

"They got me down OK too. But riding in a car on mountain curves is rough when you have bruise rings round your rear. And, no, Paul, I just ain't going to say it was barely bearable no matter how much you insist, and as for them that listened politely to my story, I can barely thank you enough.

"No I ain't bein' bearish, Paul. You should just be glad you can listen to my stories. I tell you, they're the gospel truth."

From 1873

Last night as I lay dreaming
back deep through the gray folds of time,
the clear, soft voice of a woman
called to me from 1873.
Familiar yet forgotten
through the relation connections
of the primal, spiritual mind,
it was my own great, great grandmother
calling out to me
from the year the typhoid took her,
from 1873.

I know she said very gently,
carressingly to keep me asleep,
you think that you don't know me,
I wasn't alive in your time,
and your mind can't accept
that you're hearing from me
from 1873.

Just open your heart to listen,
let me have this small piece of your time.
You can't imagine the searching
for faith in the agonies of my world.
You can't imagine how hard it all was
when the proofs of your day were not there.
For the gifts of your science
have laid the keys to know
of heaven and of hell.
How easy for you to have faith.
Why oh Lord wasn't it there for me
in 1873.

You know I cannot believe
that you listen to a box
that carries tunes through the air.
Electromagnetism you call it
that gives that thing called TV.
You talk to people all over the world
on wires or the cellular phone.
Imagine the things that surrounded us

that we had no receivers to see
here alone in the dust
in 1873.

You have machines that fly through the air,
machines that fly up to the moon.
We had trains and horses
here on the ground,
and ships upon the sea.
You even have machines
to expand your thinking.
We never had such things as you
in 1873.

You have scientists and experts
with proof for you
that all breaks down to particles
that finally converge with light
until you don't know what's solid,
and what's energy,
what's science,
and what's theology,
alternate universes and dimensions,
the relativity of time,
the proofs are all before you.
Wish to God we'd had them too
in 1873.

What's this, our connection's weakening?
But it's so easy for you to believe.
Yet you're letting me go
because you can't accept
I'm talking to you
from 1873.

Wild Willy Takes A Bite Out Of Curley Red

Gilbert Poggins had a dog on his dairy farm that made it necessary for him to tell every visitor, while he smiled, flashing over-sized white teeth, rubbing his big hairy arm, "Naah, that dog won't bite."

But the truth was, he was concerned that the half-wild dog named Willy might bite because Willy seemed to shiver nervously at times with visitors present, but somehow show no fear at all. Some people might half need biting, but what if the victim was an innocent, fragile old person, or worse yet, one of his own grandchildren. Poggins puzzled over what to do about Willy.

Willy was named Willy because one of Poggin's grandchildren misspelled Wiley, for a wiley and crafty coyote he had read about in a book, to name the dog.

Willy was large enough at 60 pounds to make even the most even-tempered visitor nervous.

He was a yellow-brown dog with a broad white collie stripe around his neck with strange yellow-green eyes that seemed to glare out at a visitor.

Willy wasn't a collie at all. He was half shepherd-collie crossbred and half coyote. Gilbert got him free from a rancher on the great open grass sections to the west, and he couldn't tell you whether the cross of dog and native animal was purposeful or a chance encounter of nature.

Willy had ears that pointed straight up when he was interested in something, which was nearly every moment he was awake. He was interested in every visitor with those ears and those eyes turned toward them, and that helped make them nervous.

From the moment a visitor stepped from a car, Willy, after looking at them through the windows, would exhibit a combination of dog and coyote nature. He was quiet. He didn't bark or growl. But he circled visitors, watching them with his nose alternately part-way to the ground or part-way in the air to catch scent, and his ears changing position to their every step.

As they walked from the car to the house, Willy continued going round and round them in a circle. He only stopped to stand a ways off, watching when a member of the Poggins family greeted a person.

"He's just different," said Gilbert," Old Willy never tried to hurt anybody."

But inside himself, Gilbert sometimes said, "Maybe I ought to find a way to get rid of that dog before he does hurt someone or causes them to panic. Naah, I've raised old Willy. He sits beside me in the front yard, and I pat his head. He sure was cute as a pup. Surely he wouldn't hurt anyone."

What Gilbert Poggins didn't know was that Willy kind of wanted to bite somebody because people who didn't belong to his home group were causing him anxiety. Just one quick bite that might cause them to run away, or establish his territoriality, seemed a natural thing to do.

Willy's number one candidate for biting was Curley Red, the milk man who drove in daily to the dairy parlor barn, where he carried empty milk cans in for filling the next day, and carried full cans of milk from the water cooler to his big truck.

Curley Red made lots of clanging noises, and his nonchalant way of ignoring Willy while the dog circled seemed to make him a threat that should be driven from the territory before he hurt a member of the home group what with all his noise and exciting smell.

And Willy's unerring nose and sensitivity were correct about the "exciting," nervous smell. Curley Red, with his red hair shaved down to nothing on a strawberry pink scalp, setting on a big square head, held by a great bull neck, didn't look like the kind of guy who could be frightened by a dog.

Curley was big, with a 65-inch chest, large shoulders and biceps built up from handling cans of milk. He exposed his build with a sleeveless shirt in warm weather. He had thick forearms and wore mud boots to the tops of his ankles.

When a person met Curley, he seemed like the type of man who ought to have many friends. He laughed easily and comfortably. But instead of lots of friends, Curley had only a couple of other bachelors who stopped to see him from time to time in his little three-room house on the edge of a prairie hay meadow. Curley seemed like he didn't have a care in the world.

But the truth was, Curley Red was terrified of dogs. A little yapper had chased him round and round a house to start it all off when he was a 4-year-old. At every farm he watched for the dogs that might come down around the milk barn. He tried various behaviors, from being quiet, to saying, "hi, pup," in a friendly way, to stomping his feet, and hollering at them to drive them away.

None of this worked very well with Willy. Curley Red was a visitor, although he came every day, so Willy wasn't going to miss a chance to look him over.

As far as Willy was concerned, the only human being that came close to being a friend was Gilbert Poggins, so saying "hi, pup" nicely had no effect on him. And the stomping and hollering got him really interested, intensifying his more savage green gaze, so he made a wider circle around Curley Red while he kicked, watching him all the more intently.

Curley Red loved the days when Willy was off with Gilbert Poggins somewhere else on the farm, and came to trying to ignore him on the majority of days when Willy circled him as he carried cans. Curley was ready to swing a can at him should the dog make a wrong move.

Willly's behavior as domestic and wild animal crossed held true in all his experiences on the farm. Like any dutiful dog, he followed Gilbert Poggins as he carried his milking machine to hook to the vacuum system at the milk parlor twice daily—once in early morning, once in the evening after field work was done for the day.

The tiger-striped orange and gray barn cats made way for Willy uneasily with the younger ones occasionally hissing as Gilbert stepped through the barn door. They could smell, and sense the wild in this dog.

Willy kept his ears up, watching the cats' every move. Here they were Gilbert Poggins' cats, safe in domesticity. But let Willy find one of them out in the pastures, and they were his. Unbeknownst to Gilbrt Poggins, Willy had killed many a cat.

When Gilbert quietly herded the big black and white Holstein cows into the lot to take their turns in the parlor for milking, Willy trotted back and forth the width of the herd behind him. He never darted in to nip a heel like a shepherd or a collie might, but stayed back like a predator watching for the animal that might fall.

One fall morning, when the aromatic smell of sweet pungent sour-apple fermenting silage permeated the milk barn area, Curley Red drove up in his big truck to find nobody around except Willy the half-breed dog, laying quietly in the building shade with his ears already up, alertly anticipating Curley Red getting out.

"So, it's you and me all alone again, is it Willy, my boy, dog or banshee or whatever you are," Curley Red muttered while he patted one hand on the steering wheel. But there was no use delaying the inevitable, so Curley threw open the door, and stepped out to get empty cans from the back of the truck for the milkhouse as Willy began to move in a wide circle around him.

Curley Red banged the empty cans together in a loud, bonging noise hoping the sound would drive Willy away, but it only agitated the dog a little so that the circle became smaller, drawing closer to the man.

Curley Red made it through the milkhouse door amidst cats that had the sense to scatter in the wake of the dog's circling. Curley opened the chest top to the cooler, and, putting his hands on the cold water-dripping handles of a chilled can full of milk, used his strong arm and chest muscles to heave it up and over the edge.

He peaked out the door first to see if Willy was there, and the dog was there with head half-lowered, ears forward, and glaring green eyes focused on the doorway. "Go ahead, get out of here, off with you,"Curley Red shouted at the coyote-cross, but Willy only lowered his head a little more, and focused all the more intently.

Curley Red came out the door with the heavy can headed toward the back of his truck as nonchalantly as possible trying not to look at Willy with any look that might draw a reaction.

But it was too late. Every instinct Willy had was screaming "threat, intruder!" The fear smell from Curley Red was too related to the aggression scent. Willy's ears went down, and he twisted his body sideways in a feinting maneuver to come in low and hard at Curley Red's ankle.

In one quick slicing bite that also allowed him to make the turn to escape, Willy's teeth cut through Curley's jeans just above the boot to open two parallell red tracks.

"Aaah! Aaah, aah, aah!" hollered Curley Red in pain, fear and sudden anger. He hurled the can at Willy causing the lid to pop loose as it hit dirt spilling the white liquid everywhere.

Willy easily avoided the throw, and moved back and forth in a half circle as Curley propped himself against his truck to remove his boots and socks, and sponge away the blood with the clean sock.

"What's all the hollering about?" asked Gilbert Poggins as Willy ran to his side. "What's happening, Curley Red? I thought you'd been killed the way you yelled.

"It was Willy," Curley explained, telling the whole story while Gilbert poured peroxide over his cuts, then stood there rubbing a finger against his weathered brown cheek as he listened.

"At least you'll be OK, Curley," Gilbert said, "Willy gets a rabies shot every year when the vet comes to work cattle. But I can't have him anymore after this. I was afraid he'd bite somebody some day. Why don't you get your boots on, and I'll be back in a minute."

"Oh, I'll drive bare foot, let the air get to my ankle a little. I'm OK. Guess I'm really a little ashamed, Gilbert. I have to admit that I have a fear of dogs, probably half brought it on myself."

"Yes, I could see that you were just a little leery of Willy, but that won't happen again. We'll fix that. You just sit here a minute."

Curley Red was taking a few deep breaths with his hands on the steering wheel when Gilbert Poggins opened the passenger door. Gilbert had a paper 50-pound feed sack that had been cut apart at the seams enabling him to fold it over Curley's truck seat, and tuck it in.

"There, that ought to keep your seat clean, Curley."

"What are you doing?"

Gilbert looked Curley Red in the face for a moment, expressionless and determined looking as though he had just made a momentous decision.

"Why I'm doing something for both of you," Gilbert said as he reached down with both hands to lift Willy, then push him down on the seat, rubbing his head between the ears to comfort him. "You live all alone, and you need a companion, help you get over your fear of dogs, and Willy doesn't have anyplace else to go now. He'll soon learn that you belong to him."

Curley's big square chin dropped below his open mouth, "Why, I don't want a dog! And, I especially don't want this spooky old dog. Look at those green eyes looking at me!"

"Give me your hand, Curley. Come on Curley Red, just let me take your hand. Don't draw back. See we're laying it right here on Willy's head. See, rub his head, that's right back and forth, let him know you're OK."

"No!" Curley said, "I can't be putting my hand on that demon dog!"

"Now darn it, Curley Red, do as I say. Quit jerking like you're so darned scared or you'll scare Willy. Give me that hand, and quit acting like a big baby."

"Hey, being a little afraid of dogs is a legitimate thing. Heck I can't help it if...."

"Sure you can help it. Don't give me that garbage. See you're patting Willy. Good dog, good dog. That's right, let him smell your hand. See, Willy, good dog. You're going to like old Curley Red .

"Easy, put your hand back on the wheel, Curley. I'm shutting the door here on old Willy, see, and you just drive on out of here. Don't look back.

"You're Willy's only chance, and if you want to open that door at a pound, or far out in the country, it's your choice. Just don't ever bring Willy back here."

Curley Red was stunned to find himself driving out the driveway with a dog in his front seat, especially one that had always been as threatening as Willy. But Willy never offered to make a move. He laid on the sack with his ears down, his head motionless cradled on his legs.

Curley Red was relieved that no dogs were in sight at the next farm. Hard telling how Willy might react if another dog came out to challenge.

When he had loaded the last can at that stop, he sliced a piece of cheddar from a big cheese among others in the truck cooler that sometimes were on order for farmers on the route. Now he'd have to buy it.

Willy didn't move when he climbed back in the cab, tore the piece of cheese in two, and ate his half while he gingerly pushed the other chunk across the seat by Willy's nose. The dog made no move.

Curley nearly hyperventilated going toward the next stop at Jackie's Jersey Farm. These people had a Doberman that they kept penned. They kept it for a relative in the city who couldn't provide enough room for it.

What if it was loose? What if it came at him? What would Willy do, try to jump from the truck to help rip him to shreds? Or, if he got away from the Doberman, would Willy be there to get him?

But the Doberman never appeared, and when he got back to the truck cab, Willy's half of the cheese was gone. But Willy never moved while Curley drove

. There was one more stop. Curley Red summoned all of the calm he possessed, reached over, and patted the top of Willy's head like Gilbert Poggins had showed him. Willy didn't move.

Yes, there was one more stop. Please God, don't let Mattie Harris turn her little mutt out of the house today. The strange little Pekinese, Pomeranian, Beagle and something else cross knew he was afraid. Please don't have it out there to yap.

But there the little dog was, running, barking, all happiness along-side the truck knowing that a very large man had to get out, and be timid of it.

Curley Red watched for a reaction from Willy, but the coyote-dog just laid there quietly with his head still down.

The Harris family didn't have many cows. He could probably just get their couple of full cans of milk, and shorten the visit by not leaving empty cans today.

Curley Red opened his door to step out slowly. Maybe he should have put his boots back on for this stop. The little hair-ball of a dog was bouncing up and down excitedly right in front of him. Curley bravely slid to the ground shivering a little. Probably even bare footed, he could deal with this little dog.

But then there was a burst of hair and muscle pushing past him from the truck, Willy gone wild again.

The coyote-dog ran behind the panicking, yelping little dog for a hun-dred feet snapping at his rear end before turning to run back just as fast toward a very surprised Curley Red still standing in front of the open truck door which had flopped open. Willy charged straight past him, straight up the truck step to jump back on his feed sack.

Curley Red had his very own dog. And it stayed that way for nearly a year.

Many evenings Curley Red sat in the lawn chair in front of his little house with Willy's head in his lap while he rubbed the dog's head, and scratched his ears.

Curley Red got a job feeding and caring for cattle where two Border Collies knew him very well, and he seldom ever had to meet new dogs.

Even his bachelor friend, Jeremy Haggins, the one with the combed back mane of brown hair, could pat Willy while the dog raised his ears to the calls of coyotes over the night wind. Curley very seldom had other visitors, so there was little circling for Willy to do.

One night Jeremy called to tell Curley Red that he had gotten a coy-ote-cross dog too, great big wolf hound female cross.

"How about I bring her over for you and Willy to meet her, Curley? If we like, maybe we could have some puppies out of them some day."

Curley Red said, "Sure." He always did have trouble turning other people down when they asked him to do something.

So Jeremy Haggins brought his wolfhound-coyote cross dog over to meet Curley Red and Willy. The two dogs met head to head, ears up, green eyes looking into yellow eyes, sniffing. They sniffed each other over entirely. For awhile they laid in the front yard grass while Jeremy and Curley visited through the dark evening from adjoining lawn chairs.

Then the two dogs began romping and playing as the southern breeze came up, and fireflies blinked from the night darkness. They ran to the prairie meadow fence together, the female quickly ducking under the fence to run on out into the night.

Willy paused for a moment before he went under too. Curley Red could envision the familiar green eyes staring back at him although they glinted bright white-yellow in animal night glare in flashes of moonlight now.

Then Willy ran out into the night too.

The two men never saw either one of the dogs again although there were rumors that for several years coyote hunters occasionally would take an animal with a white collie belt, probably the offspring of some coyote-dog cross.

Jeremy Haggins never owned a dog again.

But Curley Red made sure he got one when the Border Collies at the ranch had pups.

Wild Willy had answered the question of his origin. The cross had been a chance encounter of nature, just like this one.

The Waltz Of
Miller's Mound

Whirling in dark linens,
she waltzes through the glazed
and crystalline winter whiteness
over the spaced monolithic stones
of Miller's hundred-foot mound.

And even when
she raises her skirt
in icy morning fog,
the stones refuse to share
their memories of milennia.

Set in three-foot rows,
one-two-three,
one-two-three,
they wait,
the shells of past seas
held tightly in their grips,
for the shadowy, wispy dancers,
in bonnets darkly dancing
against the clear-cast moonlight,
who laid them there to rest.

They wait once more
for spirit world
to dance upon
the deep blackness of earth,
in waltz that takes
her winds away
in full light twirls
of endless mirth,
no clothing,
only creator nudity.

Zoom Zoom For
A Time Of Need

Big droplets of rain splashed the windshield of the car in the warm, steamy summer air outside while inside the vehicle, Abner longed to roll down the window to feel the moisture against his face.

But Jane was complaining, her voice sending incessant spasms up his throat in his weakened ability to drive.

"Abner, can't you turn that air conditioning up any more? She asked. Then she would fan her face, "Hah, hah, hah, I'm dying of heat. I should have worn a sun-dress shouldn't I? Do you think my sandals look good with this dress?"

"Just turn the fan up if you want more air. You can do it. See, there's the switch there. You'll probably be cold in a minute anyway."

Lord, but the acrid, eye-irritating smell of her hair spray was overcoming in this confined area. It would be good just to sit out under the trees in a lawn chair smelling green life while this rain dripped on you.

"There's puddles on the pavement. I just did my toe nails. Drop me off at the hospital entrance won't you, Abner? You can walk in across the lot yourself, can't you?"

He did walk, bent with it throbbing around the lumps on his neck, the heat of the pavement searing up through his shoes even with the cover of water.

Abner tried to raise his head, feeling the welcome breeze across his face ripe with the smell of life across the countryside even if he was here in the city.

"Oh, what a beautiful big building this is," Jane said as Abner entered the mechanical air through the entrance to walk with her to the desk. They had his papers ready, and they waited.

"Zoom, zoom," said a hard-muscled looking little man, elbows working quickly from side to side, as he shuffled past their seats in a half-dance to the admissions desk in his sparkling white, medical uniform.

Abner looked up, annoyed, the pain in his neck clinching him tightly with the effort. He was afraid.

No, Abner thought, afraid didn't cover the magnitude of the tightening knot in his gut. He was scared, terrified, at what faced him in this big sterile place with the big fake plastic fig trees and the faint smell of chemicals in the slow-moving atmosphere. If only one tree were real, it might have seemed a little better.

Even the breeze left by the moving little man was disturbance enough to set his nerves on edge a step further.

He looked at Jane in the next chair with the pink powdered face chewing her gum as placidly as any cow resting under a shade tree with a cud, he thought.

She didn't seem worried. Wasn't she concerned for him? Maybe in her own way, he answered himself.

"My feet really show off well in sandals, don't they Abner?" Jane asked. "I wish I didn't have a crooked toe. Do you really think my toe is that crooked, Abner?

"Haven't they decorated this place nicely? Don't you really love the way they painted the walls in stripes?"

Routine surgery for this condition, they had tried to reassure him in one breath while in the next statement they added that any surgery in the neck area was sensitive.

Abner had never been under the knife since a childhood tonsillectomy that left him vomiting from the ether so he could tell them that any surgery on him wasn't routine.

Besides, what if the malignant tumors grew again despite the surgery, like weeds that kept on coming back.

The little man was at the station, waiting on the computer printout, working his hands one over the other while he did a step in beat to music from the radio playing on the desk, bobbing his nearly bald-cut, shiny, black-haired head.

Why doesn't he hold still with more dignity, Abner asked himself? He obviously was a nurse or nurse's aid of some kind in the white clothes.

At least the little guy looked alive in this place, but he wasn't business-like.

"Mr. Duncard, Abner Duncard to the desk, please," called a woman from the station nodding at them.

As Abner and Jane walked up the woman said, "There's a room ready for you. Patrick here will take you down in the wheelchair. You'll be prepped for surgery there."

"Zoom, zoom, as fast as we can go, take'em down, Patrick now, zoom, zoom," said the small man, moon-walking backwards to the wheelchair with his arms swinging in rhythm to the station radio music while he smiled with big, bright white teeth.

"Here we go, Mr. Duncard, sit yourself down in the wheelchair, and we'll have you down to your room before you know it, zoom, zoom."

"Abner," said Jane, "Do I need to stop at the girls' room? Is my hair messed up so I need a mirror? I wonder if I really should have put that red tint in it, or just left it plain brown.

"Did we leve the hall light on at home? Maybe you ought to give me your car keys now. I'll have to go home alone you know."

Abner's intestines were empty because they had told him not to eat the night or morning before, but they still clinched and rolled. Got to calm down, he told himself, try not to be so scared.

The small man patted him gently on the shoulder when he stopped the chair, and then helped him out to sit on the bed.

"The nurses will be right in, Mr. Duncard. Got to run with this chair for another guy, but you'll see me again up and down the hallway, zoom, zoom, got to keep moving.

They had him take his clothes off, and put him in a gown with his back-end exposed. He had to take pills. They gave him a shot.

They stuck an intravenous needle in his hand connected to a bag of fluid above his bed. Abner blinked his eyes at the white ceiling, they seemed so dry.

He licked his lips, and bit one trying not to grind his teeth. The nurses smiled at him, and tried to be friendly, asking him questions about the farm.

"Oooh, look who's here, Abner," said Jane. "It's Molly come to see us before you go into surgery."

"Well, I couldn't stay away in your hour of need, Honey," said the square-built bleached blonde in the rose-patterned dress. "Oh, I like the way you've done your hair, and aren't those just the cutest sandals."

The little man was back, looking down on Abner with what seemed to be the biggest, most lustrous brown eyes.

"Came back fast didn't I, Mr. Duncard, zoom, zoom. How you doing here? Did those nurses take good care of you?"

"I'm cold, really cold. My stomach's upset."

"Here, let me pull that blanket up some for you, quick as a wink."

Then he took Abner's hand in his own warm hand. "You'll be good to go yourself, Abner. Don't worry now. It will be over quick, zoom, zoom."

In the background they could hear Molly speaking, "What are you going to do, Honey, if Abner doesn't make it? Are you set to go it alone? You know, it would have been tough when my husband died because my pension wasn't much, but he ended up having quite a few benefits."

"Oh, Abner's got a life insurance policy for $100,000. It's all up to date. I checked the file before we came in.

"Of course, we don't owe any money on the place anymore either. I don't know, I might jut move to Florida or somewhere like California or Texas you know, somewhere where you can see the ocean out of a window. I don't like winter, and you can always air condition."

"Out of here," said Abner, choking. "Both of you just get out of here if you have to talk like that. Go out in the hallway."

The little man was patting his shoulder again. "It's going to be fine, Abner, over with quick, zoom, zoom. Here, I'm going to pray for you real quick, and then you'll see me again soon before you know it, got a lot to do, zoom, zoom." He put his hands on Abner's chest while he bowed his head, and then he was gone.

They rolled Abner to surgery on a gurney, his head seeming to roll from side to side as he lay tranquilized trying to suppress a tear that rolled from the corner of his eye, Jane and Molly plodding behind with a constant volume of chit chat.

A man held his arms as he descended into a black unconsciousness, blacker than anything he had ever known. He tried to raise his arms at the last moment.

There was a noise somewhere, something that made him blink awake. He tried to focus on shiny metal, the raised rail of the surgery gurney.

"Good, Abner, you're waking up," said a voice above him from the foggy shape of a nurse's face. "You'll be coming around now. You're fine, you're fine. We'll be taking you out soon to see your wife. She's been waiting, she and your friend."

The next time, Abner could see the brown hair and rounded face of the nurse more easily, and he gasped out two words at her, "Zoom, zoom." Then he added, "I want Zoom Zoom."

When the nurse bent over Abner the next time, he made her jump when he made a major effort to take her hand. "Zoom Zoom," said Abner.

Another nurse behind her said, "I think he might mean Patrick."

After a quick kiss, Jane walked down the hallway behind the gurney chatting with Molly again. A man he called Zoom Zoom walked beside the gurney, his smaller, black hand holding Abner's big-knuckled white hand.

Two nights later, Jane tried to call Abner's hospital room from home, but received a continuous busy signal. She called the nurses' station. "I really need to talk to Abner about papers we need to have signed," she told the nurse.

The nurse looked down the hallway through the open door of Abner's room to where two men sat of different cultures who had spent most of their lives less than 30 miles apart. "It looks to me like he just has his phone off the hook.

"He says Zoom Zoom has stopped by after shift, and they've had their prayer. They're talking. I think if you'll call back in just a little bit, they'll be done quickly.

"You know, zoom, zoom."

Serenade Of Life

Serenade of life
played on strings I cannot see,
resonating strength throughout me,
carefully revealed
for glimpses of the music,
when I cannot explain,
or when emptiness abounds,
the joys and sorrows overwhelming.
Now the drums and brass
play lowly,
the sharp notes disapper,
the days are growing shorter,
low notes deeply on a giant harp,
and they call to wonder,
what did it all
really mean,
a song of empty straining,
or the tune of the future's dream.

The people I have known,
that I was meant to join,
many of them are gone,
but others have come to be,
joining to sing
in a chorus around me
that flows in sweet carressing
of a serenade of life.

But the melody
plays out louder,
comforting the waking slumber
as in His arms I sway,
in the rhythm of Creator
in this final
serenade of life.

The Cat And The Chicken Discover A Monkey's Uncle

Uncle Art was still sick.

He sat in his favorite deep-pillowed chair with his feet up on a padded stool by the hot wood stove. The stove had his deepest cooking pot on it full of water to make steam to open his sinuses.

He furthered the process by keeping a warm, wet towel wrapped around his white hair in a loose turban. Periodically he would take the towel off to it put in the hot water on the stove, wring it out, then put it on his head again.

On the book table at his side was a pile of handkerchiefs and a box of tissues, the tissues for the drizzle from his nose and the handkerchiefs for what escaped to his mustache.

The floor around him was a jumble of papers, unfolded laundry, dirty clothes, used dirty plates and silver, and a miscellany of personal items like pencils, keys and suspenders.

"Oooh," Art moaned, "what's worse, to have a headache that sucks your eyes into your head, or to have a steady stream of fluid coming out your nose that doesn't want to stop? Everything between my chin and my topmost hairs is plugged up.

"Three days this has gone on, and, still, I have to go outside in the snow and the cold in the morning and the evening to take care of all the animals. It seems like some of you could help me more some of the time—you hear me all of you out there? Oooh, I hate these aches.

"Ah, did I hear what I just thought I heard? That sounded like a car pulling in the driveway. Oh, Lord, help me get up enough just to peak through the curtain. Ah, eh, eh.

"Oh my. Yes, I did hear a car pulling in. It's that young Galatin Gilpinin with his mother, Sally, and her sister, Merci Megenpel. They're probably bringing me more goodies cuz they found out I was sick.

" I already have a half apple pie and quite a lot of fried chicken in the refrigerator from ladies. No offense to anyone, but it sure helps a man feel better when he's sick but can still eat a lot of apple pie and fried chicken. What can I say? Fried chicken and apple pie is a way of life in this country. You just have to learn to live with it.

"Oh, but hurry here, hurry, Art. What can I do with all of this in a hurry, get it half-way picked up before they come in. I know, the big walk-in closet over here, just skootch everything in there, that's right, that's right, use the feet, shove it in in piles, really quick clean-up.

"Ah, the wooden box there by the wood stove—naah, I'll just leave it there by the stove, kind of straighten up the gunny sack in it. It's kind of

nice with that big red rose on the side of it.

"That's right now, all of this stuff, all of you all of you into the closet. Careful, careful, don't get caught in the door. And, ping, I close the door.

"Now, back in the chair, get the cloth back on my head, get ready to groan, just a little bit, nothing unbecoming."

"Knock, knock, knock."

"It must be Galatin knocking. The ladies wouldn't hit the door that hard.

"Yes? Can you come in yourself without me getting up? I don't feel so well," Uncle Art called out in his best quavering old man voice. "Ahh, ehh, oh, oh."

Galatin threw the door open to let Merci Megenpel and Sally Gilpinin pass into the house, each of them holding an aromatic package, the pair of them so plump and uniform with light brown hair nearly turned full gray.

"Oh, Arthur," cried out Sally, "Poor thing, are you really that sick? We heard you groaning out there."

"Arthur, you look awful," Merci said soothingly. "Really, at our age you ought to be taking better care of yourself. Of course, it's probably nothing you could have done anything about anyway. It's the vapors. People carry them all over spreading their diseases. I hope it's not contagious, but Sally and I would risk it anyway to come to your side. You know that."

"Yes," said Sally. "Look here, Art. We brought you an apple pie and some fried chicken."

"Oh, you lovely ladies," sniffed Uncle Art. "You're just beautiful, inside and out, both of you. Whaddaya say, eh, Galatin?"

"Yeah, hi Uncle Art," replied the tall, sun-burnt young man with the black hair. "Yeah, like I could guess I might buy that it was the vapors," he grinned.

"Maybe it was the vapors out of a wine bottle, huh? I heard you and Graham Walther drank his home-made peach brandy out behind the horse barns until the snot was running out of your heads, and just never stopped."

"Galatin! What a horrible, crude thing to say! Uncle Art might be a real gentleman, but you certainly aren't. You apologize to him right now, and you can apologize to me and your Aunt Merci in the car," Sally said, her lip curled and face turning red with embarrassment.

"I'm sorry, Uncle Art," Galatin said smiling and restraining a full laugh when Uncle Art turned to look at him, and gave him a wink.

The ladies also exchanged a look when Arthur turned his head with Sally fanning her nose to mouth the word, "Whew," and Merci holding her nose to mouth "Phew, it stinks in here."

They quickly straightened their faces to looking sympathetic when Uncle Art looked back at them.

"That's OK, Galatin. I'll have to say I might wish for a little demure sip of Graham's white-hot peach brandy right now, burning out the conflagration in my throat, just to get rid of this horrible, horrible disease. Turning to the sin of alcohol would be better than dying of this stuff.

"You might tell Graham how I'm suffering over here—I could tell him a good story if he came over."

"I'll bet you could, Uncle Art," Galatin said with a couple of deep chuckles. "Only Graham seems to have the same illness you have. He says he got it pickin' peaches, only there aren't any peaches ripe now. And, by the way, you better take some time from being sick to cleaning up. It smells like you've had the chickens and cows in the house."

"That's OK, Galatin," said Uncle Art. "I suppose the illness does smell a little.

"Just put the pie and the chicken in the ice box over there If you would. Help yourself and the ladies if you all would like a little."

"Thank you, Arthur, but we brought the food for you," said Merci as Galatin returned from the kitchen biting meat off a fried drumstick, a slice of apple pie on his plate.

"Arthur, what a beautiful wooden box you have by the stove there. I don't remember it," said Sally. "What a wonderful red rose that is painted on the side of it too. It looks too delicate for a print. Did some-one hand-paint that?"

"I suspect so, I suspect so," said Art. "I got it at a second-hand store for some guests. But, I agree with you, that's a top-notch rose painting. It might date clear back to Van Gogh or some other famous fella, but then, that's another story.

"Right now, I feel an obligation to tell you the story behind the box. Of course, it's the gospel truth."

"Oh, Uncle Art," Galatin sighed, "not one of your long-winded sto-ries. We ain't got the time for a masterpiece lie. Save it for your next drunk with Graham."

"Galatin!!!" cried the ladies in unison. "Of course we want to hear Arthur's story. He's a creative genius!"

"Or something like that depending on which way the bull is turned," said Galatin.

"I tell you, it's the gospel truth," said Arthur becoming incensed as he wiped his white mustache with the handkerchief. "Go get me a drumstick too, boy, Im'a startin' in.

"Well, ladies, just sit back there, and get comfortable. This'll take me a while. You see, I always thought I might hanker to see a really big city. I've been to Kansas City quite a few times, and as you know, that's a monster of a city. You can see just about anything or get about anything you want in Kansas City. Why, one time when I sold cattle down at the stockyards, and was feeling really flush, I went to this place where they had dime dances and.....well, I better save that one.

"Anyway, I heard tell how Chicago is even bigger than Kansas City. Now, I couldn't hardly believe there was any need for anything bigger than Kansas City, but I decided to see it. I took my old jalopy in to have the mechanics go over it before I left, and I'm glad I did because it's a powerful long distance to there.

"I went through all kinds of towns, and saw all kinds of country. I even went through St. Louis. Now St. Louis doesn't seem like it's a lot different size than Kansas City, but it must be, even though I can't tell it, because the people there speak with an accent all their own. You know, just like a Frenchman speaks with an accent because he's been talkin' too much French, only different.

"I don't know what them St. Louis people been talking that makes them sound different. Only, I can tell you it's different than what the Chicago people been speaking, too, because they got a different accent. None of them sounds like normal English like us and Kansas City people do.

"When did you get that piece of pie out of the frige, Galatin? Get me a piece of it too. I hope you been listenin' to my story so far because it's got a powerful lot of information in it. Don't raise your eyebrows at me, it's all the gospel truth.

"Anyway, well, I'd been seein' lots of corn grown, but that Illinois comes by its reputation naturally. That black dirt country they got grows crops so tall they don't need trees because the birds nest in the corn tassels, and that's the gospel truth.

"Chicago is awful big, pretty near like a Kansas City and a St. Louis stuck together and then a little more. They got their meat plants and all that stuff where they don't pay people much to work long hours in some places so they can barely stick four walls together to get a house while in other places they got bankers' mansions with gardens and lawns.

"They seem to set a great store by the gangsters that robbed the bankers, so I can't tell if that's commendable or not. I got uptown to see a play about a guy that died with a bean can stuck over his head, too. Don't know if that was commendable, but it was funny.

"Now, one of the impressive things in Chicago is you go down where the tall buildings is, and notice all the wind that blows between them giving it the title of the windy city, and my God, there it is, the reason for all that wind. It's Lake Michigan, one of them great lakes, and the wind comes in putting up such big waves along the shore that a body like me that ain't used to oceans gets a terrible creeping fear that it might just wash the whole place away which would be especially tragic with me in it.

"So, there I was for a whole day just stuck between the tall buildings and that big lake that goes on and on further than an eye could ever see. I tell you, the whole landscape just struck me dumb. I couldn't have told a story then if I'da had to.

"Quit your grinning at me, Galatin. You know you appreciate my artfulness. What do you mean, Uncle Artfulness?

"The place ain't like in KansasCity when you happen to look between things, and see the Missouri River. You can see the other side of the Missouri at Kansas City or St. Louis or points between. No folks, where you might only see barges on the Missouri, they got full ocean-going ships that turn up from time to time on Lake Michigan.

"Well, the whole situation set me to thinking of home, and deciding I'd seen enough to tell the gospel truth that I'd been to Chicago. I decided to take a walk in a park down by that big lake one more time, the waves crashing along the shore, just to let my mind come to grips with the situation.

"I was eating a bologna sandwich, and carrying a loaf of bread under my arm. Food's a great peace maker. It was then I came across probably the very strangest thing I ever did see, and why you would have to be in a city like Chicago to see it, I don't know. Maybe somebody there raises smarter animals.

"I came to this place where they'd planted some bushes around a square of grass, and I thought I saw a flash of color from one of the bigger bushes. I go over there, start to pull aside the branches and leaves to see what's in that bush, and I hear this low grow.

"Uh oh, Art, I says to myself, somethin' in there ain't sure it likes you. But I pulled one last pair of branches aside, and I seen them. It was a big old Leghorn chicken hen sitting on the ground tilting her head to look up at me, her old red comb and tongue flopping to the side underneath, and under her one wing, snuggling up to her, and growling low at me, was a big, orange cat.

"The chicken gives a few low clucking noises, and then that cat begins to growl even louder. I didn't know quite what to do, but I felt I was risking immanent cat attack perhaps with chicken accompaniment.

"So, I took out a couple of pieces of my bread to give them, and the cat quit growling. They both started eating with the hen singing kind of a low, throaty little happy song. Didn't I just tell you that food's a great peace maker.

"It made me feel content too. I was saying to myself, well, Arthur, isn't this just a strange and cute sight you've discovered here. I backed out of the bush, and says to the cat and the chicken that maybe they'd like to come out, and have a couple more slices of bread.

"While they ate those two slices, I told them all about where I live, leaving out for the chicken's sake how we're all fond of eating her kin and their chicken children, fried eggs, and it was mostly the gospel truth.

"It ended up, I invited them to come back home with me, and said that when they wasn't in here experiencing congenial living conditions with me, they could stroll around the yard like any common cat or common chicken, and nobody would bother them.

"Well, the chicken and the cat face each other like two people talking, and that chicken just gabs, and clucks up a storm, puck, puck, cluck, puck, while the cat listens like he's bein' instructed. Finally, they stop, and just turn around, and look at me.

"Well, I thought, apparently I'm supposed to be getting something out of this, so I turn away, and start walking toward my car. I look back at them from time to time, and they're walking along quietly right behind me, side by side. Now, wasn't that peculiar?

"I open the back door of my car, they both jump in, and that cat snuggles up under the chicken's wing just like I first saw them only this time on my car seat.

"Then, 'Yuck, puck, puck, yawk,' goes the chicken, just as I sit down in front, and put my key in the ignition. The cat jumps up, and begins to scratch at the back door, 'yeow, meow.' So, I go around, and I let the cat out.

"He hits the ground at a run straight for a bunch of trees while that chicken keeps up a slow puck, puck, puck with her head tilted up at me like I was a snake or she was tryin' to see if she could trust me."

"Uncle Art, this is an awful long story, and I got to admit, It's about the most stupid one I ever heard out o f you. You can even quote me on that if you ever care to write it down," said Galatin. "How does this story have anything to do with us asking about a wooden box that you obviously have there to put firewood in?"

"Now, let Arthur be, Galatin," said Sally. "Let him tell his story. I know how hard it must be for him to tell it when he's so sick and all, and I'm intrigued."

"Ah, oooh, eh, yes I am awful sick," said Arthur. "Guess you'd better go get me another piece of chicken, some more pie, a glass of water, and, oh, boy, there's a coffee pot in the upper left corner. Why don't you brew us up some. I know this is a wondrous tale, and the rest of it won't take long now. And, it's the gospel truth.

"Let's see, where was I? Oh, yes, the cat finally comes running back, and right behind loping just as fast as he can on his back legs and his knuckles, his old long tale in the air, here comes a big, brown monkey. Why, he stood darn near two feet tall, and he had him a pink bare face. Now, he really looked like a fellow I saw once that had too much peach brandy.

"I did eventually get kind of fond of him lookin' everywhere with those little brown eyes like he found the whole world curious. It's disconcerting though, when you're driving, to have a monkey finally get so used to you that he'll hop out from under the chicken's wing in the back seat, jump in the front, and feel you all over to see what you're like. I didn't like them monkey hands around my eyes and nose, not to mention every place else monkey hands can go.

"We headed for home then. I guessed I'd seen enough of Chicago and the big lake, and I was carrying their most unusual sight home with me anyway.

"The chicken just sat in the back seat sleeping from time to time, and the cat stayed snuggled up under her one wing. The monkey spent half his time jumping around the car looking out every window. I didn't mind much except when he looked out my window, and would get his tail in my face.

"And, also, monkey feet sometimes have an uncommon grip to them. When he would get tired, the monkey would jump in back, and snuggle up under the chicken's other wing. It was like the three of them had been together forever. I always did hear that when country people move to the big city, it can make uncommon bedfellows out of them.

"I'd given them the last of my bread, and every time I stopped anywhere I had to pick up a couple more loaves, or the chicken would get to squawking at me. Whenever I eat, I like to get some beans. I guess you could say I like to stay full of beans.

"They always wanted me to bring the leftovers out, or even order another plate for them if there wasn't enough. I soon learned to hand any beans to the chicken. A chicken doesn't get so gassy on beans as a monkey or a cat if you want good travelling companions. The doggone monkey would sneak those hands in there for a few beans anyway. At least the cat didn't care much.

"I got so I could communicate with them pretty well. The chicken didn't want us to go through St. Louis or Kansas City on the way home because she thought I might get tired of feeding them, and dump them out—seems like that might have happened once before.

"I tell you, talking around everything to make a point, a gassy monkey, fear of dumping, going around places—it got to be like politics, and that's the gospel truth."

"OK, Uncle Art, I've about had enough. It's getting time to go home for chores. Why don't you finish this up, and I'll fill your wood box before we go home," said Galatin.

"No, no, boy, that's where the story's headed. See, that wooden box is where the chicken and the cat slept next to the wood stove when we were all here. Some times the monkey would get in the box with them, and other times, when he'd get too hot, he'd get up here on the back of my chair, or look out the windows.

"I did have a hard time getting him to do the dishes until the chicken bawled him out. I guess you can tell from history that you never can tell what will happen when you get a monkey in a white house.

"I picked that wooden box up at a second-hand store in central

Missouri on the way home. It caught the chicken's eye with that red flower painted on it. She's sensitive. I think she could be an art fancier because she's got two wings, but, yet, isn't flighty, likely to make good judgments."

"Oh, Lord," Galatin said, "the never-ending consummate liar's story."

"That isn't kind, Galatin," said Merci.

"No matter, no matter," Uncle Art said. "I'll have to finish up here in short order if Galatin needs to go do chores. I wouldn't want him not to work, and there's really not enough pie and chicken for both of us. Go get me another piece of pie, will you, boy?

"Me and the chicken and the cat and the monkey got into kind of a routine coming home. I'd stop for gas at service stations, then drive out back of the buildings so the three of them could have a toilet to themselves. They're pretty clean although the monkey slips once in a while.

" We had a good peaceful life going once we got here too, lots of cold winter days with them in the box, all of us outside around the lawn chair on sunny afternoons, that silly monkey on my knee part of the time while I sat there. I had to get rid of the puppy though."

"What puppy, Uncle Art? We didn't see any puppy out there, did we, Mom, did we Aunt Merci."

"Of course you didn't see any puppy. I told you I had to get rid of him. I gave him to some kids that live down the road. I thought the chicken, the cat and the monkey would enjoy having a puppy that could grow into the family dog. So, I picked up this free mutt pup, looked like a cross between a coon hound and a boxer.

"Well, the puppy chased the cat up trees, chewed the monkey's tail, and plopped down hard on the chicken, and tried to chew her, too, when he jumped into that box. They finally told me he had to go, or they were leaving.

"They didn't give me much time though. I got up one morning, and I didn't see them anywhere. I went out to start feeding the livestock, and was standing there rubbing the puppy behind the ears when I realized they were gone.

"I got in the car to drive out to look for them. There wasn't a trace of them on the back roads. But when I got a couple of miles up the highway, there they were trudging off to the northeast in a line together.

"The monkey was holding up a sign that said 'Need Ride To Chicago.' How they wrote that, I'll never know. Neither the cat nor the chicken have good hands for writing, and I think the monkey is intellectually challenged.

"Anyway, I just watched them walk away for a while before I came home. But that's why I had to get rid of the pup."

"Now that's a punk story, Uncle Art," said Galatin. "If they'd left, why did you have to get rid of the pup? It seems like you could have kept him."

"Yes, Arthur," said Merci, "a fellow like you could use a good dog. You always used to have a dog."

"Maybe you can get another dog, Arthur," said Sally. "But Galatin is right about one thing. We really do have to get him home for chores, and both of us have things we need to do. It was delightful seeing you, and listening to your wonderful tale. We need to do this again soon. You take care of yourself now, Arthur."

"Yes, Arthur, don't go getting such terrible colds at your age."

"Yeah, have a good'un, Uncle Art, and stay away from the peach juice. It makes your stories goofier," said Galatin.

"Galatin!!" said the ladies in unison.

"Oooh, aah, eh, yes, I'll take care," said Uncle Art. "I have to at my age."

Uncle Art drew the window curtain aside to watch Galatin get the ladies into the car. Then, satisfied they were leaving, he said, "OK, OK, they're leaving, I think you can come out now, my friends."

He went to the closet, opened the door, and out stepped a Leghorn hen followed by an orange cat and a rather large brown monkey. The chicken jumped into the box with the red rose on it, and the cat crawled in to snuggle up under her wing. He began purring almost immediately with the contentment of the place.

As Uncle Art sat down in his chair, the monkey jumped up to its top behind him.

"Well, little friends, it's good to be alone again," said Uncle Art. "I'm so happy you chose to come back when I told you the puppy had another home.

"I do apologize, chicken, for all of the fried chicken consumption while you were in the closet, but I guess you'll always find that that's just the way it is. We're a chicken consuming race."

"Yawk, puck, puck, puck."

"Yes, I suppose we would feel the same way if you ate people. And, I share your observation that it's fortunate that none of us cares to eat cats or monkeys."

Just then the door came open, and in stepped Galatin with his arms full of firewood.

"Well, I'll be a monkey's uncle!!" the young man said looking at the scene inside.

"Yes, I suppose I would be a monkey's uncle too," said Uncle Art. "At least I suppose we have a relationship of some kind."

"And, that's almost the gospel truth."

Spatsie Love

The English sparrows 15 feet high
in the hackberry tree,
we also called'em
European sparrows, house sparrows,
the little spatsies,
are fighting and chattering
above my lawn chair,
reminding me of the time
my grandmother tilted
her white-haired head
to look sideways through her glasses
down at me.
I'd told her the boy spatsie
was the one with the outlined stripes
across his eyes,
the one with with the deeper, dark cloak
and little gray cap
while the girl was that plain,
gray-faced one.

How did you know that,
my Grandma asked me?
Well, I explained to her,
way before knowing from TV,
that I'd been watching the birds and the bees,
the bull and the cow out in the pasture,
the boar and the sow down by the barn,
the big boys and the big girls,
with their arms around each other.
The roosters and hens,
where the dog poked his nose,
and you shoulda' seen
what the tomcat did out at the shed,
with the mama cat a'yowlin, Grandma,
I'd'a liked to giggle myself dead, Grandma.
It was amazing, Grandma.

Well, Grandma explained to me
that I was only eight,
and it was too soon for me
to be noticing so much.

190

But, Grandma, I told her,
you're too late,
I've learned from that little brown bird,
all the colors and differences
in the world.
That's how I know, Grandma,
spatsie love,
yeah the spatsies are'a doin' that, Grandma,
spatsie love,
Yeah, I been'a watchin' them,
spatsie love.
Everyday in the yard, Grandma,
Spatsie love.
Why are you waving your arms, Grandma?

Aunt Patricia Does Tough Times In LA

Wallace Wontevu finally got his Aunt Patricia into the car with all her baggage, and was giving a deep sigh of relief as he pulled into traffic to take her to his home in the valley.

"Oh my, look at all of this, Wallace," she said wrinkling her forehead beneath her blue dress hat adding to the furrows of wrinkles that already betrayed that she was a woman of great age.

"Look at what, Aunt Patricia?" he asked while thinking of the contrast of a woman in blue suit dress and ancient black flats alongside the young women at the airport with their low-cut blouses and bare midriffs.

"Why the traffic, it's awful. I've heard about California traffic and Los Angelas in particular. But I never thought it would look quite this overwhelming. Do you really have to drive in traffic like this every day, Wallace?"

"Yes, I do, Aunt Patricia," Wallace said sweeping his curly hair back with one hand while the other gripped the steering wheel as he accelerated to 60 to enter the freeway where another driver was kindly letting him enter the lane.

"You get used to it. From where I live in by the ocean, it's an hour and a half drive to work. I don't mind it. I don't have that long to retirement anyway if my mutual funds would regain their value, and my pension is for real, and Social Security stays in place, and I can sell our home at its current or better value so Wilma and I can move away from this rat race."

"There must be eight lanes of cars and trucks here, or is it ten? Look at that semi-truck changing lanes like that. The way he whips it, he'll crush someone."

"It's ten lanes, Aunt Patricia. You learn to watch yourself here."

"Why, when I go to town sometimes I don't meet anybody at all out on our road, and when I get to the highway, it's only two lanes. Are you really worrying about retirement? Where would you move?"

"Wow, aren't you lucky living out like that only you've no place to go anyway. Yes, I am worrying about retirement. I don't want to jump from a white collar job to being a greeter at a Wally World or flipping burgers at a Mickey D's just to make ends meet. I suppose we might move upstate, or maybe even back to the Midwest near you."

"Wallace, I have places to go. I'm only an hour from a movie theater or a play, just like you are. I go to my clubs, I play cards, I rent movies, I go to the grocery store, and I go to church. Do you go to church, Wallace?"

"Oh, yeah, sometimes I do if I think of it from time to time. Guess I haven't been to a church for a while now......maybe five or six years ago."

"I was hoping your brakes would work coming down that exit ramp like that."

"Don't let it bother you, Aunt Patricia. You keep your car up, and it does what it's supposed to. You have to drive them hard here to keep up with the pace."

"Maybe if you went to church more, Wallace, you wouldn't worry about your future as much. You could leave it in the hands of the Lord."

"I don't guess I know for sure what the Lord's stance is on high priced oil and a down economy, Aunt Patricia. There's a lot to worry about even for a true believer."

"Wallace, do you like home-fried chicken?"

"Sure I do, Aunt Patricia, if I can get it. It's easier to buy Chinese food here than American fried chicken that's any good."

"Well, I'll fry some for you and Wilma while I'm here, but I want you to think on something else when I do it."

"OK, I can sure do that for some of your chicken."

"Well, Wallace, I know things are tough right now, and don't look too good to a lot of people. There were tough times in the 1950's and the 1980's got a little hard. But the 1930's, oh those Thirties, now there was a time.

"When I was a kid, we bought the groceries with the eggs from our flock of chickens. But a dozen eggs got so it wouldn't buy a loaf of bread. Sometimes there wasn't even a price for pigs. They couldn't pay for them.

"We're better off on the farm than we were then. Our real income's better even though our prices fluctuate, and are usually too low. There's a constant worry about fuel and fertilizer prices. But all the kids can usually make wages somewhere too.

"But the thought always scares me. Oh dear, if we have to go back to those times. I remember too well having a mortgage on the cattle. When we sold them, the bank got them. We didn't get anything. That's where the chicken comes in.

"You know, we have money in the bank now, money in savings. But when I hear the news, sometimes I think we should take the money out, and bury it in a can. They say if times get really bad, the money won't be worth anything anyway. But those who had cash back then sure got along better than a lot of people who didn't.

"There wasn't money around for anything then. That's why there wasn't a price for pigs. The pigs were there, but the money wasn't.

"But on the farm we were better off than some of them. We could raise a few chickens, and have a garden. We had cows, and we'd have home-made cottage cheese, you know.

"That fried chicken—that was some darn good eatin'—but I got tired of it. I'd think, oh my God, how good roast beef tasted when we could have it. We'd butcher that beef in winter, and keep it in a cold room.

"There was good times but hard times, desperate times for a lot of people. We had each other and a lot of family around. I guess it's a little tougher for you that way, Wallace. I hope to goodness we are pulling out of these times.

"I guess some of those stock brokers are having a hard time of it. On the news it showed a stock broker and his wife, an interior decorator from Chicago. They went to the farm in Iowa—a couple there had them in their home. They helped do chores, tend cattle and pigs. They found out what it was like, but they still sang a mighty hard song about food prices and their own problems.

"Of course, they could take the time to see those farmers, and they want the farmers to come back to Chicago to see them. But the farmers can't find anybody to do their work for them while they're away.

"I hope they can eat some good beef, and count their blessings."

"Well, those are some interesting facts and observations, Aunt Patricia. I guess it was really hard for people back then thinking about retirement too."

"Retirement, Wallace? No, they were thinking about surviving. When you get close to standing naked with what you believe in, it changes your viewpoint. You can have a whole different attitude about the importance of where you're at and who's around you in different kinds of times, even right here in LA.

"I don't know which way we're better off, Wallace. I hear lots of people planning for retirement, but very few of them planning for what comes afterwards."

Polar Bears A' Go Go

Where did the polar bears go?
Where will the polar bears go?
I really need to know.
And you tell me that you
want to know too.
So here's another dire warning
about global warming,
where will the polar bears go?
Where did the polar bears go?

Once northern lights,
danced over mountain heights
where forests of new oak trees grew
before the melting glaciers
of a bygone older age,
a bygone colder age,
when the mountains
were always covered in snow
that never, ever melted,
so, where did the polar bears go?

The Norwegians sailed in ships
over the melting green expanse
of the great Northern Sea
to Iceland, Greenland and Vinland.
They found land for farming,
for grazing their cattle and sheep
before the melting Greenland glaciers
of a bygone older age,
a bygone colder age,
when their lands
had been covered in snow
that never ever melted.
So, where did the polar bears go?

Then the little ice age
set the world stage
that melted the Norwegians away,
starving, dying and suffering,
on their little Greenland farms.
The spruce drove out the oaks

on their growing mountain glaciers
new-covered by feet of snow
that never, ever melted,
building on top of a bygone age
a bygone colder age,
but where had the polar bears been,
my friend,
where did the polar bears go?
We really need to know,
because we're doing it all again,
my friend,
the world is warming again,
so, where will the polar bears go?

The snow is melting away,
the glaciers turn to water each day,
the spruce of Norway are still here,
But soon might disappear,
when the oaks come back again.

So, we're burning our gas for Norwegians.
soon the Norwegians will plow
Greenland again,
maybe tomorrow, maybe in 10 years,
but where will the polar bears go?
Because the ice of a bygone age,
the ice of an older, colder age,
that may be slow to come back again
is melting away, my friend.
So, where will the polar bears go?
Where will the polar bears go?

If it isn't obvious to you now,
I don't know what to tell you,
holy cow!
You're focused on the ice,
thawing all around you,
in all the earth's warming regions,
but the polar bears are busy too,
they're turning into Norwegians.

The Hanging Of The Greens

If you had been able to focus your eyes closely, you might have seen through the chilled, misty rain turning to ice an apparition of a sorrel mare bobbing up and down at a trot with the figure of a man in broad-brimmed hat on her.

Garvey Oliphant rode down out of the hills where he normally tended cattle that freezing, cold, wet day in November, 1924, in a way that seemed more characteristic of times 40 and 50 years before that because he was heavily armed.

At his side hung an old Colt revolver fully loaded except for the sixth cylinder he left empty as a safety for the ride. The shotgun in a scabbard on one side of the mare's saddle was loaded with large shot that could tear a man apart, and the rifle in the opposite scabbard was there for long-range shots. He had a long-bladed World War I trench knife with brass knuckles for a handle in a home-stitched leather case attached to his belt.

Garvey's brother, August, had set off an hour before he did for the area 40 miles away, where the other relatives of Henry and Milicent Green lived, to tell them of their plight. August would have to rest his horse periodically, but it was better for him to ride with little sleep than to risk the news with a postal letter.

Justice was still swift with the crime only last week, the trial set for next week with the scaffolding already being put together for raising in the courthouse yard to carry out the possible hanging at the end of that same week. The owner at the lumberyard figured it could still be used for a barn bracing in the unlikely event the verdict went the other way.

"Too bad, too bad," the merchants in town were saying. The Greens had had a rough time with their weak-minded grand-daughter, Agnes Colwich, and such a thing had been bound to happen sometime given her good looks.

The merchants were torn. The Greens had been good people to have in the community, and they always paid their bills. On the other hand, a basket dinner after everybody went to the hanging might be just the way to kick off the Christmas season.

Good entertainment could be hard to come by, and the hanging of a woman was far more unusual than the hanging of a man. A movement was already underway for the community chorus to sing some songs of mourning followed by the usual Christmas carols.

The merchants' executive committee voted five to one to proceed with the basket dinner, Gerald Bogdon against because he thought they ought to wait for the verdict since a chance decision where only one of the Greens hanged, that being Henry of course, could considerably lower the merriment of the situation. It might be unseemly to begin early holiday celebrations right in front of a mourning widow.

Boulder Billings, the undertaker, abstained because he felt he stood to make good money anyway considering he already had been able to work on the body of the alleged victim, Monte Peathscheit.

Peathscheit's body had been tough to patch up with the shotgun wounds to get him presentable for viewing, but all the coins and a little

folding money in the collection jar from the curious who came to look testified that it had been a wise decision.

Plus that, the county still would be paying him its share for Peathscheit's burial. "Life could be wonderful when you dealt in death—that would be another person's death," Billings sometimes observed to his wife.

Everybody agreed it probably was a fine touch for Billings to put a black mark on Peathscheit's forehead so Saint Peter and the Lord would know the public sentiment on which way the man should go.

And they all also shared Billings' sentiment when he said, "Poor beautiful, half-witted Agnes Colwich, so fortunate when her grandparents decided to raise her when her mother and father died of the typhoid. How strange it is, that the misfortunate among us sometimes are blessed with attributes all of their own. She is so sweet, so simple in her great beauty, so voluptuous. She looks so natural. Is it any wonder Peathscheit noticed her?"

James Geitche, the hardware store owner whom the county intended to employ for the hanging because he knew his ropes and was a steady hand for butchering other people's livestock, wrote out the final statement for the merchant's executive committee which they decided best briefly expressed their sentiments after a couple of them became tearful, and expressed a few righteous statements.

It read, "We the members of the Merchants' Executive Committee, being people of great values with concern for the welfare of our fellow citizens, declare that Henry and Milicent Green have been fine upstanding members of our community, and the possible loss of them grieves us all. They have been upstanding hard-working, God-fearing, commendable members of their township and their church. They always paid their bills.

"It is a relief and a public service to have Monte Peathscheit removed from said community. He was a bully, a thief and a scoundrel. He seldom paid his bills. He more than once threatened members of this community with the knife he carried, or otherwise promised bodily harm, when collection of bills was attempted. He frequently attempted to force his presence and attentions on our young ladies which was resented by everyone. His attentions to Agnes Colwich were especially disgraceful, and this committee commends, understands and thanks Henry and Milicent for their righteous disposition of Monte Peathscheit.

" Monte Peathscheit seldom did his work as a farm hand or general laborer in the community well. Therefore, this committee recommends to the county that no public money be spent on a headstone or otherwise marked grave for him, but that his remains be placed in the unmarked portion of the cemetery usually reserved for vagrants, suicides and the poor."

All of the committee members agreed the statement was a fine piece of work and it passed seven to zero.

At about that same time Garvey Oliphant had succeeded in circling the town, where he had no desire to be seen, and was arriving at the Green farm south of town, his horse kicking up the half-frozen mud when he came into the farm driveway.

Sheriff Jewel Blackstone heard Oliphant riding in, and stuck his face through a corner of the farmhouse front door. "Garvey, we've been expecting you. Just sling your gunbelt and pistol over the saddle horn, and come in for the moment unarmed, will you? Sorry to bother with that, but that's the way I have to operate. "

Milicent Green got up from her chair to hug Garvey as he came in the door. "Hello, nephew, "she said. I knew you'd come as quick as you could when the sheriff sent for you. Thank you for being here in our time of need. Your cousin, Agnes, went to stay with the relatives, probably Hank and Erma, yesterday. The Bogglemans took her in their wagon. They'll explain what happened, and she'll be fine until this is over. I think she scarcely knows what it's all about."

Then Sheriff Blackstone had him turn as he patted him down for other weapons. "Garvey, you should have told me you had the knife!"

"Sorry, Sheriff, I didn't mean anything by it. It's on my other belt, and I got used to the feel of it."

"Well, I have to take it until we leave."

Garvey thought Milicent looked good considering everything that had happened, a bit gaunt and gray in the wrinkled elderly face if anything, but the blue eyes were still sharp and bright below her white hair and flowered house cap.

Then there was the sound of wagon wheels churning through the mud and the slopping clock of horse hooves as Deputy John Humboldt drove to the front gate with Henry Green already on the seat beside him.

"Well, Garvey," said the sheriff, we'll be leaving the rest of that pot of coffee and the farm to you. The deputy and I have to get Henry and Milicent to the jail for their own good, and just because it's the law. Don't worry, we'll take good care of them. We think a lot of them too."

Garvey followed the others to the wagon, and helped Milicent in. "Don't fret about anything, Uncle Henry, or you either, Aunt Milicent. I'll feed your horses, cattle, pigs and chickens, and check everything several times a day to make sure nobody's messing around here to take advantage of the situation. I came prepared.

"The relatives probably will know all about it before our little cousin gets there, bless her heart having to go through something like this because of someone like that. I should have been here to shoot him myself. Anyway, you take care, me and August and the folks love you both."

Henry didn't look as good to him. His eyes were swollen and red, set in big black circles on his round face. As a matter of fact, he seemed a little pathetic slumping wearily in the seat with the cold rain running off the brim of his hat. It seemed like the county ought to be able to afford a better cover on its wagon.

"Tell you what, Garvey," said Sheriff Blackstone. "Raise your hand, and I'll deputize you right quick. I'll put it in the books when I get to town. That way if you shoot somebody thieving around here, it's legal. You'll just have to come to file a report with me."

That night as the sun went down, as Milicent and Henry Green settled down in adjoining cells after eating meals of beef stew, August Oliphant rode his tired horse in at the home of Hank and Erma Hembel.

They were home, and after everything was explained twice over, Erma began to make up the extra room for Agnes with a pretty calico quilt on the bed with a doll that once had belonged to her daughters. August explained, "I saw them coming with the wagon a couple of hours back. Agnes was already asleep, just like a baby, with her chin down between the Boggelmans'."

Hank Hembel wasted no time. He was the first person in the clan to own a motor vehicle, and he started up his Ford truck with the flat bed to begin the drive from farm to farm, arousing all of the men who might want to go with him to the trial.

When they gathered the morning before the trial, there were 14 of them to take turns riding with their bed-rolls and lunches on the flat bed or in the truck cab with Hank.

They would all get off to wade if they had to if the truck seemed to get boggled down crossing creeks. They would all have to push if the wheels got to spinning in the mud. They all agreed that it was nice to have the speed of the truck, but it had a long way to go in replacing horses in rough country.

It seemed that nearly every one of them had brought a shotgun, and some of them had two or three weapons. They agreed it would be unseemly to ride into the town all heavily armed, so Hank had a couple of them help him drag out a big wooden box with a padlock to put the guns and ammunition in. They put one tarp over the gun-box and added another big tarp for all the men on the back of the truck in case the weather turned worse.

The Hembels and all of the rest of the family along agreed they would abide by the law and the court's decision, but they would bring the guns out if their cousin, Milicent, or her husband, Henry, were threatened with early lynching. They would be there for the Greens, innocent or guilty, but probably guilty they were afraid.

"Now, fellows," Hank Hembel asked, "do we all agree we can just sit there while maybe the legal authorities are hanging Henry and

Milicent? Or, is it better for some of you to go out to the Greens' farm to wait for those of us who can?"

Perhaps Jim Hembel said it best, "Hank, there's not a one of us can back out of going to a legal hanging if there's to be one. We owe it to Milicent and Henry to see them through whatever happens."

Everybody nodded their heads except tough August Oliphant who stood contemplatively with the ends of his sandy-brown mustache dripping with water because he had just come in.

Finally, Hank said, "August, you'd better put your guns in the box too, and you ride first in the front with me to talk this over."

August said, "I guess you all know that Milicent did well when she married Henry Green. There's no finer people than the two of them. They are saints to do what they've done for our Agnes."

They all agreed, but they also all agreed that they had to stay within the law except in the case of a lynching.

They were all just as excited as the townspeople were the next morning when it was time for the trial after sleeping out, and eating pork belly with fried potatoes. It was a nice day for a public event, crisp and cold, but bright and sunny with a light that seemed slowly to penetrate with its heat.

The merchants' committee members and many among the townspeople were taken aback to see such robust relatives of Henry and Milicent Green arrive, but they seemed to relax when Sheriff Blackstone seemed unconcerned. The sheriff even deputized August Oliphant as an extra hand to uphold the law, and had him strap a handgun on besides carrying a shotgun.

Judge Barnaby Matsken was at the courthouse to preside over the trial. His stomach growled with the fruit and coffee he'd had for morning meal, his head hurt, and he swore to himself that he would have that new deputy with the big mustache shoot anyone who got out of hand.

The Greens sat at a table with their public defender, Norman Pfiester, who took a subtle look at his watch from time to time. He hoped this didn't take too long. Everybody knew the Greens were guilty as sin, and the county didn't pay him enough to be here very late even though he knew he had to do his best with what little material he could muster. He had coached the Greens to be evasive when questioned whether they had actually shot Monte Peithscheit because they had little other defense.

That would especially be true given the formidable attorney they had against them, Ikeston Bainesworth Goodfellow, better known as old I. B. Goodfellow himself. I. B. was feeling grouchy himself because he had stayed up late the night before playing checkers with his grandson, Oscar Bainesworth Goodfellow. The kid would probably be an attorney, too, given that he played checkers that well already, good head, good head. But I.B. Goodfellow was tired—best if he got to the chase of this matter quickly. Old men want peace.

Even the 12 men of the jury were tired. They had been sequestered for two days playing five card and pinochle at the courthouse plus devouring everything the county would feed them. Grown men rarely got such a vacation, and they stayed up late.

But they had no chance for a nap here. Old I. B. Goodfellow thundered out his opening statement saying the Greens were guilty of premeditated first degree murder, and justice demanded that they be hanged by the necks until they were dead. The Greens stared in fascination as much as anyone at I.B. Goodfellow's contorted face and oratory skills, but their heads tilted backwards a couple of notches like they'd been struck with blows.

August Oliphant tapped the handle of his revolver with an index finger, and looked around the room.

Pfiester said the Greens were good people, and that they were responsible for the welfare of their grand-daughter, Miss Agnes Colwich.

Goodfellow roared out that being responsible for a granddaughter was no defense for murder. Then he asked the judge for a recess that was granted to take the jurors over to the mortuary to see the shotgun holes in Monte Peithscheit.

Boulder Billings was irritated when I.B. Goodfellow told him to get his collection jar out of there, but he decided the publicity and donations to come later from this event made it worth it to reveal the tortured body to the "I'll be's" of the jurors.

The prosecutor called Henry Green as his first witness. "Now, Henry, Mr. Green it has to be in this case," the old attorney smiled. "Mr. Green, tell us about the evening before the shooting of Monte Peithscheit. You discovered Peithscheit and your granddaughter, Agnes, in your barn, didn't you?"

"Yes, I did Mr. Goodfellow."

"Now raise your eyes, and look at the jury when you speak, Mr. Green. We want them to hear clearly what you say. Now, Mr. Green, what state was the clothing of Peithscheit in, and in what state was the clothing of Agnes in? Just tell us very clearly, Mr. Green."

Henry Green gripped the arms of his chair. His face turned pale, and his eyes became glassy as he looked at the jury. "Our Agnes had her dress off, and Monte Peithscheit was pulling his pants down, Mr. Goodfellow."

"And, Mr. Green, what did you say to them?"

"I told Peithscheit to get away from Agnes, to get out of there, and never come back again. I told him he was not to ever come near Agnes again. I told Agnes to get her clothes on, and she showed me her dress was torn."

"Did Agnes say anything, Mr. Green?"

"Yes, she said she loved Monte Peithscheit, and that Monte Peithscheit loved her."

"What did you think of her statement, Mr. Green?"

"I thought that my Agnes loves anybody who pays attention to her, and that she's sweet that way. I thought that Monte Peithscheit probably never loved anyone in his life. He only considered his own pleasure."

"What did Monte Peithscheit say back to you, Henry, Mr. Green?"

"He told me he was leaving because I had messed up his mood. But, that he would be back tomorrow, and he would be with Agnes when it pleased him. He said If I got in his way, he would give me a beating, and maybe worse."

"Did he do anything else before he left, Mr. Green?"

" Yes."

"What was that, Henry?"

"He slapped my face, and pushed me down on the floor. He called me a stupid old man, and he kicked me."

Deputy August Oliphant's knuckles were turning white as he gripped his gunbelt. Many persons in the courtroom were sitting with open mouths.

"Now, Mr. Green, when did you see Monte Peithscheit again?"

"I saw him again the next evening, Mr. Goodfellow."

"Where did you see him?"

"He was walking down my driveway toward me, coming into the farm."

"Were you carrying anything?"

"Yes, my double-barrel shotgun.

"Was it loaded with bird shot?"

"No, it was loaded with big game shot."

"Had you been watching for him all day?"

"Yes."

"What did you say to him?"

"I said I'd told him to stay off my place, and never come back, and that he better get on down the road."

"What did he say?"

"He said I was an old fool, and that he was going to take the shotgun away from me, and stick it down my throat. Then he said he was going to stick my craw to my backbone. Then he started walking toward me."

"What did you do?"

"I raised my shotgun, and fired one barrel into the front of his body, and he flipped over backwards."

"That's all for that witness, your honor."

Judge Barnaby Matsken sniffed. Good thing old Goodfellow knew how to bring along a trial quickly. Of course he'd had an easy self-incriminating witness. "Defense," Matsken said, "you got any questions for this witness?"

"No, your honor," said Pfiester. The old man certainly hadn't done much to be evasive. So much for honesty.

The sheriff decided to order August Ornsby outside to watch the door.

"The prosecution calls Millicent Green to the witness stand."

Millicent Green swore to tell the truth, and gripped her dry throat with her hand.

"Mrs. Green, you heard what your husband just told us, didn't you?"

"Yes, I heard him, I. B."

"Were you there behind him?"

"Yes, I was."

"What did you do?"

"I asked Henry if Peithscheit was dead, and he said he didn't know for sure. So, I took the shotgun out of his hands, went up to Peithscheit, and kicked him in the side, but I couldn't tell anything. Then I aimed the shotgun at his chest, and fired the other barrel just to make sure he was dead."

"Did you know if he had his knife on him?"

"No."

"Well the sheriff said in his report that he had his knife on him. Don't you think you should have looked to see if his knife was on him? Were you afraid he would do something anyway?"

"I was afraid he'd kill Henry, and maybe me too if I got in the way, and that then he'd take our Agnes."

"That's it, your honor," I.B. Goodfellow said. "The prosecution rests."

Judge Barnaby Matsken yawned, and swatted at a fly that was bothering him. "Defense, do you wish to question this witness, or call any witnesses yourself?"

Pfiester only had the merchant's statement about the situation read to show what the community thought of Peithscheit, and had one farmer stand up to open his shirt to show how his ribs were still taped up from a beating by Peithscheit.

"Then," said the judge, "prosecution, do you need a recess, or do you want to go right into your closing statement."

"Your honor," said I. B. Goodfellow, "I'll just go right into my closing statement so we can all go home early.

"Gentlemen of the jury, I think you can tell readily enough that a verdict of first degree murder is called for from you by state law given that the defendants have confessed to this murder themselves. We can be brief here, and you can let us all call it a day.

"Now, I suppose the defense is going to call this justifiable homicide by reason of self-defense since he'll probably say the Greens were in immanent danger of their own lives from the hands of this threatening and known town bully. But, we all know this was premeditated, that they thought out what would happen if Monte Peithscheit ever crossed the sights of that shotgun."

Pfiester listened intently. What's this that Goodfellow was saying?

Goodfellow continued,"He's probably going to tell you that the Greens were acting to protect their grand-daughter when they killed poor Monte Peithscheit because how were they to know all he would do to her, or even if he might kill her after he ravished her given his foul reputation.

"But, I tell you, gentlemen of the jury, Monte Peithscheit was a human being, and he deserved the full protection of the law, even if he was a thug and we all the know the Greens are outstanding citizens. The prosecution rests."

"Very interesting, Goodfellow," said the Judge. "Defense, what do you have to say."

Pfiester said, "Well, gentlemen of the jury, I call upon you to exercise your righteous consciences, and declare both of the Greens innocent by reason of justifiable homicide for self-defense. The case speaks for itself in the case of this villain."

Judge Matsken gave a long pause, and stared at one attorney, then at the other one. "OK, gentlemen, most unusual.The jury will be sequestered at least one hour to consider a verdict while the rest of us recess. Sheriff, go talk to that Deputy Oliphant about peaking in the doorway like that. It's unseemly."

The jury decided the verdict in 10 minutes, and had time for one hand of pinochle before the judge called them back.

"Chairman of the jury, do you have a verdict?" the judge asked.

"We sure do, Judge," said the chairman sticking his thumbs in his belt, rocking back on his heels, and giving a big smile. "It pleases the jury, your honor, to find both of the Greens innocent by reason of justifiable homicide for self defense."

Milicent Green hugged I. B. Goodfellow, and thanked him for his fine prosecution.

Henry Green shook his hand too.

They both shook hands with Norman Pfiester, too.

Judge Barnaby Matsken called Norman Pfiester into his office to advise that he really didn't know if his talents were directed well in the practice of law, but that he was willing to give him another chance.

Pfiester ran for congress then, but folks say he didn't prosecute his campaign well enough. He didn't seem able to defend the criticism, so he went into corporate law.

The merchants' committee members agreed the community chorus Christmas season concert the first week of December was a huge success. The Greens and some of their relatives, the Hembels, attended too. Agnes had a beautiful voice, so she began it all by singing Silent Night with the chorus joining in when it was obvious she wasn't going to remember any more than the opening lines.

But Agnes was beautiful with her blonde hair and high pink cheek bones. Everybody agreed that when she smiled at a person, it could melt them to butter.

She went back with the Hembels and a more extended family to live.

The Oliphant brothers didn't attend any of it. They had been away from their solitary lives in the hills too long, and their cattle needed attention.

The ladies of the community brought in their home-made wreaths and garlands of cedar. Everybody agreed it was the finest hanging of the greens ceremony they had ever seen.

Henry and Milicent Green sold their farm a year later, and followed Agnes to live closer to the Hembels.

Nobody checked to discover that Boulder Billings saved Monte Peithscheit's casket for a later funeral, but still collected from the county for it. Nobody was there to see him put Peithscheit's body in the hole. Sheriff Blackstone could have been there, but he told Billings to go on ahead by himself because he had a cold. The preacher Billings contacted said he was under the weather too, but he'd say a prayer for Peithscheit.

Nobody could find Peithscheit's grave now because decades later the county unknowingly put an asphalt street over it, even though the poor remains of the bones are only a foot below where the graders dug.

"Such is the ephemeral nature of every human being." At least that's what I. B. Goodfellow told O. B. Goodfellow before he passed on.

Chickens of the Serengeti

Chickens of the Serengeti,
Settle down, and let's get steady,
Chickens to the left,
Chickens to the right,
Chickens to the middle,
And fight, fight, fight.

Chickens of the Serengeti,
Save your eggs like
J. Paul Getty,
Circle round that corner pullet,
Do-si-do her,
Work your gullet,
And stretch your legs,
Make really sure you
Lay those eggs.

Set very tight
On substantialities,
You hatch your eggs
With chicken ease.

Puck, puck, puck
In chicken rage,
Circle to the left,
Circle to the right,
Feather your nests,
Really, really tight.

Hold your beaks
In grins then nasty pout,
This is what chicken dancing
And elections are about.

Auntie Beastie Provides Roland's Rhubarb Succor

Ricky was ready to go, sitting out in the shade of his front porch with his big broad face occasionally sinking to his chest as he closed his eyes in brief naps.

He startled himself totally awake at the sight of his friend, Roland, striding out with his long slender frame down the sidewalk toward him.

"Roland, Roland, where are you going in such a hurry?" he shouted. "Carol's almost ready to leave."

"Hi, Ricky! I thought about stopping to see you, but I thought you might be out doing something for the holiday. What do you mean, what am I doing? It's Labor Day Monday, like Sunday without church or get-togethers, so you can do whatever else you want to. Nancy's been reading, and for the last hour she's been rummaging around going through clothes or something. I decided to slip out the door for a quick walk."

"Nancy's probably getting ready to go just like Carol has been. It's so close to time to leave, Roland, that she's probably wondering where you are. You must have not been aware of the time. I guess what you're wearing will do to go to Auntie's anyway. You look pretty good."

"What do you mean go to Auntie's? I'm not going to Auntie's. This is my holiday."

"Roland, you have to go to Auntie's. Have you forgotten? We've had a date to go to Auntie's house for evening dessert for nearly a month now. Auntie invites far ahead because she expects absolute punctuality. You know that. I'm really looking forward to it."

"I don't have any invitation to Auntie's, Ricky. It must just be you and Carol. Yeah, it has to be just you and Carol. It's not me. I'm taking a real Labor Day holiday this year."

"Roland, you have to go. Just ask Nancy."

"I don't have to go. I don't want to go to Auntie Beastie's house, Ricky. I won't go."

"Roland, Nancy is your wife. She'll tell you that you have to go, and you'll go. Besides, it will be fun."

"Fun for you maybe, Ricky. Auntie always did like you better. I don't like to go to Auntie Beastie's house. I never would have been going there when we were little boys if it wasn't for you, Ricky. I want that part of my life where Auntie is in it over with. I'm not wanting to go even if Nancy tells me to."

"But, Roland, Auntie loves us. She loves to fix us dessert. My mouth is just watering with the hope that she'll have her rhubarb pie, good, green, sour rhubarb with barely any sugar in it, just the way she fixes it."

"Yuck, I hate rhubarb. I don't ever want to eat that garbage again, Ricky. Auntie's rhubarb stinks, the slimy, strangling stuff. Also, she's liable to poke me hard in the ribs with her nasty, square little finger with just enough nail on it to cut like she always did when I was a little boy, and say, 'Roland, you need to get some meat on those ribs.' She always said that to me, Ricky. 'Roland, get some meat on those ribs.' I can't stand the thought of it. Besides that , remember the time she force-fed me until I threw up on her brown hair rug, and I had to clean the whole rug. You're mistaken, Ricky, Auntie doesn't love us, and I don't want to go to Auntie's."

"Auntie does love us, Roland. She always says so. And she won't poke you now because you're a grown man. Carol, Carol, can you hear me in there? Honey, call Nancy, and tell her Roland is over here ready to go. She can come over, and we'll all leave from here."

"Ricky, I don't want you to call Nancy because we aren't all leaving from here. I don't want to go. And, what do you mean Auntie loves us, Ricky? We aren't even related to each other let alone her. She's just some old neighborhood woman who asked all of us kids in to feed us desserts, and play cards with us because that's what she wanted.

"Sure I appreciate it that she taught us pitch, canasta and five-card stud, but don't you remember how she used to lean over when I made a mistake at cards, and poke me in the ribs, 'Roland, you need to get some meat on those ribs?' nasty, foul old woman.

She only told us we had to call her Auntie to draw us in, Ricky. If she was related to us, we'd call her Aunt Beatrice, not Auntie. Haven't you ever wondered at the possible motivations of a woman named Beatrice Beastie? No, I don't want to go. She'll poke me."

'You have to go, Roland."

"No, no, I don't want to go, Ricky. She'll poke me. She'll tell me I have to eat her rhubarb pie, nasty stuff sticks in your teeth. And, if I don't eat it, she'll poke me several times, so I might throw up on the brown hair rug without eating too much."

After Nancy told Roland he had to go to Auntie's, it was a quiet ride in the back seat of the car. Carol and Nancy sat together in the front seat discussing everything from children to clothes very happily. But Roland wouldn't even talk about the fall football schedule with Ricky.

Roland only spoke one time on the ride, "She'll poke me. I know she'll poke me."

Auntie greeted them at the door, her flowered apron over a rotund fig-ure, her little square teeth clinched in a tight grin, her square glasses set on a Roman nose in a big, square face, her carefully parted down-the-middle gray hair, all squared up to spell domestic epitome.

"Yeah, the iron, square Auntie Beatrice Beastie, that makes sense," Roland later was to say to Ricky.

"Oh, I'm so happy to see you all," said Auntie in her low, gravelly yet feminine in a curious way voice. She hugged each of the women, and added a kiss on the cheek for each of the men. Everybody pretended not to see when Roland got a tissue out to rub his cheek.

"Well, sit down, sit down," said Auntie Beastie. "Your Auntie doesn't really like to play cards with five people, makes the partnering awkward, so we'll probably refrain from that tonight, children, unless you ladies want some action with some five-card? No? Good, we'll just visit then before we sit up at the table for your special favorite, Auntie's good, sour rhubarb pie, stuffed four inches thick with rhubarb chunks, and covered with a thick sugar crust. There's no other sugar to it other than the crust this time. Auntie promises you, you can taste it all of the way down, sour and pithy."

"Oh, my goodness, that sounds so delicious, Auntie," Ricky said. "I can hardly wait."

"Yeah, Auntie, I can hardly wait until I wait again," said Roland. "It sounds like one of your greater efforts."

"Ricky, you still have such pretty, blonde hair, not a gray strand in it," said Auntie Beastie. "And, you girls, such figures, if only your Auntie could have stayed so trim over the years. You children have done very well. Roland, you poor little thin thing, you still have such dark hair. Are you coloring it?"

"No, Auntie," said Roland, "that's just the way it is."

"Well, you know how concerned Auntie is for you, you're such a small-framed boy."

"Yes, Auntie," Roland said while rolling his eyes, and sticking out his tongue at Ricky when she turned to smile at the girls.

"All four of you have such beautiful children. Roland, I'm sure you must be pleased to see that your children have their mother's good looks."

"And, Ricky, I keep hearing such good things about your career, Dear. You are quite an upcoming young executive. Roland, I guess you have a job too?"

"Yes, Auntie, actually I'm very successful at it."

"Yes, Dear, I'm sure you have good friends, too."

"How are you doing, Auntie?" Carol asked, trying to steer any more conversation away from Roland.

"Oh, I'm fine, Dear, I just always stay the same as long as I take care of myself. I am blessed with a great constitution."

"Yeah, like the USS Constitution," said Roland, "able to plow through all of the waves, and sink anything that gets in your way. You're very durable, Auntie," he added grinning. "We all celebrate how able you are."

"Yes, I know you celebrate, Roland," replied Auntie Beastie. "Auntie knows you very well. Now, everybody, let's sit up at the table, and eat our rhubarb pie.

"I have very good news. Not only do we have a pie with one slice for everybody, but Auntie has made a second rhubarb pie. I know you girls may not be able to eat two pieces of pie, but I know equally well you boys will eat two pieces."

"You bet, Auntie," said Ricky. "You know I love your rhubarb pie. To have two pieces of it instead of one is a joy indeed."

"Yippee, yes, a joy indeed," said Roland.

"And beyond that, Auntie has another surprise, dear children. There is a third pie and a fourth pie, so each couple can take one home."

Nancy said, "Auntie, you are wonderful. You are so thoughtful."

"You certainly got that right, Nancy," said Carol.

"What a thought, rhubarb for a week," said Ricky.

"Yes, thoughtful," whispered Roland.

"Would you each like a scoop of vanilla ice cream on your rhubarb pie?" asked Auntie.

"Yes, that would be great," the girls said in unison.

"Not me," said Ricky, "I want pure, sour, green unadulterated rhubarb pie."

Auntie looked at Roland, and Roland just sat there looking at his pie.

"Roland, what about you, do you want some ice cream on your pie? Roland, Roland?"

"Good night, Roland, answer her," said Nancy, "have you gone into a trance."

"No, no, just anticipation, I'm thinking," replied Roland. "Auntie, would you have any strawberry ice cream?"

"Well, yes, Dear Boy," said Auntie. "You can have strawberry ice cream on your rhubarb pie if that's what you really want."

"Thanks, Auntie," said Roland. "How about we put my pie in a bowl instead of on a saucer if that's OK."

"Why, certainly Roland."

"May I have a second scoop of strawberry ice cream on it, Auntie?"

"Well, yes you can."

"Auntie, would you happen to have any strawberries?"

"Just some frozen ones, Roland. But I can get you some from the freezer to crush up if you really want them?"

"Yes, I want strawberries on my rhubarb pie."

The others had already been eating as Roland stared at his strawberry and ice cream inundated pie."

"Auntie, how about having some chocolate syrup for my pie? Do you have chocolate syrup?"

"Yes, I have some chocolate syrup, Roland. But I'm afraid you really won't enjoy your pie. You'll hardly be able to taste it."

"Oh, I'll enjoy it alright, Auntie," said Roland. "It's a rhubarb pie split, just like a banana split. I got the idea from a Dairy Freeze where they have both banana splits and cream pie shakes, very good, very original."

Roland began eating big chunks of his concoction looking as much like he was strangling as enjoying it as he gulped, and coughed.

"Does anyone else want to make a rhubarb pie split?" asked Auntie.

The others all shook their heads in the negative while watching Roland gulp like an ostrich swallowing bricks. "No, Auntie, we're fine."

"Ricky, Roland, the two of you are eating your pie right down. Here are your seconds! Roland, here are more fixings for your next split."

"Oh, thank you, Auntie, this is such a treat," said Ricky. "I love your rhubarb pie so much. I hope we can do this again."

"I'm sure we will," said Auntie who was staring at Roland as he bobbed his head with a hand on his throat while pulling at his stomach.

"Roland," said Nancy in a low tone, "do you realize that with all of those additives you are eating about four helpings?"

"Ummm, umm, umm," said Roland. He looked down at the brown hair rug. Could it really be looking back at him? He was eating in big chomps now with his mouth open to hold all of the contents. The others all turned away except for Auntie who stared in more intense fascination.

After the treat and a brief visit, they all got up to leave, Auntie following them to the door. Ricky, Carol and Nancy lead the way with Roland trailing behind as he held the very swollen pooch of his stomach, and took small steps.

"It was so wonderful to have you visit, children," said Auntie, hugging Ricky, and patting him on the back, then hugging the girls in turn.

As they began walking out the door carrying the special extra pies, she turned with a special smile for Roland. As Auntie hugged Roland, squeezing herself against his full belly, she bared her little teeth, and growled lowly into his ear, "You didn't fool me a bit, Roland."

Then she stepped back to jam a square finger into his ribs. "Auntie got you to eat quite a bit, didn't she skinny boy. We'll put some meat on those little ribs!"

"Aaah, oh, oh," groaned Roland as he waddled to the car. But at least he had kept from looking at the brown hair rug again. He gratefully slid into the back seat shoving everything toward the far door as he leaned over his taut stomach softly moaning while the others stood one more moment outside waving goodbye to Auntie Beastie.

The girls got in the front seat. Ricky sat down in the back seat by Roland, splat!

Ricky sat for a moment, raising his hands in the air, then said, "Wait, girls, don't start the car yet. Roland, I think you set that extra pie under me in the car to sit on, on purpose. We didn't load it like this. We have to scrape it off my pants, and off the seat into the pan for Roland and I to eat later if it kills us."

"Roland! You did that to poor Ricky!" both women said in unison.

"No, it wasn't on purpose. But, Ricky, she poked me. I told you she would poke me, and you really didn't listen to me. She poked me. She really, really poked me, and my ribs actually hurt, and my belly hurts.

"You sitting on that pie must have been divine retribution. That's what it was, rhubarb pie retribution.

"As for retribution, I got mine too, ah oooh, Auntie Beastie."

The Ruthie Wrap-Around

Russet-haired Ruthie
wore a wrap-around
that showed she
really was quite round,
rotund and robust,
if not unusually rapturous
in all the most regarded regions
of relative physical rotation.

But, Ruthie rated highly
with all the boys in town,
who remembered most repeatedly
the day her wrap-around
came unwound,
twas unsound,
that wrap-around
when Ruthie
respirated roundly.

I remember Ruthie
most routinely
when I'm messin' around,
with words naturally.

Jimmy Schleighbottem Cranks Central A Second Time

"Hello, Central, can you hear me?

"Why, yes, Central, this is Jimmy Schleighbottem. You knew my voice?

"You did? And here it's probably been a whole couple of weeks since I talked to you last. You're really smart, and good, Central. And, you can hear me just fine, Central?

"Good, Central, I thought you might be able to hear me even better than last time cuz I've learned something new. I don't just use the catalogues on the chair to get up here to talk in the mouthpiece, and crank the phone to get you any more, Central

"What am I doing? Why, Central, I go into the living room, and get the little stool to put up on the chair first, and then get the catalogues. It's a little wobbly, but I got a fine sense of balance, let me tell you, Central. I've turned six now, and I can do an awful lot of stuff for a kid.

"Yeah, Mommy says I hadn't ought to be doing things like that either, Central. But then, Mommy says I hadn't ought to be calling you either. I guess she called you about that.

"She did, huh?

"You told her I wuz your little boyfriend? I spose you wuz tryin' to be nice but that's a awful thing to say about a big kid like me, Central. Mommy says Daddy's awful some of the time too, and I just spose he is. You know, I even had a third grader run away from me when I made fists.

"You say you're a little busy, Central?

"Well, yes, I did have an emergency, Central, but it's not one now. It's all over. I wuz just callin' you to tell you about it since we got to be friends cuz there ain't any other grown-ups around to tell about it. Of course, just like always, I wouldn't be allowed to use the phone if the grown-ups wuz here cuz of all the stuff I done, mostly cuz of my little brother fallin' off the stool. And, there wuz that time I shocked him and me both layin' the screw driver across the phone batteries. It wasn't my fault, Central. I didn't know 'bout electricicals bein' insulted on the handle but not the blade.

"Sure I know it's electricity. Ain't that what I said? In-sul-a-ted, now that's a powerful big word, Central. Mommy said she got insulted once,

216

and I sure felt that way after them electricicals.

"You have to go for a minute? Central? Central? You didn't hang up on me did you now? Oh, there you are.

"You say you're really busy, and you don't have time to listen to me if there's no emergency now? Well, you'd listen to my Daddy if he called in sayin' he'd had an mergency, or I mean emergency, wouldn't ya , Central.?

"I thought so. Now, Central, I am just a little kid, but I'm a human bein' too, so I think you really ought to listen to me.

"You'll give me five minutes. Well, that's not very long seein' as how you have so little to do. Least-wise that's what Mommy said cuz you are a lonely spinster that likes to listen to everybody else.

" Do I even know what a spinster is? Well, I'm not real sure, Central, but I think it has to do with sewing too much on account of it's about spinning.

"It means you ain't married, Central? Well, heck, what is wrong with that? I ain't ever going to get married either, Central, cuz Mommy says if I did I would have to marry some stupid old girl. Imagine that, Central, me marryin' some old stupid girl. Why, girls about make me puke, Central, all yappy, and wantin' to dress up, and stuff.

"You're a girl too? Well, I spose you are, Central, but you're an old girl, a grown-up, so you really don't count when it comes to me, and we're friends anyway. OK, if you are really fixing to get married to somebody a lot of years from now, Central, I guess I'd marry you if I had to, but you got to wait on me to grow up cuz I got some other stuff to do first. And don't you tell Eddy Hilbert that cuz he might get me down, and rub mud on my face like he did the other day.

"Wait a minute? You got somebody else calling? You always got some-one else calling, Central.

"Ah, you're back.

"You really need me to get goin' with telling my emergency, or you're going to have to hang up.?That wouldn't be very nice, Central. But, OK, here it is.

"Well, you see, I'm comin' home on the school bus like I do every night now since I got so big, and the bus comes to a stop at our cattle crossing. I get up, and look out the windows like all the other kids, and it's a awful, terrible sight. You see, my Daddy has the dairy herd on one side of the road with the Holstein bull, and the beef herd on the other side of the road with the Hereford bull. Them two got themselves out, and they were fighting like fury, right there in the middle of the road, Central, butting their big old heads together, pushing one another, and trying to stick each other with their horns. They're terrible big animals, Central.

217

"Ah, yes, you know cuz you've seen big bulls before. I hear you there, Central.

"Well, anyway, the school bus driver steered the bus around them two honking his horn, and he made it, but it was like they didn't even hear him. They got to spinning around the road there, even down on their knees, and we thought we could hear their tough old skins scraping on the gravel. It was awful, Central, worsen' than a car wreck or a dog fight, but we got around it.

"You're happy to hear that, and you have to go now? Wait a minute, Central. I haven't even told you the half of it.

"The bus went on up the road, and dumped me at my house. Mommy and Daddy weren't there, so I knew it wuz up to me to do something about those bulls.

"What do you mean I should stay away from them, Central? Somebody had to do something.

"You see, Central, I had the main weapon. Our good, old dog, Rudy, wuz there to meet me. You'd remember him, Central. He's tougher than Rin Tin Tin, Lassie and Kazan, Wild Dog of the North, all stuck together. And, he's a natural heeler. Daddy says that's the best thing about him. That way he ain't going to make any mess tearing something apart.

"Rudy's really got sharp teeth, Central. I touched them with my fingers, and pushed down on his tongue to put it between them to figure how he could bite without slicing his tongue up, especially since he's got his tongue laid over them panting and smiling at me about half the time.

"Well, I put my books in the house, and did some figuring on how fast I might be able to run to make it back to the house from the cattle crossing. Then I went across the front yard to the lilac bush where I got my private crawl hole to the middle of it, and figured on how I could make it to there from the cattle crossing if I couldn't quite make it to the house. You know, a bull can run powerful fast.

"Oh, you do know that? I see I got your interest now, Central.

"Well, my secret to the whole deal is old Rudy. I knew I could count on him to break up them bulls. But to make sure I got back alive, I didn't go quite all the way with Rudy. I just went part-way with him, and old Rudy wuz powerful interested in the bulls just seeing them there fighting still.

"Central, it was scarey. Them bulls had blood running on their necks, and their shoulders, and their sides. It wuz really neat if I hadn't been just a little scared,too. They had foam running out their mouths, but I don't really think bulls bite each other do they, Central?

"You agree with that? Good.

"You should have seen all the snot and dirt, and heard them terrible

218

moans and growls, Central. A bull is powerful mean. But I did my plan then, Central. I sicked old Rudy on them. After I said 'Sick'um real loud, I hollered 'Get'em, Rudy,' over and over.

"Well, Central, old Rudy run in there, and bit one bull on the heels, and then the other. And, when them bulls wouldn't pay attention, he'd jump up, and bite them in the sides. Central, Rudy wuz so fast that when a bull finally would turn to try to get him, he wuz already biting the other bull. He got them so mixed up, and scared, he broke them up, and they both run into their own pastures, and on down the hills with the right bunches of cows, Central. Me and Rudy really did it, and I wuz breathin' proud, but I guess I wuz still a little scared.

"Now, Central, I'm kind of sorry to say I'm not quite strong enough to close them gates. Daddy can close them, and I think maybe even Grandpa can. Of course, Mommy and Grandma can't because they probably aren't even as strong me cuz they all say I'm powerful built for a little kid, Central. The gates were all bent up, and yucked up on the wire too from them big bulls pushing on them, and leavin' their hair and blood on them.

"I stuck my finger in some bull blood, Central. It wuz real yucky. And, Central, I hope this ain't too dirty for you, but there wuz bull poop all over the road. People are going to have to drive their tires through it. I suppose Daddy will have to clean it up, don't you think?

"The rain will wash it off? Oh good. So, anyway I figured I had to make it so them bulls wouldn't want to come back for a while, so I told old Rudy to chase first one bunch further away, and then the other bunch further away. That way, Daddy's got time to get home, and close them gates. Then Rudy and me ran all the way home so I could call you.

"Why, no I didn't try to call Grandpa and Grandma, Central. They're too old for bulls, don't you think?

"You're going to call them. Now, Central, just cuz I told you all about it don't mean I think you ought to call Grandpa and Grandma, especially not Grandpa cuz once he gave me a spankin'.

"And you don't want me to ever go near those bulls again? That's powerful friendly of you, Central, but you just don't understand how it is with Rudy.

"What do you mean you don't want me crawlin' up here on the chair and the stool to call on the phone anymore.?? That's no business of yours what a man does in his own house, Central, least-whys, that's what Daddy says. I don't hear you sayin' anything to him when he smokes behind Mommy's back.

"Well, sure you can call Mommy and Daddy to tell them what I been doing, Central. I'll be tellin' them myself before you do anyway, and they'll be proud of me. I don't think I like your tone. You're bossy. Betsy at school is bossy too, and I just call her Betsy the heifer. You don't want to be a Betsy the heifer, Central.

"I hear you. And if you really got to call them, Central, you just crank the telephone handle two shorts. Even a little kid knows that, old Crank.

"Click!"

Contentment's Forge

We are forged
In the trials of life,
beaten upon the anvils
with the hammers
of death, destruction,
disaster, mistakes,
lost opportunities,
betrayals, disease
and injuries
that make
the inner steel.

Inward strength
we discover
while we pass
through the
smithy's fires
that holds us up,
bears us through,
not, as weak bullies think
to spread the pain to others,
but for that heart
that brings us joy,
that lets us
find contentment
when the confusion
of this state
might overcome us.

Indeed we can
celebrate when
we have learned
to let today's cares
suffice for today,
when we have discovered
that inner peace
which passes understanding.

Then are our
Inwards gathered
for what
we were meant to be.

Burford Gets His Wings With the Pet Maniac on Philly Square

It was Georgia Wayford who called him this time from the backwards house.

The Reverend Wolford Wongamuff had come to think of it as the backwards house because instead of facing the road like most homes did, it faced the pasture with its picture window so Hermes Wayford could watch his cattle gaining weight.

Whooey, Reverend, Hermes had said to him once, gives me pleasure to think every time a calf takes a bite of grass it could mean another penny goin into my pocket.

Then he had paused to stare at the Reverend with the eyes behind thick spectacles that seemed a bit small for the broad face, Of course, every thousand bites could be a penny goin to your church too, or, well, maybe every couple thousand bites, at least every 10,000 bites. I believe in givin the Lord his do, just got to figure how big a do it is. Hey, you want some extra spray cheese on that cracker?

The Reverend Wongamuff also associated it as a backwards house because of its backwards thinking.

And, yes, whooey, he was going to have to hear that word many many times over the next hour to two hours in the backwards house. Just the thought of the repeated word, whooey, began to make his stomach knot.

He stopped the car, and stepped out in the dust of the gravel road on a warm, autumn day, bent over the roof of his car, pounded it with his fist, and said, "Whooey, whooey, whooey, whooey, whooey, whooey!"

There that might get it out of the system, Lord give me the strength. He turned to prop the car door to get back in only to confront another car that had somehow pulled alongside his without his hearing it.

Kermit Douglas leaned over his wife, Kitty, in the passenger s seat to speak through the window. "Reverend Wongamuff, are you OK?"

"Oh, hello Kermit—Kitty. Yes, I was just having a prayer. Thank you."

"Having a little prayer, huh?" Kermit said as they watched the Rev. Wongamuff's car speed away.

"Yeah, huh," said Kitty. "Hollering whooey, whooey, whooey over and over again. Sounds to me like the reverend is on his way to see Hermes Wayford."

The Reverend Wongamuff got out of his car at the backwards house to step up on the front porch which was really the back porch. "Why, hello, Burford," he said as he looked down at the Wayford's little black and white Feist terrier who was laying there stretched out with his head between his front paws, and his ears hanging low.

Why, what was wrong with the little dog he wondered. This was easily the smartest dog he knew of anywhere, a dog that normally wagged his tail immediately upon seeing him with his ears up, eager to inspect the visitor.

Why, his ribs sagged and poked out so he looked as though he had lost a third of his weight. His hair coat wasn t glossy. Good Lord, this must be the problem. The dog had to be terminally ill.

What would happen to the Wayfords if Burford was dying? Yes, Reverend Wolford Wongamuff told himself, Georgia Wayford might need more life insurance on Burford than she did on Hermes.

Georgia Wayford opened the door, rubbing her palms together, knitting her brows, and saying, "Oh, thank God you re here Reverend Wongamuff. We've been needing you."

"Are you and Hermes getting along OK?" the reverend asked while glancing and pointing at Burford.

"Yes, yes, we re fine, sssh, sssh," she said putting a finger to her lips, and rolling her eyes toward Burford.

Oh, yes, he had forgotten that Burford seemed to understand a great deal of English.

Georgia ushered him into the living room by the picture window where Hermes Wayford sat, his great thin-haired noggin sagging down into a face wrinkled, and creased around downcast eyes in classic signs of profound depression.

Why, the little blue parakeet was even perched on his head without Hermes slapping at him. The cattle were out there grazing, and Hermes showed no sign of looking at them.

"Hello, Hermes," the Reverend Wongamuff said.

"Hi, Reverend Wongamuff, Hermes replied with a lips together wind sucking sound that sounded highly atypical."

What was this, the reverend wondered? No whooey? No wide-mouthed launch into a big tale of the latest trip?

"Let me explain, Reverend, Georgia said in a moderate, evenly spaced tone. Basically our problem is Burford's depression since his incarceration, and that's what's bothering Hermes, too, they are so linked by friendship, mutual tastes and psychology."

"Incarceration?"

Hermes looked him in the eye for the first time, and nodded his head in sober, tight-lipped affirmation. "Burford s done been in the big house."

"The big house?"

"You see, Reverend," Georgia said, "We decided to take another one of our big trips. And, since we had never gone clear to the east coast states before, we decided we would see Philadelphia. So, we went to Philadelphia."

"No, whooey, that ain't the way you do it, Georgia," Hermes said. "You don't go tellin' no trip story that way. Let me tell the story, Reverend, cuz whooey, it wuz fun, whooey, yes, it started out fun."

Control, control, the Reverend Wongamuff whispered inside his mind. You don t go jumping and flinching at the first few whooeys. This is good that Hermes is responding so quickly.

"You see, the calves wuz all worked, and I figured the old cows could be out on pasture at least another month, so I says to Mama, that would be my Georgia honey bunch here, and Burford, let's go on a trip, Hermes continued, his face beginning to glow and animate to follow the speech pattern.

"Now, ya see, Reverend, we just don't go on trips just anywhere. Whooie, no sir. We go through some mighty sophisticated selection processes to decide where to go.

"I could tell Burford had powerful urges to go to Texas cuz I ain't ever been to Galveston Island before, and Georgia was hinting we ought to see California before it gets shook to pieces. Then Burford got to scratchin' hisself behind the ear, and slapped his paw down on Philadelphia.

"Reverend Wongamuff, it wuz a piece of brilliant thinking that goes to show my Burford is a certified purebred Mazzoura Feist terrier even if he wuz bought off a crazy man.

"You see, we got a set of relations in the City of Brotherly Love that we figured would love to put us up free for a few days, Lazzus and Louisa Wayford."

"Lazarus?"

"No, Reverend, Lazzus. Remember, Lazarus come back from the dead, and our Lazzus ain t ever been dead yet, I don't think. I'll have to ask him since his mama did come up with a most peculiar name. But she wuz dumb, Reverend, whooey, not educated like you and me.

"Heck, I almost had a high school degree if my folks hadn t made me take algebra and home economics the same year. There's too many girls in home economics, Reverend. Why, whooey, that Sally......

"What? Yes, Georgia, honey lamb. I won t go talkin any more about home economics girls in front of a reverend.

"Now, where wuz I? Well, we had ourselves three coolers for this trip, Reverend. Three coolers! And, whooey, one of them wuz full of nothin but spray cheeses, cheddar, pepper jack, extra sharp, cream cheese, you name it. We had three sacks of chips to go with it. Of course, Georgia don t eat a lot, doesn t much go for spray cheese on dill pickles, but me and Burford hits it pretty hard, especially the sharp cheese on the Ritz crackers, whooey.

"We got it all stacked in nice so Georgia could stretch out in the back seat with her ear phones on listenin to her Beetoven, and me and Burford could listen to our latest CD in the front that alternates Louis Armstrong, Guy Lombardo, Elvis Presley and Mel Tillis all in one handy package.

"Darned if that Burford don't crack you up when he tries to do his imitation of Mel Tillis stutterin' when he s talkin'. Or, I don t know, maybe Burford just gets the heaves from all the spray cheese. The veterinarian says that all might not be good for a dog, but Burford sure loves it.

"We got there by and by, Reverend. I won't go into all the meat of the story since we need you to heal our Burford. Whooey, do we ever need you to cuz we is oppressed.

"But we had ourselves some adventures, and did ourselves some zig zagging on the drive. Burford even had two altercations along the way, once for what he did on the St. Louis Arch, and again with the dinosaur bone at the Field Museum in Chicago. So, when you counsel him, whooey, you might want to consider he ain't always as pure as he seems, me neither. I confess, it s possible for me and Burford to be rascals.

"Now, Reverend, whooey, we had ourselves a swell time the first three days stayin' at Lazzus' and Louisa's big old house what wuz built before the revolution but George Washington never stayed in. Just atween you and me, Reverend, I don t think old George slept around as much as they think he might have. Whooey, guys in wigs just didn't do that, too high class.

"We ate lots of spray cheese and sausage, and Louisa tried to tell us about how a fruit diet could be beneficial, but, Reverend, that woman's nearly skin and bones. We even saw Betsy Ross's house where she commenced with flag sewing.

"Anyways, after three days, Lazzus and Louisa got to yawnin' a lot, and explainin' how we wuz ready, with our abilities, to see some of the big city by ourselves. Besides that, whooey, wuz they ever jumpin' every time our Burford ran one of their neutered cats to the top of the refrigerator. You wouldn t think elderly fat cats could climb like that, Reverend, like bankers clawin' for their interest.

"That's how Burford and I got to be sittin' alone on a park bench right below the Philadelphia library. Lazzus dropped us off there on his way to work to look at the suits of armor in the library while Louisa took Georgia somewhere to get her hair done.

"Just Burford and me, whooey, him on a leash waitin' for a squirrel to get close, and me eatin' a spray-cheesed cracker, blendin' in with the

225

native populace in dear old Philly neither one of us wuz lookin' for trouble.

"Well, now, Reverend, Burford might have caused a little ruckus if he'd been able to dispatch a squirrel. He could have, too, if he hadn't been on a leash snarling at it. Burford's got a powerful snarl when he's miffed. And, whooey, wuz he ever miffed with them big ol' fat squirrels baiting him to the end of his leash.

"Now, whooey, I d been tryin' my best to follow Lazzus' instructions, Reverend. He told me never to look people in the eye in Philly cuz they might think you're a'gonna mug them or panhandle them in some way. And, he told me you don t say good mornin' or hello to people you meet on the sidewalks like we do at home because they might think the same thing.

"But, I can t help it, me and Burford are just naturally friendly fellows, and them Philadelphia people get to sounding so much like Kansas people, you get to thinkin' they're just normal every day Americans instead of almost a whole different country what happens to be in the same country, whooey. You know, they got the Liberty Bell, and we celebrate it, and I'll bet you half the hot dogs got meat in them from out our way.

"Why, whooey, we got free trade with them folks, and we ain't supposed to look'em in the eyes?

"Anyway, like I says, me and Burford are just sittin' there on the bench, him snarlin' at squirrels at the end of the leash, me eatin some pepper jack cheese on a cracker, gettin' powerful thirsty, whooey wuz I dry and sweatin' in that humidity, when this thin-haired, blonde fellow in a red necktie and blue suit comes along.

"Well, whooey, Reverend, I m a mindin' my Philadelphia manners when this fellow looks me in the eye just like he ain't supposed to as if he never seen a fella eatin cheesey crackers while holdin' a powerful, snarlin' Feist from squirrel killin'.

"Whooey, I says to him, and he curls his lip like he never heard anyone use a word like whooey, you know you ain't supposed to look folks in the eyes in Philadelphia.?

"He smiles then, and I say, my cousin, Lassus, says so on account of you could think I wuz a mugger. I explains that back home I say hi to everyone I meet, and nod my head at them and stuff.

"Then, he laughs, and says, 'I know what you mean. I m native to Philly, but I spent some time in North Carolina, and the small town people there say hello and good morning to everybody, too.'

"Then I says to the fellow, whooey, I m about famished here, I could sure use me a pop.

"He looks at me real strange, and says, 'A pop?'

"Yeah, I says, you know a pop, a coke.

"'You want a pop of coke,' he says.

"Yeah, I says, a pop, a coke, just anything will do, somethin' to wet yourself down with, ya know.

"Well, whooey, Reverend, this fellow steps back like I tried to hit him in the gut or somethin', and he takes off down the sidewalk. By this time I'm tired, and so's Burford although he had stopped to listen to the conversation.

"Let s go where I can get me a good cold drink of pop, Burford, I says to my little Feist, and maybe we can get you a little cup of ice water too. Burford don t care much for pop, Reverend. It makes bubbles come out his nose.

"Whooey, we just walked and we walked, over an interstate with a guy livin' in a tent beside it, and down through some brick buildings, and we're gettin' powerful dry.

"The desperation wuz settin' in, I guess, and, whooey, I forgets myself. There s this young woman comin' down the sidewalk all dolled up with high heels on, and I says to her in my best manner, pardon me, Ma m, but I'm fair to desperate dry here, do you know where I might buy a pop?

"Even Burford is wagging his tail, and trying to poke his nose into her leg when, whooey, she swings her purse at him, and marches off like we tried to hurt her. It wasn t any problem for Burford to dodge her cuz he's way quicker than a human bein'. Go figure, Reverend, it wuz powerful strange.

"But then when I turns around, whooey, what do you think I saw. It wuz a little brick shop window front across the street in a brick building that I hadn t noticed cuz it wuz all blended in with all the other brick buildings.

"Well, we went in the front of the shop, and there wuz this young woman with blue-black straight hair there that made me pause right inside the door she wuz so strange.

"Whooey, Reverend, she had blue and red tattoos everywhere she wuz exposed, and that wuz in plenty of places. She had holes poked all over her with jewels hangin' out them in plenty of places besides the several in each ear, in her nose, on her eyebrow, in her cheek, by her belly button, and when she opened her mouth to talk, there wuz even one in her tongue.

"Whooey, she made me real uncertain, Reverend, and Burford wuz standin' in front of me, tiltin' his head, his ears up, goin' uuurgh, uuurgh, kinda whinin' like he didn t know quite what we were lookin' at either.

"Finally she says, 'Can I do something for you?'

"And I says to her, well at last, whooey, you can, I m powerful famished, I need a pop.

"Well, she looks at me a minute, and asks, 'You want a pop?'

"Yeah, I says, a pop, a coke.

"Well, whooey, Reverend, she just stands there lookin at me a minute, then says, 'You re asking me for a pop of coke?'

"Well, yes, Ma am, I says, a pop, a coke, however you want to say it. I d likely pay whatever you want for it if it s OK for me to come on in. Pardon me, but whooey, this place is a little different than what we got at home—I wuz lookin at some bunches of garlics hangin' from hooks.

"Whooey, Reverend Wongamuff, that s when old Philly started comin' unraveled for poor Burford and me. That hole-poked girl pulls a spray can of somethin out from under the counter, and points it at me and Burford, and says, 'You get out of here. I m calling 911.'

"Reverend, I didn t argue with her, and neither did Burford. I don t know what wuz in that spray can, but, whooey, it wasn't spray cheese, and all them jewels in the poke-hole girl wuz glowin' like she wuz some sort of demon.

"Burford and me stepped across the street, and we wuz just standin' there a while tryin' to decide where to go next. Burford wuz pullin' like he wanted to go back to the park, and have another crack at killin' squirrels, and me, whooey, I wuz so dry my tongue felt like I d been spray cheesin' it directly.

"It wuz about then these two young policemen pulled up on bicycles. They had their white helmets on, all their gear hangin on their belts, and they had on shorts so you could see the muscles in their legs. I says to Burford, 'Now, whooey, Burford, them is some good lookin' young cops all dark haired, and matchin like they could be twins.'

"Well, the poke-holed tattoo lady comes out of her shop then, and points at me all pouty and nasty, and says, 'That s the one officers. The nasty old man asked me for a pop of coke, and his nasty little dog gurgled at me like he might be having a fit. The old fool probably gives it to him, too.'

"Well, 'Whooey, I says to Burford, what's that evil lookin' woman talkin' about?'

"Then there wuz the blonde-haired fellow in the suit and tie from the square across the street, and he calls out, 'He tried to get me for a pop of coke, too, officers, and that little dog was snarling at everything in the park like he was half-mad.'

"Then there wuz the young woman in the heels walkin' up, too, and she hollers, 'Me, too, officers, the old man tried to hit me for a fix, too, and the little dog tried to get his mouth on me.'

"Well, whooey, them two young cops wuz lookin at me then like I wuz fish bait or worse yet, Reverend. And, I says, 'I ain't old, and I ain't tried to fix anything for that woman. Never would either, let her do her own fixin'.'

228

"The one cop popped his holster then like he might try to quick draw on me while the other cop walks up to me, and says, 'Steady there, Pops, you're goin' to have to come with us.'

"Then he pulls his handcuffs out, and takes hold of my wrist, Reverend. Well, I just naturally says , 'Ahhh, what the heck!' when he does that, and that seemed to be Burford's call to action.

"Whooey, no sir, no quarter, ain't ever gonna be any way that my Burford tolerates anybody tryin' to manhandle the poppa Wayford of the family, Reverend. He growled, jumped up, and gave that young cop a good pinch with his teeth high on the inside of his thigh, whooey did it ever make the fellow jump.

"The other cop tries to grab him, but Burford is powerful quick, and he dodged around to open him up a scab on the bicycle muscle.

"By that time I wuz wavin my hands, and callin to Burford to calm down. This one cop pulls a deal out of his pocket then, and sprays me and Burford both in our faces.

"Whooey, my God the tears, Reverend, you wouldn't have believed it. The stuff wuz mace, just like tear gas if you wuz ever in the service. I yowled, Burford yowled, and Burford found some dirt to bite around a little tree, and tried to yowl some more. He got it worse than I did because I at least had my glasses over my eyes to help a little.

"About that time, a squad car pulled up for them to shove me into with the handcuffs on, and a pound paddy wagon pulled up for Burford. He doesn't seem like he'll ever get over the humiliation of them puttin' a little muzzle on him.

"Whooey, that wuz a long ride, Reverend Wongamuff. I wuz half worried to death about Burford, and I wuz wonderin' over and over again what I had done to stir up all these people so. You'd have thought the poke-holed tattooed girl wuz the normal one.

"Well, they put me on a bench, and since I wasn't seein' too well, one of the cops runnin' around there wuz kind enough to call Lazzus for me. I sat there for over an hour, but at least they had a water fountain there where I could get a drink. Whooey, I must've drunk a gallon.

"Finally, my two young bicycle cops come in, and they took me to where this old policeman with a bald head and short, white sideburns sat at a desk. He looks me over, and says, 'Soliciting drugs, huh?'

"And then, he shakes his head at me. 'I guess they come in all looks and ages.'

"Well, whooey, I says, I don t likely understand this, your honor, we did stop at a Walgrens out by Lazzus' place so Georgia could get some headache medicine. She gets sick when she travels with Burford and me, but that s the only drug I got in Philly. Otherwise, I wuz just powerful thirsty.

"Whooey, this old bugger looks me up and down, then looks at the two young cops with me.

"He says, 'Thirsty, huh, and don't call me your honor. I'm a police officer, maybe a sergeant, but still an officer. You call me officer. Where are you from anyway?'

"'Well, officer, sir,' I says, 'I'm from out on the West Kansas border, and I been enjoyin' most of my stay here in the City of Brotherly Love. But I m worried about my dog, Burford, and I figure he and I have had about all the love we can stand now. We wuz just thirsty, but we sure offended someone in a big way, whooey.'

"He looks me up and down again, and says, 'Thirsty huh?'

"'Yes, we wuz. I wuz askin people where I could get a pop, and they wuz actin' like I wuz speakin' Chinese. So, I d say to them, you know, a coke, but it didn t help none. Whooey.'

"Well this police sergeant looks me up and down again, kind of smiles, and says, 'Did you ever think of asking them for a soda?'

"I says, 'Well, whooey, why would I ask them for soda when I'm dry? I wasn't gonna bake anything, and I don't even have a refrigerator here to get stunk up. Oh, granted, the one at home might be stinking a little when we get home, so we might pick up some Arm & Hammer when we get there.'

"The old cop wuz really grinnin' then, and he looks at the young cops, and he looks at me, and says, 'Tell me, my whooey friend, have you ever had a cold soda pop to drink?'

"'Well, whooey, I guess so, otherwise I wouldn't have been tryin to get me a cold sody pop to drink all afternoon.'

"Well, he looks me up and down one more time as Lazzus, Louisa and my sweet Georgia, all dolled up with her new hair cut come up.

"He kind of curls his lips, and says to the two young cops, 'Just let Mr. Wayford go, and give these folks directions on where they can go to pick up his little dog. I hope you have a wonderful time the rest of your stay in Philadelphia.'

"Whooey, well, Reverend, we did just that. We went down, and got poor Burford out of the big house. But he wuz mighty glum, mighty glum.

"They had him in a big cage on concrete with that muzzle still on him in the middle of a whole bunch of other dogs. God knows what those regular convict dogs might have tried to do to him, whooey, my poor Burford.

"He just laid in the back seat with his head down the whole ride home, didn t even get up to do mimics when I played our disk of Alvin and the Chipmunks, never ate no more spray cheese. Our lives seemed forever changed.

"Burford has been like that ever since, Reverend. He knows his reputation is soiled, whooey. He is a scarred pooch. I don t know if I can ever get him up for the next trip to Philadelphia if we can t snap him out of it. Whooey."

"Let me go out on the porch, and talk to him for a few minutes," said the Reverend Wongamuff. "You folks just stay in here."

A half hour later, the reverend opened the door, and in trotted Burford at full prance with his ears and tail cocked up. He promptly jumped into Hermes Wayford's lap, licked him in the face, and snapped at Joseph to scare the blue parakeet away. The reverend stood there grinning as he watched.

Then the reverend made his way the door, stepped out on the porch, and paused a moment to pray just as the music inside started up.

Georgia came out behind him. "Reverend Wongamuff, whatever did you say to revive Burford. It's a total transformation. Burford and Hermes are dancing to their favorite tape. They started the shimmy to Guy Lombardo's rendition of 'If You Don t Like My Peaches, Why Do You Shake My Trees,' and now Burford's shaking his tail to Elvis and 'Blue Suede Shoes.' What happened?"

"Well, Georgia, everybody comes to a crisis point in life when they realize they must be here for a reason to make it worthwhile to push on despite all the obstacles of this existence.

"I simply, in so many words, explained to Burford that he has been put here in the position of a kind of a guardian angel to take care of Hermes.

"If you'll pardon me for explaining this to you bluntly, I told him it isn't his fault that his master is a sort of a maniac, and he simply has to adjust his life's mission to take that into account, and do the best he can.

" It gave Burford a reason for living—whooey."

"Yes, whooey! Reverend, why don't you stay a little longer, and have some soda pop with us."

"I'd like that, Georgia."

Earth Flower

A yellow flower grows
amongst the close-clipped grass
on the family graves,
more beautiful by far
than the silks and plastics allowed there,
Perhaps also more precious by far
to the reborn souls of those
whose remains lie below.

For it tells of their tenacious roots,
their closeness to the soil,
their persistance
through the turmoils of life,
the glow of their faces,
the like service to feed creation,
not only food but biting wine,
of hope and wisdom,
their recognition
that dominion
meant care for creation,
not plunder, cruelty and ruination.

The landscaper comes
to remove you soon,
what's left mouldering down
to join the remains,
even though you release
a hundred seeds before him,
persistence, tenacious you,
lovely, lowly earth flower.

God bless the dandelion
of new spring.